The Man Behind the Bridge

The Man Behind the Bridge

Colonel Toosey and the River Kwai

PETER N. DAVIES

With a Foreword by
HRH Prince Philip

ATHLONE
London & Atlantic Highlands, NJ

First published 1991 by The Athlone Press Ltd
1 Park Drive, London NW11 7SG
and 171 First Avenue, Atlantic Highlands, NJ 07716

British Library Cataloguing in Publication Data

Davies, Peter N. (Peter Neville)
The man behind the bridge: Colonel Toosey and the River Kwai.
1. South-east Asia. British prisoners of war, 1939–1945—Biographies
I. Title
940.547252092

ISBN 0–485–11402–X

Library of Congress Cataloging in Publication Data
Davies, Peter N.
The man behind the bridge: Colonel Toosey and the River Kwai / by
Peter N. Davies.
     p.   cm.
Includes bibliographical references.
ISBN 0–485–11402–X (cloth)
1. Toosey, Philip.   2. World War, 1939–1945—Prisoners and
prisons, Japanese.   3. World War, 1939–1945—Conscript labor.
4. Railroad bridges—Thailand—Design and construction. 5. Burma–Siam
Railroad—History.   6. World War, 1939–1945—Atrocities.
7. Prisoners of war—Thailand—Biography.   8. Prisoners of war—
Great Britain—Biography.   I. Title.
D805.T5D38   1990
940.54'7242–dc20
[B]

Frontispiece: A portrait of Philip Toosey in the mid-1950s as Honorary
Colonel of his Territorial Army Regiment, the 287 Medium Regiment RATA.

Typeset by J&L Composition Ltd, Filey, North Yorkshire
Printed in Great Britain by Billings & Sons Ltd, Worcester

*This book is respectfully dedicated
to the memory of those who did not return.*

Contents

BUCKINGHAM PALACE.

Those of us who took part in the last war are only too familiar with the story of the campaigns against the Japanese, and particularly with the inhuman treatment of both civil and military prisoners by their Japanese captors. Much has been written about these events and I hope that future generations will find the time to read what their predecessors suffered and achieved.

The story of the bridge over the river Kwai in Thailand has become a legend, but the legend does not include many details about the life of the remarkable man whose leadership in the prison camp did so much more than just maintain morale.

It seems to have become the fashion to belittle heroes and to denigrate leaders. Philip Toosey deserves better than that, and I am delighted that Professor Peter Davies has written with such sympathy about a man whose courage and example in very dangerous and difficult circumstances gained the respect and affection of all who came in contact with him.

1990

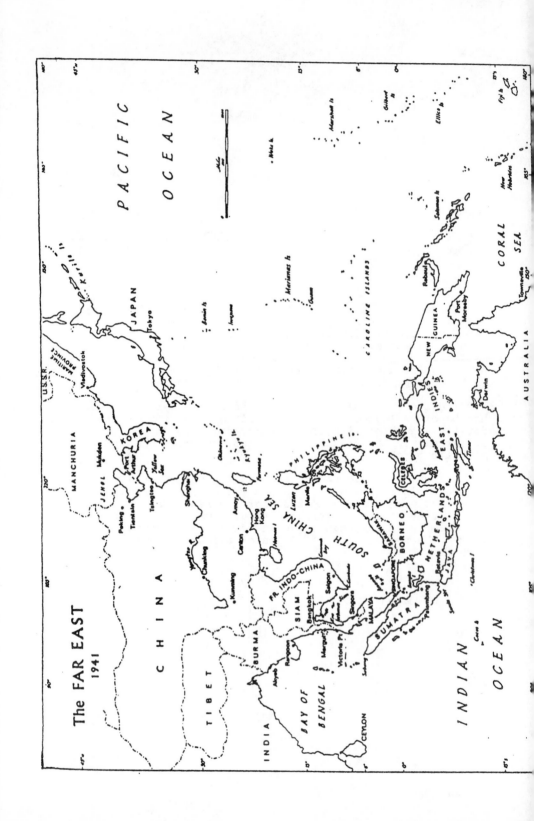

The FAR EAST
1941

Preface

The many thousands who knew how Colonel Toosey stood up to their Japanese captors at great personal risk were incensed by Alec Guinness's brilliant portrayal of 'Colonel Nicholson' in the film version of Pierre Boulle's *Bridge over the River Kwai*. Although the film was released in Britain in 1958 it was its subsequent showing on television in the late 1960s that brought it into national prominence. It then appeared to many ex-prisoners of the Japanese that this excellent piece of fiction was being accepted by a wide section of the public as a true representation of what had happened during the building of the Thai–Burma Railway. As Toosey was both the president of the Far East Prisoners of War (FEPOW) Federation and had also been the senior British officer at the bridge camp (the part played so convincingly by Alec Guinness), pressure developed for him to attempt to correct the misleading image that had, quite innocently, been presented.

Toosey had already spent much time in writing an autobiography. Although this was regarded by all who read it as an excellent piece of work, Toosey himself felt that it had little merit except as a personal account and refused to consider its publication. However, in response to the publicity generated by the film, the insistence of his friends and the knowledge of his own frailty, he finally agreed that a biography should be prepared by a professional author. At this time his work with FEPOW still kept him in touch with Sir John Smyth (one of the trustees) with whom he had many links during the early days of the federation. Sir John's background as a commander of the 17th Division in Burma during 1942 and his subsequent career during which he had produced several military histories of the Second World War made him an obvious candidate for this task and he gladly accepted the commission.

Sir John's other commitments permitted him to devote only a limited amount of time to this work. Thus he concentrated on presenting

Colonel Toosey's own autobiography in a more acceptable manner and added only a small amount of material. The finished draft showed Toosey in a broader light and included an account of his part in the formation of FEPOW, but it did not supply the kind of 'in-depth' study that it had now been agreed was what was really required. Consequently a decision was made that it would not be published. This meant that the original objective, that of preventing the film from assuming the mantle of reality, remained unfulfilled, so Toosey was again pressed to secure an account that would enable future generations to distinguish between entertaining fiction and the true facts.

It was at this point that Colonel Toosey attended a meeting of the Elder Dempster Pensions' Association (of which he was then the chairman) at which I gave a talk on the background to the writing of my recently published history of their company. The venue provided a useful opportunity for discussion and led to a further meeting at which the possibility of a new and fuller biography was carefully investigated. The immense scale of Toosey's collection of letters and official papers and his vast library of books on POW matters proved to be strong inducements. Consequently the decision was made to attempt a comprehensive study of the man and his achievements and to place them both in the correct historical perspective.

The present work is thus designed to provide a more accurate account of the terrible events during which more than 16,000 POWs died while building the Thai–Burma railway of which 'the bridge' formed an essential part. There is no desire to glorify an essentially modest man. Toosey made what stand he could against Japanese brutality and indifference and established a style of command which gained him a tremendous reputation. But, as he was at great pains to point out, many other brave men did what they could in the particular circumstances of their own captivity without seeking or receiving any recognition for their efforts.

Tamarkan camp, where Toosey was in command, was only one of a large number of sites where the prisoners were forced to work under barbaric conditions. It was not in any sense either the largest or the most important work centre and it is certain that camps on the more remote northern sections of the railway were infinitely worse in every way. But along the whole length of the track it gradually became known that Toosey was the 'man to handle the Nips', and the thought that one man could do it inspired others to try and gave some small crumbs of comfort to all.

It was a pure accident of fate that placed Toosey on the Kwae in a position of authority. He was not a professional soldier. In peacetime he had worked as a merchant banker although he had been a particularly successful gunnery officer in the Territorial Army (TA). Furthermore, while he had undoubtedly enjoyed a distinguished career on active service he was outranked by literally hundreds of the officers who had been captured in the Far East. Japanese policy, however, segregated all senior officers (colonels and above) from their units so the lieutenant-colonels were forced to assume command. Even then, Toosey was frequently not the senior lieutenant-colonel in his camp but invariably he was encouraged to take charge by the wishes of his fellow officers or, in some instances, at the express desire of the Japanese.

Colonel Toosey was forced to ponder on the realities of life and death when he found himself in charge of the POWs responsible for constructing the notorious 'Bridge over the River Kwai'. But his dilemma was not that presented by Pierre Boulle in his novel. Toosey understood from the very beginning that the only real issue was how to ensure that as many of his men as possible should survive their captivity. He appreciated to the full that the bridges would be built with or without his cooperation and set himself the task of mitigating the terrible conditions under which the work was to be completed.

This, then, is not intended to be a tribute to the deeds performed by Colonel Toosey during the harsh days of the Second World War. If it turns out to be one, it will not be by design, but only as a true reflection of the actual events.

Peter N. Davies
December 1990
University of Liverpool and Visiting Professor at Hiroshima Shudo University

Note on the spelling of River Kwai/Kwae: The popular spelling of the River is 'Kwai', whereas the proper Thai term for 'river' is 'Kwae' (as in 'Kwae Noi'). The spelling 'Kwai' has been used in association with the legend created by the film *The Bridge over the River Kwai*. Otherwise the spelling 'Kwae' has normally been used.

Acknowledgements

My sincere thanks are due to the former prisoners of the Japanese who have so kindly placed their specialized knowledge at the disposal of one who was not there. While many have been mentioned by name in the text, others might have inadvertently been omitted and to these I wish to freely acknowledge my enormous debt.

I am particularly grateful to the following who have generously assisted by commenting upon various sections of the original draft. These include Pharaoh Adams, W. L. Davis, Jack Edwards, the late Ewart Escritt, Carl Fritsche, Keith Trace, Douglas Williams and Harold Payne – the latter, as President of the NFFCA, has also provided considerable, additional support over many years.

A special acknowledgement is also due to Patrick Toosey, the eldest son of Sir Philip, for his constant encouragement, while Captain Will Harris also deserves my deepest gratitude – without his determination and single mindedness this study may still not have seen the light of day.

The maps for this book were based on material provided by Mrs Escritt and G. P. Adams. I am pleased to give my thanks to Mrs Escritt and Mr Adams for their help.

Note on place-names

Allied POWs building the Thai–Burma Railway often gave the sites names of their own, or, like the Japanese, pronounced the original Thai names in their own way. Some alternative versions of the POW names used in this book are given below.

Ban Khao, Bankao, Bangkao
Banpong (Ban Pong), Banponmai
Chungkai, Kao Poon, Kaopon
Hintok (Hintock, Hin Tok), Hintoku
Kanchanaburi, Kanburi
Kanyu, Kanu
Kha Khannat, Dha Khanum, Takanun, Takunan
Kin Saiyok (Kinsaiyok), Sai Yoku
Konkuita, Konkoita, Concreeta
Lat Ya, Laddya
Lum Sum
Nikhe, Nike, Nikki, Neekey
Nong Pladuk, Nonpuradokku
Purankasi, Plankashi, Brankassi, Prang Kasi
Rin Tin, Rinten, Lin Thin
Tamarkan, Tha Makham
Tambaya
Tardan, Tha Manao
Tha Muang, Tamuang, Tamoan, Ta Mueng
Thanbyuzayat
Tha Soe, Tarsoe, Ta Soe: *now* Namtok
Tonchan
Wampo (Wam Po), Wanpo, Wang Po, Wang Pho
Wang Yai, Wanyai

Prologue
A journey into the unknown

Lieutenant Colonel Philip Toosey breathed a sigh of relief as his train pulled out of the battered station at Singapore. Since his arrival on the island in January 1942, some 9 months earlier, he had survived the dangers involved in fighting against an experienced and vicious Japanese army, endured the humiliation of a disastrous surrender and been obliged to witness the execution of many innocent Chinese civilians.

Toosey had also been forced to begin the gradual adjustment to a new role – that of prisoner of war. At first his captivity had been in the Changi area of Singapore Island where the vast majority of European servicemen had been confined, but he quickly volunteered to move to a working camp and from June onwards was in charge of what had formerly been the site of the RAF HQ at Bukit Timah. Here he commanded some 3000 men including about 500 from his own unit – the 135th Field Regiment, Royal Artillery (RA). The work, that of loading ships in the docks and helping to build a shrine to commemorate those Japanese who had fallen in the fighting, was not unduly arduous and food and shelter were good by later standards. But relations with the Japanese and, in particular, with the renegade Sikhs they employed as guards, were always brittle, and violent punishments for minor offences were becoming a regular part of the way of life. Consequently it was with some relief that, early in October, Toosey received orders to prepare to move to the north.

These instructions were extremely vague. Toosey was to form a group of 650 men into the equivalent of a battalion and report with them to Singapore station on the morning of 22 October 1942. Not surprisingly he selected the bulk of this force from his own unit together with detachments of Norfolks, Suffolks and RASC of the 18th Division. No one was told and few were able to guess their ultimate destination but Japanese suggestions promoted the rumour that they 'were going to a

1

land flowing with milk and honey, plenty of good food and light work'.[1] A more jaundiced view was that the Japanese had decided that it was unwise for them to keep such a large body (over 80,000 men)[2] in such a small area and had therefore begun a policy of dispersal.

The march from Bukit Timah to the centre of Singapore indicated a changing attitude towards the prisoners of war. Instead of the hostility that had been apparent at the time of the surrender the local population now showed a great deal of sympathy by the gift of many small presents of food – clearly membership of the Japanese 'Co-prosperity Sphere' was not so attractive as it had first appeared. Consequently it was with a cheerful heart and a lighter step that the column of men made its way to the station and came to a halt in one of its outer courtyards.

After a lengthy delay a Japanese officer appeared and Colonel Toosey was given his first instructions. He was informed that the ensuing journey would take 4 days and 4 nights; that no man was to leave the train without permission; that prisoners were not to sit with their legs out of the doorways; and that two men per truck were to stand by at each main station to collect the food that was to be provided. Toosey was also told to place in charge of each truck an officer who would be responsible for its discipline and it was made clear that in the event of any trouble the doors would be kept locked – a very severe threat in conditions of great heat and overcrowding. However, when Toosey learned that the escort was to consist of only a sergeant and four men he quickly appreciated that it was unlikely that these orders could be strictly enforced so he made no particular protest at this time. He was then taken into the station proper, shown a long line of not-too-clean steel railway trucks normally used for the carriage of rubber and ordered to get his men aboard.

A simple calculation indicated that each truck would need to accommodate thirty-one prisoners together with their baggage and a share of the group's heavy equipment. It seemed to Colonel Toosey and his fellow officers that this was going to prove a virtually impossible task, but the Japanese provided unlooked-for aid by insisting that many useful items, including rice boilers and ovens, be left on the platform for later transmission. Of course they never arrived and were sadly missed and it was subsequently felt that the cost of additional discomfort for a 4-day period would have been a small price to have paid for their convenience in the jungle camps.

By admitting the men in groups of thirty-one through the barrier Toosey easily allocated them to individual trucks and, after several abortive efforts, they and their possessions were tightly packed on board. After a further lengthy delay a shudder ran along the line of trucks and with a great deal of noise from the engine and a loud cheer from the troops the train began to move. The hot and bored passengers then gradually came back to life as the sights of Singapore drifted past their open doors and even the most blasé took note when the locomotive slowed to a walking pace to cross the damaged causeway which connected the island with the mainland of Malaya. Memories of earlier crossings were relived at this moment, for many of the men on board had fought the oncoming Japanese in Johore before retreating back to Singapore to face the final attack. Soon, however, the train had passed through Johore Bahru and was making its way north at an irregular speed through mile after mile of pineapple groves and rubber plantations. Occasionally there would be a brief stop at a tiny station and, at first, only the very brave or desperate descended to the track and stretched their legs. Then, finding that the guards took no notice, more and more of the prisoners began to climb down at each halt and in many places were even able to purchase fruit, hard boiled eggs and cigars from the local population. Unfortunately no one could anticipate the length of any particular stay and as the train restarted only a few seconds after a warning whistle there was great confusion as the men sought to regain their places. Although some were only just pulled on board in the nick of time, no one was actually left behind.

By nightfall the train had passed through Gemas and the overpowering heat of the day had been replaced by bitter cold. This, allied to the cramped sitting position which was the best that could be managed, meant that few of the men achieved anything more than brief snatches of sleep – on each occasion waking in extreme discomfort. The dawn provided a welcome relief but this feeling gradually evaporated as the temperature rose to over 100° and, with water bottles nearing exhaustion, accentuated the thirst which was rapidly becoming a major problem. By mid-morning, when Kuala Lumpur was reached, everyone was desperately hot, tired and hungry, so as soon as the train had stopped, two men from each truck were quickly despatched to collect their rations. These consisted of rice and boiled vegetables which, when supplemented with a small quantity of the bully beef which had been issued at the beginning of the journey, provided a reasonably satisfying meal. The provision of a pint of hot water per head was even more welcome but was clearly insufficient for current and future needs. Consequently, as soon as the food had been consumed, many of the prisoners made their way to the locomotive and filled their bottles with boiled water which, if somewhat oily, had the virtue of being sterile. With Japanese approval, full use was made of both the gentlemen's and ladies' toilet facilities within the rather ornate station and most managed to enjoy a brief wash before it was time to respond to the insistent whistle of the engine and return to the train.

3

The next stage of the journey, which took about 5 hours, passed fairly quickly, for the changing scenery provided a useful stimulus to jaded minds and bodies. Ipoh was reached on the evening of the second day and, once again, the routine of collecting rice and (largely) vegetable stew was completed. The indifference and, perhaps, the limited number of Japanese accompanying the train then permitted an increasing number of prisoners to sample the delights of the station buffet and large quantities of very sweet coffee and tiny cakes were consumed. This was followed by another night of sheer misery and discomfort before the train arrived at Prai opposite the beautiful island of Penang. Breakfast on the third day was provided at this point and, with the addition of the carefully hoarded items still retained, a moderate meal was achieved. Water remained the chief difficulty and in spite of Japanese curses and blows dozens of individuals besieged the locomotive during every brief stop. Some relief was obtained by the purchase or barter of fruit and drinks when the train halted at local stations but the supply was seldom equal to the demand and everyone remained permanently thirsty.

The journey north then continued under gradually worsening conditions. Apart from the increasing exhaustion caused by a lack of sleep and inadequate supplies of water, the spread of dysentery was beginning to make life absolutely intolerable. Sufferers from this disease frequently need to retire to the latrines fifty or more times a day. In the particular circumstances of crowded wagons and irregular stops this was not possible and the interior of the trucks became indescribably foul. To make matters even worse, some time after leaving Prai the train was halted and all the doors were fastened from the outside. Fortunately this was for only an hour or so but at the time it seemed to be the final straw. It later transpired that the reason for this was that the railway passed close to the former British airfield at Alor Star and the Japanese were worried in case some of the prisoners subsequently escaped and provided useful information to Allied intelligence.

Soon afterwards the original border between Malaya and Thailand was reached and those still alert noticed a distinct alteration in the character of both the inhabitants and the country. Apart from the change in currency from dollars to ticals there was no practical impact for the now weary travellers, and as the train plodded on, the main topic of conversation was where and when the next meal was to be served. It came during the third night when a short stop was made near Singora and then the journey was resumed through the darkness.

The fourth day was one to endure. Even the brightest of spirits was weighed down by a combination of heat and exhaustion and the majority were content to doze quietly in whatever position caused them least pain. Some trading took place at convenient stops but the most attractive activity continued to be the acquisition of water from the locomotive whenever the opportunity presented itself. Equally desirable but more difficult to achieve was a shower, which could sometimes be managed while the locomotive was filled from a water-tower, or even a swim if the train happened to stop near a suitable pool or river. As the heat of the day gradually subsided the passing scenery received rather more attention. The interminable paddy fields were quickly finished as a topic of conversation but the more exotic sights of a temple, an elephant working, or even a passenger train loaded with prosperous-looking Thai men and women were certain objects of mass curiosity.

Towards evening the usual meal was provided and was followed by a final attempt at sleep. The best that most could accomplish was a series of brief naps punctuated by long periods of cold and despair, but as morning approached a new atmosphere of hope gradually emerged. Everyone knew that these were to be their last few hours on the train and looked with increasing interest through the half-light at what they anticipated would be their new home. The countryside was now showing increasing signs of civilization and a number of villages and small towns were entered and subsequently left, though at each one the expected end of the journey was confidently forecast. Then, at about 4 a.m., the locomotive stopped at the tiny hamlet of Banpong and the order was given to leave the train.

Throughout this nightmare of a journey Colonel Toosey had been unable to relieve the hardships being endured by his men. His repeated requests for more drinking water had been received with non-committal noises and his appeals for information had been greeted with silence. Appreciating that the Japanese *gunso* (sergeant) was making little attempt to enforce the rules so rigorously laid down before their departure at Singapore and not wishing to spoil the working arrangement that had evolved, Toosey did not press his arguments too strongly. Instead he made it his business to show himself as prominently as possible at every stop – rightly believing that the presence of a senior officer would both raise the morale of the prisoners and inhibit the activities of their guards.

On arrival at Banpong Colonel Toosey continued with this policy, making his way up and down the line of wagons on several occasions – each time urging the tired and hungry troops to unload their possessions and prepare to move away. His efforts and those of the guards were redoubled when it was noted that a party of Japanese officers had appeared and it was indicated that they wished to inspect the new arrivals. The effect on the attitude and bearing of the prisoners was miraculous. All ranks came smartly to attention to half-hear a few incomprehensible words delivered by Colonel Ishi of the new Siamese

Command and then marched off in good order through a crowd of Thais and Chinese along the main road.

Within a few hundred yards the column of troops, led by Toosey and a Japanese guide, had passed beyond the confines of the built-up area and had left behind the rows of tiny shops which, even at that early hour, were fully open for business. The enthusiasm generated by these fresh sights was lost as the POWs entered open country and the nearly exhausted men found it difficult to carry their packs and share of equipment. Fortunately their destination lay quite close and after about a mile the column turned off the main road and entered what was clearly a transit camp.

The delight with which the troops received the order to halt was tempered by the awful conditions which they saw all around. Toosey later recalled that the area had originally been a paddy field so was naturally wet and had degenerated into a sea of mud:

> The latrines were overflowing and excreta [were] flooding the camp. In the 'Hospital', which consisted of the normal bamboo huts and bed stagings, the water in some cases was above the level of the bed platforms and generally was only 6 inches below. It was full of filth and excreta of all descriptions. No arrangements had been made for our reception and in my opinion the British POW staff in the Camp had lost [their] grip and given up hope.[3]

Toosey was then informed that his party was to move on the following day, so he passed on this information to the men and told them to rest as much as possible. They then 'fell out' and struggled through the heavy mud to find what space they could in the 'atap' huts constructed of bamboo and leaves which provided the only accommodation. For the next few hours most of the exhausted prisoners were able to sleep. The conditions on the bamboo shelves along each side of the hut were extremely cramped but at least the men could stretch out fully and in their tired state they were able to ignore the many different types of bug and fly that pestered them.

By mid-afternoon many were awake – still weary, but anxious to find their way around. An essential visit to the latrines was a traumatic experience which many regarded as the nadir of the whole trip. It was basically a morass covered with flies and maggots and totally open to the general view. After this, things could only get better and even the long walk to the only well was quite a relief. This was made all the more interesting by the presence of many local people, all of whom seemed anxious to buy whatever valuables were available. In turn they were happy to supply items such as bananas and boiled eggs and these, together with the rice which Toosey had managed to extract from the camp staff, meant that all ranks settled for the night with reasonably full stomachs.

At first light a meal of rice and stew was provided and shortly afterwards the Toosey party was called out on parade. Several hours' wait then followed and although the men were allowed to 'stand easy' and eventually to sit down, no one was permitted to leave the area. The heat of the sun allied to the uncertainty gradually began to have its effect. At last, however, a number of motor lorries turned up and the prisoners climbed on board with feelings of relief. By then they had begun to realize just how unpredictable and inefficient was Japanese organization but also understood very clearly that if the transport had not appeared they would have been forced to walk as, indeed, did many of the parties that followed them.

The vehicles took the prisoners along a surprisingly good all-weather road for a distance of nearly 50 kilometres. For most of its length the highway passed through largely cultivated countryside and many small hamlets, following the wandering path of a large river. After about an hour at what appeared to be breakneck speed, the town of Kanchanaburi was reached. This stood at the confluence of two rivers and proved to be of substantial proportions, containing many brick buildings and two modern mills that were busily occupied in processing the timber which was floated down from up-country.

The convoy did not stop in the town but went on for a few more kilometres along a road that quickly deteriorated into little more than a country lane. It then pulled over and came to a halt on a site overlooking a broad river and the men were instructed to get down from their vehicles. Once they had done so the trucks quickly moved away and the party and its kit were left in an untidy line at the edge of what had originally been a clearing in the jungle but which now showed signs of human habitation.

Toosey was then greeted by a British Army officer who introduced himself as Major Roberts of the 80th Anti-Tank Regiment. Roberts told him that three weeks earlier he had brought a party of 200 men to the area and had been ordered to clear the site between the road and the river. A number of Thais had subsequently appeared and had started to construct a series of atap buildings and the prisoners had been encouraged to learn and help. It was from these local people that Roberts had discovered that their camp was known as 'Tamarkan'[4] and had understood that the river was named the 'Kwae'. (It was, in fact, the Mae Khlaung but the Thai term for river is 'Kwae' and it was this that registered in the prisoners' minds.) On 20 October a second party had arrived at the site. This consisted of 110 men of the 2nd Battalion of the Argyll and Sutherland Highlanders under the command of Captain

David Boyle and these, too, were quickly put to work improving the camp.

On looking round, Toosey could see the progress that had already been made. Five long huts were complete together with what was obviously a cookhouse and, standing a little apart, some buildings of a more superior construction, which he rightly guessed were the Japanese quarters and administration centre. However, no Japanese made their presence known at this time and the remainder of the day was spent in allocating accommodation to the new arrivals and in their familiarizing themselves with their fresh surroundings.

Once Toosey had seen that his party was fed and settled, he spent some time in discussing the situation with the two officers he had found on his arrival. His rank and inclination made it certain from the start that he would take charge and he quickly discovered that, as Roberts had recently suffered a severe beating at the hands of the Japanese, he was only too pleased to relinquish his responsibility. Toosey also found that Boyle had been held in Pudu Jail, Kuala Lumpur, from the time of his capture in late January until his move to Tamarkan a week earlier and that he had spent much of this time in learning to speak a simple form of Japanese.

Early next morning Toosey, accompanied by Roberts and Boyle, made his way to the camp office and waited outside, at attention, for the commanding officer to appear. After a brief interval a Japanese, whom Toosey knew to be Lieutenant Kosakata, came out of the building and they exchanged salutes. He then listened carefully as Captain Boyle haltingly explained that Colonel Toosey was now the senior British officer through whom all instructions should be given.

Lieutenant Kosakata then turned and spoke directly to Toosey and, as his words were translated, everything became suddenly clear to the British colonel:

Koko ni nihon no hashi o kakeru rōdōryoku o teikyo seyo.

Your task will be to provide labour to build two bridges here.

Kosakata saluted and it was clear that the interview was at an end. Toosey therefore responded and, while the Japanese officer returned to his quarters, Toosey was left to reflect on how best he could, and should, obey these orders, which were obviously against both the spirit and the letter of all international agreements. Japan had signed the Hague Convention of 1907 and the more humane Geneva Convention of 1929, both of which laid down that POWs must not be used for any tasks that would help their enemy's war effort. Although Colonel Toosey was not aware that the Imperial government had never ratified the second of these treaties and did not feel bound by it, he did appreciate that this was not a time for legal niceties. He therefore decided against making what he understood could only be an empty gesture and adopted a policy of limited co-operation which he thought would give the men under his command the best possible chance of survival.

1

Sound foundations

The Toosey family

Philip John Denton Toosey was born in Birkenhead on 12 August 1904. He was the eldest son of Charles Denton Toosey, proprietor of a successful shipping agency (Ross, Skolfield & Company) and Caroline Percy, daughter of a former governor of Dublin Gaol.

The profits from Ross, Skolfield & Co. were never enormous partly because its founder (Philip's grandfather) and later his son (Philip's father) spent a great deal of their time working and travelling on behalf of the Catholic Apostolic Church in which they were both Elders. Nevertheless, the income was sufficient, with careful management, to enable Charles Denton Toosey to live in a comfortable house in the Oxton area, bring up seven children, pay for their education and employ four inside servants and a gardener. In addition a local woman, Miss Williams, acted as a part-time governess, for Caroline Toosey believed that one of the main keys to success in life lay in education. Although Miss Williams was regarded as 'very severe', she undoubtedly provided a useful form of pre-school training. Her ideas on discipline were reinforced by the children's nurse, Ethel Kirkdale, who, although greatly loved, also believed that her charges should be kept strictly under control.

However, it should not be thought that the Toosey children were totally repressed. Philip's father was a quiet and serious man and his paternal grandmother was a typical Victorian lady with austere views on how children should behave. But his mother was essentially a happy, cheerful woman with a strong sense of humour and she and Philip achieved a great rapport. Her parents, too, were quite liberal by the standards of the time and Philip grew fond of the bearded Captain Percy who had been wounded in the Afghan War and who could tell marvellous tales of death and glory. His maternal grandmother was another kindred spirit with a casual and informal nature that was typical of her Irish upbringing. Consequently although Philip may have been in the process of acquiring a strong sense of self-discipline he was quite capable of being extremely naughty.

Philip and his father were great friends when he was young and the two frequently went on walking holidays together. But a permanent cloud was to mar their relationship and that was caused by religion. Philip's father was completely devoted to the Catholic Apostolic Church while his mother was a sincere member of the Church of England. This led to a certain rift in the family and Philip's attendance at the Protestant St Saviour's one week in four was a compromise that never really satisfied his father. This disruption never affected his relationship with his mother, although she undoubtedly regretted the regular visits made to his father's church. Clearly Caroline Toosey was an exceptional woman who, apart from managing the family budget, bringing up her children and directing her domestic staff, also found energy to pursue her particular interests in gardening and furniture. Caroline was a cultured lady with a concern for all things artistic but although she encouraged her children to follow her example in these matters her real aim was for them to equip themselves so as to be able to take advantage of whatever opportunities came their way.

Schooldays and apprenticeship

When Philip was 7 or 8 he went as a day boy to the Birkenhead Preparatory School, which was conveniently situated about a mile from his home. Then at the age of 11 he moved across the road to 'Big School'. In her quest to improve the prospects of her children, Caroline Toosey frequently discussed their schooling with her friends and although it was clear that Philip was making satisfactory progress at Birkenhead she was advised that a boarding-establishment of the right calibre would provide even greater advantages. There the matter would probably have rested but for a specific recommendation by her husband's partner who had a nephew at Gresham School and knew both its fine reputation (established under the headship of J. W. S. Howson) and (most importantly) the modest nature of its charges. The result of his suggestion was that Philip took the common entrance examination when he was 13 and at the beginning of the Michaelmas term in 1917 moved to Gresham School in the village of Holt, in Norfolk.

As in most public schools at the time, the living conditions were deliberately spartan. Each day started with a morning run and a cold shower before breakfast even in the depths of winter and there was a great lack of creature comforts. This normally austere regime was further worsened by wartime shortages of fuel and food. However, even

11

poor-quality bread, sometimes containing weevils, was welcome if one was hungry enough and Philip learned at an early stage that if the food did not suit you and you did not eat it you just went without.

When Philip had attended Birkenhead Prep he had encountered an unpleasant youth who had delighted in bullying smaller boys. Philip was eventually provoked into striking out. Fortunately he succeeded in hitting his tormentor very hard between the eyes and the bullying then ceased; Philip had learned the important lesson that it always pays to face up to difficult situations. With this attitude and background Philip found it relatively easy to adapt to the wider challenge presented by Gresham School and his growing prowess at games also helped to get him accepted by his peers.

Philip also had to come to terms with the code of discipline imposed by the school prefects, who enjoyed great autonomy and were at liberty to beat their juniors if they felt it to be necessary. Philip himself received a severe thrashing after an incident in which he 'borrowed' the changing-room blind in order to provide a sail for a boat he had purloined on a local lake. Though painful at the time the caning was not unduly resented as it was regarded as being fair and just. This was another lesson that was well assimilated, so that when Philip was in turn appointed a prefect and experienced the responsibility of power he clearly appreciated how carefully it needed to be exercised.

Philip was at Gresham when the First World War reached its climax and he had happy memories of the armistice. He was, automatically, a member of the school's Officers' Training Corps and it was there that he learned the rudiments of infantry warfare. This was, of course, taken quite seriously at the time because many of the boys went straight into the army when they became 18 – some even before they reached that age. The highspots of the war were a Zeppelin raid and the visits by uniformed old boys. But the reverse of these excitements and welcome diversions from school routine were the inevitable casualty lists that were read out in chapel each Sunday. In a closed community like Gresham where personal relationships were all-important and every boy was well known to the staff, the loss of so many promising young men cast a long shadow. The older boys realized that their time to enlist was approaching but with the optimism of youth looked more to the opportunities which this presented. Mr Howson took a different view and the rising death toll eventually led to his breakdown and early death in 1919.

The new headmaster was J. R. Eccles, who had previously been Philip's housemaster. The two had shared a great rapport and, by a strange coincidence, Eccles later turned out to be a relative of the girl that Toosey was to marry. Eccles exerted a significant influence over young Toosey throughout his school life and saw so much potential in him that in spite of relatively poor examination performances he was prepared to recommend him for a Cambridge scholarship. Philip was not allowed to accept this offer, which was always a matter of regret to him, but, in the event, he quietly followed his father's plan for him to go straight into his uncle's business. There was no discussion about his future. In those days one's elders knew best and in the difficult days of the post-war slump Philip realized that he should be grateful for a position that promised a good living and a degree of responsibility.

Thus it was that Philip was apprenticed to the cotton merchants Newall & Clayton of Liverpool, which was run by John Souter Clayton and Grierson Clayton, together with Philip's uncle, Philip Brewster Toosey. There were two other apprentices – Philip Glazebrook and Derek Clayton, son of Grierson Clayton – and together the three young men were gradually instructed in the mysteries of the cotton trade. There was no risk in this type of work but only a low rate of commission. Consequently the partners would frequently engage in both the American and Egyptian 'futures' markets and by backing their judgement would hope to secure high returns. When Philip joined the firm these gains were always sufficient to offset occasional losses but it was clearly a dangerous game.

Philip's duties as an apprentice were to learn something about office administration, to follow the fluctuations of the 'futures' markets and to walk round the Exchange with a parcel of cotton samples and attempt to sell to (usually) unwilling spinners. He was appointed, in the first instance, for a five-year period during which he was to receive a total remuneration of £150. Living at home with his parents meant that his expenses were low. Philip's main hobbies were rugby football (he played for Birkenhead Park), which cost nothing, and shooting, which, if one received the right invitations, cost very little. In fact, it would appear that money played very little part in determining his activities at this stage in his life.

As a strong-minded individual, Philip was always prepared to speak his mind if provoked. But his customary good humour was such that he could take most disagreements in his stride. It was a different matter if his integrity was questioned. On one occasion, after an incorrect telegram had been sent to America, Grierson Clayton blamed Philip and concluded by saying: 'One of us is a liar and I know it is not me!' At this Philip lost his temper. Had he made a mistake he would have admitted it, but he was sure that he had not and was not going to be accused of lying by anyone, even a partner. The ferocity of the ensuing discussion was such that it was said to have stopped trading in the Futures Market room in the Cotton Exchange. The incident resulted in Philip and the other apprentices threatening to leave the firm but the remaining partners would not accept their resignations and, in effect, reprimanded Grierson for his action.

This event was untypical of Philip's time as an apprentice, for it was really a period in which he worked hard and played hard. The only other incident that broke his routine came during the General Strike of 1926 when he, together with a gang made up of members of the Birkenhead Park Rugby Club, worked to unload the cargo from a refrigerated ship.

By and large Philip's pleasant home and family together with his sporting and social activities were sufficient to offset what he regarded as a rather mundane job. Then, as he gradually acquired more responsibility, he began to take a really serious interest in his work and with the promise of a partnership when his uncle retired felt far more sanguine about his future. Against this growing contentment developed something of a feeling that there should be more to life than just the pursuit of a comfortable life-style. He therefore decided to follow the example of many of his friends and applied to join the Territorial Army (TA).

Philip's education and connections were sufficient to ensure the necessary introduction and on 1 November 1927 he was commissioned as a Second Lieutenant in the 359th (4th West Lancashire) Medium Regiment, Royal Artillery (RA). The choice of this unit was somewhat arbitrary. It was commanded by a Liverpool businessman, Lieutenant-Colonel A. C. Tod, and as most of its officers were employed in the city they were, at least, slightly known to the new recruit. In addition, the brigade's HQ was less than two miles from the Cotton Exchange, so it was quite convenient for both the evening and weekend training sessions.

Second Lieutenant Toosey entered into this fresh activity with his customary enthusiasm. His membership of the Officer Training Corps at Gresham's School provided him with some half-forgotten experience and his interest in shooting stood him in good stead. However, he had never learned to ride and this was a major disadvantage in a battery that was only partly mechanized. Consequently his first task was to repair this omission. His other progress rapidly made him a valuable member of the unit and it was, therefore, a great disappointment to all concerned when, in the summer of 1928, he was forced to tender his resignation.

Visit to South America

The reason for Philip's decision to relinquish his new-found interest in the TA was bound up with events in Peru. Messrs Newall & Clayton had successfully operated a cotton-buying agency in Lima for a number of years but it had recently begun to make huge losses. The partners had therefore decided to send Philip out to investigate the situation so at the age of 24 he sailed from Liverpool on the PSNC's passenger liner *Oroya*.

On his arrival in Lima, Philip was met by Newall & Clayton's manager. He was then taken to this gentleman's home in the suburbs where he quickly discovered that both the agent and his wife were alcoholics. A professional investigation of the accounts uncovered faked invoices to the amount of £50,000 and as these could have been forged and accepted only by the agent he was clearly the guilty party. Philip then put a great deal of effort into reorganizing the business and was rewarded by signs of a steady improvement in profitability.

Philip made a large number of friends in Lima and spent much time in travelling round the country so that after nearly a year he felt that he was beginning to understand both his job and Peru. It was at this stage that Philip received a message from Liverpool that Newall & Clayton were in financial difficulties and that he should cease trading. A further message confirmed not only that the partners had gone bankrupt but that they had no funds to pay for his fare home. However, he was given full authority to dispose of the firm's assets and eventually, after selling the office furniture, was able to raise sufficient funds to buy a passage back to Liverpool on the *Orbita*.

The early thirties

On his arrival at Newall & Clayton's premises, Philip found that the firm was in the final stages of liquidation. He was warmly thanked for his efforts but with their own problems the partners were in no position to offer him further employment.

The fate of Newall & Clayton was typical of numerous firms who were caught out by the deepening of the post-war recession. Worse was to come, however, and the effects of the 'Wall Street Crash' were crippling investment and employment opportunities just when Philip was beginning to look for a new job in October 1929.

It was at this point that Philip's brother Arthur happened to meet Alan Tod, Commanding Officer of their Territorial unit. When he heard that Philip was back from Peru and looking for a job he suggested that he should call and see him. The subsequent interview proved to be a favourable one and as a result Colonel Tod asked Philip to work with him at Baring Brothers.

Barings were, and remain, highly respected merchant bankers. Their main business at that time was the financing of cotton, grain and other commodities by means of bills of exchange. As Liverpool was a major centre for these imports, Barings maintained a branch office in the port and Tod was their agent. Philip immediately agreed to become his assistant, for he appreciated that this was a marvellous opportunity to join a first-class firm and work with a man of 'powerful character and great integrity'.

Thus began an association that was to last for forty years. Together they were to make a formidable and well-balanced team – Tod having a keen and analytical business mind while Toosey had the imagination, ability to mix and the enthusiasm to follow all proposals with flair and panache. Philip's first six months were spent in the Liverpool office and during this time he rejoined his original Territorial unit. It was then decided that he should spend a year with Barings in London.

On his return to Merseyside in 1931 Philip moved back to his parents' home in Birkenhead. After a brief period, acting on Tod's advice, he acquired a flat convenient for the centre of the city and from then onwards spent most of his working week in Liverpool. However, he continued to use his parents' home as a base for his weekend activities, which were still largely concentrated on rugby and shooting. It was against this background that Philip was to spend his remaining time as a bachelor.

Marriage

While he had been in Peru, Philip had made the acquaintance of Kay Eccles, daughter of one of the partners of Messrs Alexander Eccles & Company who, like Newall & Clayton, maintained a cotton-buying agency in Lima. He already knew her cousin, A. S. Eccles, for both had served together as junior officers in the 59th Medium Regiment. Then, when he returned to Liverpool, he found that another member of the Eccles family usually formed part of his circle of friends. This was Muriel Alexandra Eccles and Philip's links with her brother and cousin provided useful common ground when they first met.

'Alex', as he was to call her, was the daughter of Henry Eccles (Kay was the daughter of the other main partner, Percy Eccles) and the family business was one of the largest of the Liverpool cotton firms. 'Alex' was very much part of the Liverpool social scene and she and Philip met on numerous occasions and took to attending many functions together. In time their friendship deepened and when they attended the Red Rose Ball at the Adelphi Hotel he proposed by writing on the back of the menu: 'Will you marry me?'.

The wedding took place at Christ Church, Linnet Lane, Liverpool on 27 July 1932. The young couple then set up home in a flat adjoining Sefton Park. Although this appartment was comfortable and convenient in many respects, Philip never liked it, so after their first son, Patrick, was born the family moved to a small rented house in Willaston. This had a garden but it was not big enough to satisfy Philip who, by then, was

16

beginning to take a serious interest in growing flowers and vegetables. Consequently he used the birth of his second child, Gillian, as an excuse for saying that they must look out for a larger home. Knowledge of this situation spread amongst their friends and, by chance, reached the ears of a junior partner in Alexander Eccles & Company. This gentleman's son had purchased a substantial house close to where the Tooseys were living, after becoming engaged to an American girl. The subsequent breaking of this arrangement left the son with 'Heathcote' somewhat embarrassingly on his hands so he offered it to Philip for the very reasonable figure of £2000.

Philip and his wife took only 24 hours to decide and 'Heathcote', standing in large grounds in the rural setting of Hooton, was to be their home for the rest of their lives. There can be no doubt that the acquisition of 'Heathcote' was an excellent buy from every point of view for it provided a congenial background for the Tooseys to make their lives and they were able to bring up their children in a happy atmosphere in beautiful surroundings.

Philip's own, much later, assessment of his marriage provides a valuable insight into his private feelings:

> I do not think that two people could be so diametrically opposed in character and life interests as my wife and myself. I am an extrovert, she is an introvert. My interests are catholic and very widespread; I love business, the open air, gardening, shooting and meeting people. She loves her children and grandchildren and the home which she has run in a quite admirable manner. She is a very strong character and is known to all her family as Mrs T. or 'The Regimental Sergeant Major'. We all deeply respect her. I fear I must have been a great trial to her, like a hen with a duckling when it first takes to water, but we have been married for 39 years and have had a very happy married life, even though I have been absent without leave for a large part of it.[1]

'The King's Cup'

Amidst the excitement of the birth of Gillian and the impending move to 'Heathcote' came Philip's involvement with the competition for the King's Cup. This was an annual competition aimed at finding the best battery in the British Army and was designed to improve the efficiency of both the regular and territorial units of the Royal Artillery. Under the new rule introduced in 1935 the National Artillery Association laid down that henceforth entries must be by brigade. This meant that

> the figure of merit entitling a brigade to complete in the Final was to be ascertained by taking the average of marks obtained by all batteries

in the brigade. The Commanding Officer of the successful brigade would then nominate a battery for the Final.'[2]

The 236 Battery which had been commanded by Toosey since 1931, when he had been promoted to captain, was then nominated to represent the 359th Regiment.

The final was to be shot at Larkhill on Salisbury Plain at the end of September and was to be between four field batteries equipped with 18-pounders, and the 236 Battery which operated 6-inch howitzers. As the latter weighed nearly 3 tons they were almost three times heavier than the 18-pounders and it was mainly for this reason that a medium battery had never won the competition. Major Toosey (he had been promoted to this rank in 1933) realized, therefore, that a massive effort would have to be made to offset this disadvantage and he organized an accelerating series of drills. Nothing that could be anticipated was left to chance and in the event it was this thoroughness plus the keenness of everyone concerned that won the day.

Preparations for war

The victory in the King's Cup was followed by congratulations from many sources and by a visit to London by the entire unit to receive its trophy. Philip's life then returned to something approaching normality, although the demands of two small children – the third, Nicholas, was not to be born until February 1940 – undoubtedly kept him fully occupied. This meant that there was less emphasis on the military side, although his wife still claimed that she was married to 'guns both large and small' as he continued to follow his interests in the TA and in shooting. At the same time the improvement in world trade which developed from the mid-1930s meant that Philip's role with Barings was becoming more demanding and productive. This involved a tour of South America which culminated in a lengthy stay in Brazil where he was seconded to the chairman of the Banco do Sao Paulo. The other side of this enterprise came in the way of increased business for the Liverpool office and towards the end of the 1930s it was estimated that Barings were financing over a third of all cotton imported into the UK.

There was no competition for the King's Cup in 1936 but in 1937 the 359th Regiment proceeded to West Down on Salisbury Plain with the clear intention of qualifying for the final. This they did and in the process earned the following comment from General Langhorne, the Inspector of Artillery:

I should like to say that there is no regular regiment in England that could put up a show approaching what I have seen today, perhaps one or two in India, but certainly none in England.[3]

Once again 236 Battery was the best of the four within the brigade but Major Toosey was asked by the Commanding Officer, Lieutenant-Colonel Hubert Servaes, to stand down in the overall interest of the regiment. Servaes eventually nominated 235 Battery under Major Douglas Crawford to compete for the Cup and as Hubert, Philip and Douglas were all close friends, it was to their immense relief and joy that the trophy was retained.

The winning of this prestigious award in successive years marked the 359th as one of the country's leading territorial units and, as such, it had an important role to play when rearmament began in earnest after 1937. By then the regiment was completely mechanized and had been largely re-equipped with Scammels. These were much superior to the Fordson tractors they replaced but the guns were still the same 6-inch howitzers, fitted with iron-shod wheels, with which the unit had ended the war in 1918. In an effort to simulate war conditions, a series of 'dry' (i.e. not shooting) camps was organized in 1937 and 1938 and experience was gained of living in the open air. The art of camouflage, especially against aircraft, was rehearsed with the use of newly issued nets and gradually a momentum was built up which further accelerated after the Munich crisis. This process culminated in April 1939 when the brigade doubled its strength (and thus spawned the 68th Regiment) in a period of under five weeks.

Throughout these last pre-war years Major Toosey was actively concerned with the build-up of the preparations for war and by 1939 he was spending three or four nights a week with his unit. The tempo further increased during the summer months and a hectic practice camp was held at Redesdale. Philip's battery performed particularly well, as usual, and he personally set a marvellous example by competing in, and winning, the regimental cross-country race, an exceptional achievement for a man of 35.

The regiment was ordered to mobilize on 26 August and key parties at once began to assemble at its Edge Lane depot. As more and more men arrived the scene may have appeared chaotic but the long years of preparation reduced confusion to a minimum. Officers were not all required to stay overnight at this stage and on 1 September Major Toosey and Lieutenant A. S. Eccles (his brother-in-law as well as a member of his battery) were dining at 'Heathcote' when they were recalled by telephone:

> They both had to leave at once and Toosey did not return permanently to his house for another six and a half years. It was a dramatic evening for his wife and two members of her family.[4]

2

On active service

The war in France

Early on 2 September 1939, the 59th began to move from its peacetime base to its mobilization area at Tarporley in nearby Cheshire. A wide variety of motor vehicles were used to transport the personnel and equipment, some, being modern Scammel gun-towers and others merely civilian trucks pressed into service. In practice this did not matter a great deal because the artillery dated back to 1918 and with its steel-shod wheels could proceed only at 4 m.p.h.

Thus when war was actually declared on the following day the regiment was already established at its wartime base and had started to receive additional equipment and replace its 18-year-olds with Regular Army reservists. By then the Officers' Mess had been conveniently sited at the Swan Inn and the men had been billeted at two huge unoccupied houses. The next month was spent in learning how to deal with such new apparatus as the latest '360° Director' and modern wireless sets, while the existing items were painted and greased and prepared for action. During this period everyone was extremely busy and no leave was possible for the men. In view of this, Toosey resisted the temptation to return home himself, so he kept in touch with his wife (and his firm) by telephone and she visited him several times.

The pre-war reputation of the regiment was known to have marked it out for early embarkation so it came as no surprise when orders arrived for it to move and the 359th were, in fact, to be the first TA Gunners to land in France. A small billeting group left on 24 September, two days later the guns and transport departed by road for Newport in Monmouthshire, and the main party travelled by rail to Southampton on 3 October. After a rough crossing they were landed at Cherbourg without experiencing any interference from the enemy.

The regiment then came under the command of 11th Corps Artillery and within a short time had moved to St-Jean-sur-Mayenne near Laval. There it was reunited with its transport and guns. Major Toosey had good reason to remember his brief stay at this rendezvous. While the 359th found its feet he, together with the other officers, enjoyed the hospitality of the local château, which belonged to a member of the Rothschild family. The following three days were not so pleasant for they were spent on the road, but if not exactly comfortable they were at least stimulating and the experience was to prove invaluable in the future.

The regiment had been given the task of helping in the preparation of a strong defensive position which was being constructed to fill in the gap between the sea and the end of the Maginot Line. Thus the 359th was directed into the region near Lille. Regimental HQ and 235 Battery were established at Herrin, while 236 Battery, under Toosey, was billeted at the mining village of Chemy. The troops were then required to learn how to live in the field and with the early onset of a particularly harsh winter they suffered many hardships. On occasions it was so cold that fires had to be kept burning all night so as to prevent the guns from freezing, and for long periods the movement of heavy vehicles and artillery was prohibited as the severe frost had taken much of the surface off the *pavé* roads. Nevertheless the appointed tasks had to be completed and each day parties were sent up to aid in the construction of gun pits and their supporting field works that would be large enough to cater for 6-inch howitzers. These were eventually built to such a high standard that they were extensively photographed so that they could be used as examples on training courses in England.

This period of 'acclimatization' during which most of the men slept in barns and outhouses involved a great deal of hard, physical work and considerable effort was necessary just to stay warm. In these circumstances the visit of His Majesty the King on 6 December was most welcome and gave a valuable boost to health and morale. However, it was the prospect of the Christmas festivities which aroused the most lasting interest and, in the event, these surpassed all expectations. Large numbers of gifts arrived from home and many of these were shared with the local people (especially the children) at a series of entertainments and parties. However, the highlight was to be a 'grand Christmas dinner' and to this end a number of piglets had been acquired and specially fattened.

The continuation of the 'phoney war' in the early months of 1940 saw the regiment complete the preparation of its defensive positions along the Franco-Belgian border. The main task was then to raise the unit up to the highest possible level of efficiency but as only one visit could be made by each battery to the local artillery range this involved a

21

considerable amount of repetitive and routine work. Inevitably some degree of boredom arose in spite of the pre-war training and resulting friendships which gave each man the feeling of belonging to a well-organized team. However, Major Toosey's enthusiasm and ingenuity were equal to the strain and the troops were still in good heart when, on 1 March, they moved to an industrial suburb of Lille.

The new quarters in Fives Lille provided better accommodation and more scope for sampling the excellent meals that were still to be had in the city's many restaurants and cafés. A number of courses, which included motor cycling and surveying, were then organized and the old steel-shod artillery wheels were finally exchanged for ones fitted with solid rubber tyres. These activities and the improving weather encouraged all ranks to take a more optimistic view of their capabilities and news of the German invasion of Belgium was received with ill-considered delight.

Two days later, on 12 May, the regiment loaded its guns on to railway trucks destined for Brussels and then set off to follow by road. Much of the journey was undertaken in the hours of darkness, and in the absence of lights there were a number of accidents and breakdowns. Then when dawn arrived the column of vehicles found itself to be tightly bunched with German planes frequently passing overhead. In spite of these rather frightening incidents the guns were located, safely unloaded and moved without damage or casualty to a rendezvous to the east of the Belgian capital. Major Toosey later recalled that during this process the battery received a most wonderful reception. Flowers, drink and food, indeed everything that the Belgians could possibly offer, were made available. He also remembered that this was when they first witnessed the sad sight of refugees attempting to move to safety.

The following day the regiment was instructed to advance so as to provide artillery support for Allied forces that were attempting to defend the approaches to Louvain. Its progress to the village of Berthem was accomplished with much difficulty due to the ever-increasing numbers of refugees and the general state of panic, which was not helped by the sight of numerous Belgian soldiers bicycling at high speed in the wrong direction. Major Toosey had first-hand experience of this terrifying atmosphere, for while leading his battery he accidently bumped into a Belgian HQ and found that the Regimental HQ's intelligence officer was locked up in a room having been accused of being a fifth columnist. After a great deal of persuasion in broken French, Toosey managed to prove that he was a British officer and they let him go. This was in the middle of the night and as the party came out of the building they saw a blue light flashing about 500 yards away in front of the HQ. There was an immediate panic amongst the Belgians and they said: 'There you are.

There is somebody signalling telling the enemy exactly where we are!'
At Toosey's suggestion four or five of the group – all heavily armed –
carefully stalked the flashing light only to discover that it was the
reflection of a very full and bright moon on the top of a glass frame.
Such was the existing state of mind and nervous tension!

When the 359th arrived at Berthem they found that this lovely little
village had been deserted in a hurry. The houses were empty with meals
still on the tables and the unmilked cows were making an appalling
noise. Fortunately one member of Toosey's battery had been a farm-
worker so the troops were able to enjoy a plentiful supply of fresh milk
for the duration of their stay. This, however, was not to be for long.
When it was learned that the French on the right had fallen back it was
necessary for the regiment to move quickly. Then, as vehicles and guns
pulled back towards Brussels, the unit was bombed for the first time.
This was by an aircraft flying at only tree-top level – a pattern of
withdrawal and bombing had commenced that was to last all the way to
Dunkirk.

The return journey through a nearly deserted Brussels was characterized by many scowling faces – clearly the Belgian population had not
been impressed by the Allied armies' performance – and by the need for
speed. Once across the great canal a halt was called for a meal but
before it was ready the column was ordered to move and it then
continued for most of the night until after crossing the River Dendre it
reached the village of Terwarent. Thirty-six hours later, fortified by a
good night's rest and solid meals, the regiment was again ordered to
withdraw and by 19 May was close to its original position at Ascq on the
Belgian border.

All of this activity had taken place without the 359th firing a shot or
suffering any casualties, but this situation was soon to change. On the
following day there was a forward move to Templeneuve and Major
Toosey then went into action for the first time:

My Battery had an extremely good gun position in the gardens of the
small houses surrounding [this] village and they must have been very
hard to see. None the less they were discovered because shortly we
were shelled and I had my first casualty, my best No.1 being hit in the
back by a shell splinter and receiving a very nasty wound indeed.
However, fortunately, I got him to the local dressing station and he
got back to England safely. We were fairly heavily shelled in this
position and I was very proud and pleased to note that the Battery
stood up under shell-fire very well indeed even though it was their
first experience. I went forward to my Observation Post to find out the
situation. We were at that time supporting the First Battalion the

Grenadier Guards. As I went up there was obviously a certain amount of panic. An RASC Sergeant stopped me and told me that the German tanks had broken through and they were all over the place. He then pointed out what in fact was a British [Bren gun] carrier which was simply going to its own wagon lines in an orchard and said, 'There's one of them.' I didn't tell him not to be a B.F. but made him come forward to see exactly what it was. However, as we approached the wagon lines they were heavily shelled. I do not think he thought much of my advice.[1]

The action at Templeneuve was succeeded by a withdrawal to Flers and then, on 26 May, to Neuve Eglise. This involved a night drive through (and in some cases round and round) the empty streets of Lille and along roads that were an absolute nightmare. The route was choked with masses of refugees, dead horses and abandoned French and Belgian equipment together with large numbers of somewhat elderly French troops retiring as best they could on any form of vehicle. The 236 Battery was dive-bombed several times and its Commanding Officer spent an uncomfortable quarter of an hour in a roadside ditch filled with stinging nettles. The Stukas appeared to have a kind of whistle attached to their wings and in the absence of air cover presented a frightening spectacle and noise even to trained troops.

A further brief journey saw the 359th arrive at Killem Linde where, after a night in the open, all unwanted vehicles were destroyed. The regiment now came under the command of Major-General H. R. L. Alexander (later Lord Alexander of Tunis) and his instructions made it clear that the situation was now desperate:

> When you are behind the canal, only personnel will be evacuated to England. Therefore, if owing to road blocks you are unable to get across the canal before you are surrounded, spike your guns and save your personnel.[2]

It was fully understood that the route to the sea would be extremely difficult and congested. Arrangements were made, therefore, for the second-in-command (Major Douglas Crawford), who was regarded as the best map reader, to lead the way while Major Toosey brought up the rear by motor cycle. This teamwork proved to be highly successful and the regiment got through with all of its guns so that it could take its place in the defensive perimeter that was being formed around Dunkirk. The unit was sited near to the village of Ghyvelde with 235 Battery on one side of the canal and 236 on the other, and an observation post was manned in a nearby windmill close to the HQ of the Grenadier Guards.

Both batteries then opened fire, 236 from a position in a field full of abandoned French vehicles. It was anticipated that these would give some degree of cover but in a very short time the German artillery began to drop its missiles uncomfortably close. A sideways movement of above 400 yards proved to be an effective remedy, for whenever the battery fired, the enemy continued to shell its old position. Altogether the regiment fired nearly 2000 rounds – its entire stock of ammunition – from Ghyvelde before it was obliged to move to the beach. The 235 moved first, for their site was gradually being flooded by water released from the breached dykes. Its personnel, including Philip's brother Arthur Toosey, then made their way through the position held by 236 Battery, which stayed on for a further 24 hours. Then, when the last round had been fired, they reluctantly drove their vehicles into the nearby canal, spiked their guns and started to march to the shore.

The men were so tired that whenever the column stopped for any reason they fell asleep at once and were exceedingly difficult to wake. Major Toosey realized that anyone who was left behind at this stage would have little chance of escape so when verbal abuse failed to obtain a response he resorted to the use of a shovel to emphasize his point! The net result of these tactics was that every surviving member of the battery safely completed the 10 miles to Malo-les-Bains and in spite of the most incredible confusion reached an appropriate position on the sand.

It had been originally planned that the regiment would be taken off from the Mole but this was already in the possession of a large number of disorganized French troops. In the circumstances it was decided that the best policy would be to form an orderly line and wait for space in the many small boats that were moving between the beach and the larger vessels waiting offshore. Major Toosey placed John Tilney,[3] who was the tallest officer, at the head of his battery which then waded out into the sea while he brought up the rear. For the next 2 hours the unit stood in the water, each individual getting deeper and deeper as he worked his way to the front of the queue. The fact that Toosey and Tilney kept their men under strict control encouraged the sailors to give their column some priority for they were always fearful of being overloaded or upset by undisciplined groups and the battery spent much less time in the water than many others.

It was a most eerie sight ... this long column of men standing patiently in the sea waiting for someone to pick them up. Fortunately, there was a very calm sea and a sort of diffused moonlight ... all the time there was sporadic shelling but we were so tired that we really hardly noticed it.

I suddenly realized that my good friend the Commanding Officer, Hubert Servaes, was not with us so I sent the Adjutant to find him.

He failed to do so and the CO was left on the beach for another 24 hours.

Finally, Tilney said to me that all had gone and I must come too. So I was hauled aboard what appeared to be a Thames barge already three-quarters full of water ... it was quite clear that considerable bailing out had to be done and Tilney organized it and told us to bail with our tin hats. I was so dazed that I did not get on with the job until he gave me a great thump and was told to 'Bail you bugger', so I did.[4]

It was fortunate that a determined effort was made to keep the incoming water in check, for the barge was over-full and had very little freeboard. Consequently, it reached the side of the minesweeper HMS *Llyd* with much difficulty and, as the last man climbed up a rope ladder on to the deck, it gave a final gurgle and sank. Once on board the naval ratings took Major Toosey's clothes to be dried. When they were returned he found that all the buttons had been removed for souvenirs but thought that this was a cheap price to pay for his passage. This began at about 3 a.m. and only 2 hours later they had arrived at Margate after an uneventful voyage.

Much to Toosey's surprise the troops received a hero's welcome from large crowds which cheered them all the way to the railway station. There they were quickly placed on board a waiting train and by noon had arrived at Ashton-under-Lyne, not far from their original camp at Tarporley. Every man was provided with a billet and fresh clothing but no leave was to be granted. Major Toosey took it upon himself to ignore this instruction. Instead he called the battery together and told them they could have 24 hours off to go home – Liverpool lay only 1 hour away – providing they returned without fail. By making it clear that he was the one who would suffer if there were any absentees, he placed each man on his honour and not a single one went missing.

At Margate all ranks had been able to send telegrams to their next of kin but now Toosey was free to telephone his wife for the first time. She was waiting anxiously for his call, for 236 were amongst the last of the troops to be evacuated from Dunkirk, only leaving the beaches in the early morning of 2 June. Having established the fact of his own safety, Philip then enquired about the fate of his brother Arthur, whom he had last seen when 235 withdrew, and was reassured to learn that he was already at home. Arrangements were then made for a reunion at Manchester, which lay conveniently between the family residence and Ashton-under-Lyne, and that night the Tooseys shared dinner together at the Midland Hotel. It seemed incredible that the previous evening Major Toosey had just finished the last of his ammunition at Ghyvelde.

Picking up the pieces

Major Toosey returned from his brief leave the following day and waited for further orders. These quickly arrived and as a result 236 Battery reassembled at Larkhill on Salisbury Plain and discovered that only three of its men were missing, killed or taken prisoner. The unit was then issued with small arms and after only a 24-hour stay moved on again – this time to Wimborne in Dorset. The lack of heavy weapons and vehicles meant that little useful training could be undertaken, so apart from a certain amount of guard duty there were few military tasks to be performed. Knowing the danger which usually befalls idle or bored hands Toosey organized a series of sporting events, which included cricket, swimming and golf. He also arranged for men to help the local farmers with their haymaking and as this was a time when the nation was being urged to 'Dig for Victory' much assistance was given to individual gardeners. A programme of lectures, route marches and visits to a miniature rifle range was slowly introduced but the main benefit of their four weeks' stay at Wimborne was to the battery's health and morale.

On 5 July 1940, the whole regiment left to take up its position for the anticipated invasion of Britain. At this time the 359th was divided, with the Regimental HQ and the two batteries being based at various separate locations in East Anglia: 235 were given the task of helping in the defence of a line which stretched from Lowestoft to Felixstowe, while 236 were to support the second defence line which lay inland along the course of the Cam and the Ouse. Thus Toosey found himself established at Wittlesford, near Cambridge, close to the Duxford fighter aerodrome from where Douglas Bader was operating. His battery had still not been re-equipped with their normal armament and, like the 235, had to make do with a wide variety of odds and ends including 4-inch naval guns and 6-pounders. The latter had an interesting history for they had been designed and manufactured for the navy but in 1917 had been shortened and adapted to use in tanks. They had subsequently lain in Woolwich Arsenal for over twenty years before the emergency after Dunkirk had led to an almost literal scraping of the barrel.

Major Toosey was not unnaturally concerned about the likely performance of these guns so put up an enormous block of sandbags, painted a target and invited the neighbouring 'top brass' to a demonstration. Unfortunately his first shell went straight through the sandbags and 'disappeared into Cambridgeshire'[5] so the exercise had to be called off at that point! What opinions may have been expressed by the local

27

population is not known but the performance of the weapon gave at least some confidence to their potential defenders.

An event that was later to have a dramatic effect on Philip Toosey's subsequent career and life took place at the end of July. The regiment's Commanding Officer, Hubert Servaes, was promoted and moved to a larger unit. He was succeeded by his deputy, Douglas Crawford, and in turn Major Toosey was appointed as second-in-command. The work of the constituent parts of the 359th still continued, with the main emphasis being on training and the strengthening of their sector's defences. There were a number of air raids and the regiment witnessed a little of the aerial battle which eventually ended the threat of invasion. The slight slackening of tension then permitted Toosey to attend a course at the Senior Officers' School and, on his return, he found that he had acquired an additional job.

Toosey's fresh task was to train, from scratch, the newly formed 902 Home Defence Battery at Cambridge. He took with him Captain A. I. Crawford (brother of Douglas) and three senior NCOs and, together, they set about turning these raw recruits into soldiers:

> At the start I would not allow them to wander about Cambridge in uniform because they did not look in the least like soldiers so I kept them in their barracks until they began to show some sort of shape and also we decided that we would not allow them to wear the gunner's cap badge until they had passed certain tests. It all worked very well, the only thing that went wrong was that in my enthusiasm to get them fit we all went for a ten-mile run and practically 90 per cent of the battery was lame when they got back.[6]

In spite of this particular incident the training programme went well and in the period from September 1940 to February 1941 the standard rose to an exceptionally high level. Thus when the battery completed its passing-out parade the inspecting officer warmly congratulated Major Toosey on his fine achievement. As later events were to prove, Toosey's performance had so impressed General White that he was later to offer him the command of a regiment in his division, but in the meanwhile Toosey returned to the 359th on a full-time basis.

While Toosey had been so busily and successfully engaged with 902 Home Defence Battery his own unit had moved into billets in Cambridge. This enabled him to keep in close contact with all its activities and made it easy for him to resume his duties at its second-in-command. Shortly after his return came news that the regiment was to move again, and by the beginning of March it was occupying defensive positions in East Sussex.

The batteries, now issued with 60-pounders of 1901 vintage and a

French 75-mm gun, were placed in the Polegate and Battle areas with Regimental HQ being established in Battle Abbey itself. Preparations for the expected onslaught then proceeded at a great pace and resulted in the construction of a fine network of gun-pits and observation posts. Reports of heavy enemy raids on Liverpool led to much apprehension and distress and contrasted sharply with the peace of the Sussex countryside. In these circumstances the maintenance of morale was always a problem so once the defences had been completed a high priority was given to constant training and 'war games'. During July a practice shoot was organized at Sennybridge, but by then it was becoming clear – following the German attack on Russia – that an invasion was unlikely and a sense of anticlimax gradually developed.

At this stage additional exercises and training tended to be counter-productive so they were progressively replaced by various forms of sport. As might have been expected, Major Toosey played an important role in organizing these activities and his enthusiastic participation further enhanced his reputation as an officer who really cared for, and understood, his men. These methods ensured that the 359th became an extremely fit and efficient unit and with the steady arrival of new equipment its potential as an effective fighting force gradually increased. Toosey was not, however, to see the culmination of this process, for at the end of August 1941 he received two offers of an independent command. The first of these came from General White, who was in the middle of organizing a new division and who had clearly remembered the capable artillery officer who had impressed him at Cambridge. While Toosey was considering this invitation he was approached by Hubert Servaes, his old friend and former Commanding Officer, who asked him to take over a field regiment in the 18th Division. Both offers provided equal opportunities, including promotion to Lieutenant-colonel, and it was only his affection for Servaes that was the deciding factor. The result of this decision was to have momentous consequences for Toosey – had he accepted a position with General White his entire army career and, indeed, his life would have been vastly different.

Lieutenant-Colonel Toosey's new command was the 135th (Herts Yeomanry) Field Regiment, which was based at Macclesfield. On his arrival he quickly discovered that he faced a fresh challenge of substantial proportions. The quality of the officers and men was high and included several members of the nobility and many who had occupied responsible positions in civilian life. But the unit was largely untrained and when it visited the Royal Artillery practice camp at Trawsfynydd in North Wales this became abundantly clear. It is reliably reported that during the whole of the day's firing the only things that were hit were two villages outside the range! This may have been an exaggeration but there can be no doubt that the results were extremely depressing.

Toosey's response that evening was quite blunt – he told the officers that if they could not do any better Britain would certainly lose the war. This statement was received with some degree of shock and Toosey then withdrew in silence. Later that night, however, he was invited by his officers to an informal meeting and with the aid of a bottle of port a vigorous discussion took place. The conclusion that gradually emerged was that Toosey was right, but what could be done to remedy the matter? Toosey's solution was simple. He claimed that there was no substitute for hard work and enthusiasm and when these principles were accepted he gladly agreed to a fresh start. Thereafter, under his leadership, a new spirit of co-operation and dedication developed and as a result the 135th regiment rapidly increased its efficiency.

Toosey's understanding that the 18th Division, of which his unit formed part, would soon be sent overseas lent urgency to his efforts to produce a well-trained fighting force and he dealt swiftly with anything or anybody that hindered this process.

In spite of some minor incidents the training programme and preparations for a move made great progress. This was indeed fortunate, for in mid-October, only six weeks after his taking command, the 135th was ordered to Gourock and Toosey soon found himself on board the Polish ship *Sobieski*, *en route* to an allegedly unknown destination. At the time, however, the whole unit was quite confident that it did know where it was going, for not only had its vehicles and guns been painted a sandy colour but some of its equipment had been labelled 'Basra'.

The move to the east

As *Sobieski* sailed from Scotland, Toosey gave little thought to the possible end of the voyage. The roughness of the sea and the unfamiliarity of the hammocks added to the inevitable problems caused by the need to pack his men tightly in the confined spaces available below and it took great effort to reduce the appalling confusion. Toosey, as usual, was most anxious to see to the welfare of his troops and until he had made the best possible arrangements for them he had no concern for anything else. It was only after the ship's routine had become firmly established that he was able to take a more balanced view of his surroundings.

As a senior officer, Toosey was welcome on the ship's bridge and was able to note *Sobieski's* progress to the north of Ireland and out into mid-Atlantic. *Sobieski* proved to be one of an eight-ship convoy which was escorted by two destroyers and a flak-ship. There were no incidents to cause concern and the ship's captain, with whom Toosey became increasingly friendly, laughed at his apprehension, frequently commenting: 'Soon we meet a powerful friend.'[7]

Toosey could get no more than that out of him and came to the conclusion that it was some kind of Polish joke. One morning, however, he saw an American plane through his port-hole and when he went on deck found that what appeared to be a substantial part of the US Navy had taken over the task of escorting the convoy. As this event took place before the United States entered the war, Toosey was somewhat surprised as well as delighted to see these vessels. Neither Toosey nor many other people at that time fully appreciated the extent of the arrangements that had been made between Churchill and Roosevelt to help Britain survive. One major aspect of this was the granting of lease-lend; another was the patrolling of the western Atlantic by the US Navy, and with its aid *Sobieski* and the remainder of the convoy successfully completed their voyage to Halifax on the Canadian seaboard.

Once in port the men and equipment of what Toosey now learned was the whole of the 18th Division were trans-shipped to three large American vessels. The 135th formed part of a complete brigade which was accommodated on a former passenger liner now renamed *Mount Vernon*, and after the briefest possible stay the three ships moved south along the American coastline.

Conditions on *Mount Vernon* were much superior to those on *Sobieski* and once the initial difficulties caused by a lack of familiarity with the ship and its (American) crew had been overcome the troops settled down well. This process was considerably aided by the abundance and quality of the food, and these attractions more than made up for the unaccustomed use of a 'cafeteria' system. It was appreciated that a long voyage lay ahead, so detailed arrangements were made to keep the men as fit and alert as possible. These owed much to the guidance provided by Brigadier W. L. Duke, the Commanding Officer, who ensured that training schedules were rigorously enforced. Toosey developed a sincere admiration for Duke and followed his lead with much enthusiasm. This meant that, in addition to the compulsory physical exercises undertaken by all on board, the 135th also took part in special courses designed to improve their skills as gunners. These took place on 'miniature ranges' which on Toosey's initiative were constructed out of canvas in two commandeered 'empty' spaces. They became so sophisticated that it was possible to teach men how to range and fire a gun – with a puff of cigarette smoke blown up through the painted canvas to show where the shell had landed! For a change, the same model could be used to demonstrate infantry tactics and such items as the value of camouflage and how to take advantage of the ground when moving.

31

The organization of these activities and the establishment of a daily routine took much time and concentration so the days passed quickly. Then, as the ships reached warmer climes, swimming-pools were erected on deck and the men were able to enjoy periodic, brief dips. Toosey thought that the voyage (apart from the congestion) resembled a peacetime cruise, but in spite of all effort a feeling of boredom gradually began to emerge. This was intensified when the little convoy reached Trinidad but the troops were not allowed to go ashore. Although the reason for this always remained a mystery to Toosey it was a fact of life and as *Mount Vernon* departed from the West Indies it was he and his fellow officers who were left with the task of maintaining morale. The only favourable factor in this respect was that HMS *Exeter* – victor of the Battle of the River Plate – joined the convoy at this time and her presence was to remain a valuable reassurance on the long journey which lay ahead.

The general belief that the 18th Division was destined for Basra led to a universal expectation that Cape Town would be their next port of call. This indeed proved to be the case, but before it could be reached the troops had to endure a further month of increasingly wearisome travel. The crossing of the South Atlantic seemed to last an interminable time to men who were cooped up in hot and crowded quarters for most of the 24 hours and then, just when the sighting of the African coastline gave some promise of relief, came news that Japan had entered the war.

Japan's entry into the war

Until the middle of the nineteenth century Japan was an isolated and largely feudal country. For several centuries successive emperors had been little more than figureheads; real power had been exercised by various hereditary shogunates. At the beginning of the seventeenth century the Tokugawa shogunate established a stable political system that continued with only the smallest of changes for over 250 years. This was achieved by sealing Japan off from the rest of the world, imposing extensive controls and stifling all innovation.

The basis of the shogunate's authority lay in its traditional military strength, which was not challenged until a US naval squadron under Commodore Perry arrived in 1853. The shogunate was not able to resist the American demand for port facilities, and other western powers were quick to follow. This intrusion engendered a bitter debate between the isolationists and those who wished to see Japan open to the outside world.

The matter was finally resolved in 1867 when the Tokugawa regime was overthrown by a coalition of *samurai* who restored the monarchy under the 15-year-old Emperor Meiji. His government planned the complete modernization of Japan's armed forces and of her political, economic and social institutions, using western nations as models. In 1889 the Emperor granted a constitution giving legislative powers to a two-chamber parliament, although he retained supreme command of the armed forces. A dispute with China over Korea in 1894 resulted in victory for Japan's westernized forces. The Chinese were forced to accept Korea's independence and to cede Formosa (now Taiwan) to Japan. Ten years later Japan fought Russia and gained a decisive victory on land and sea. This gave Japan control of Korea, which was annexed in 1910, as well as many concessions in Manchuria.

The death of Emperor Meiji in 1912 ended a reign that had transformed Japan into a modern industrial state. During the era of the Emperor Taisho (1912–1926) which followed, Japan emerged as a Great Power. In return for naval assistance to the Allies in the First World War, Japan acquired Germany's colonies in China and the Pacific, and concessions in Shantung. Her troops also occupied eastern Russia after the Revolution. In addition, Japan gained immense economic advantages from the war. Her manufacturers were able to replace most of the items still imported into Japan and to fill many of the gaps that opened up in the Asian and African markets. They were even able to sell to the western nations.

Once the war was over, however, Japanese exporters lost most of these gains. Despite considerable economic progress through the application of modern techniques, Japan was hit hard by the world economic depression. Increased food prices, a rapidly expanding population and growing unemployment led to mounting social and industrial unrest, which was intensified by the Tokyo-Yokohama earthquake disaster in 1923.

During the early 1920s Japan had adopted a more conciliatory diplomacy, but some Japanese, especially the military elements, thought this policy unlikely to secure the rights and interests regarded as essential to Japan's development, and they wanted to extend Japanese influence and power on the Chinese mainland. Japan's economic problems were exacerbated by the world slump of the 1930s. Her overseas trade, on which she was so dependent, was so reduced by western tariffs that she could not afford to pay for essential raw materials. This increased the determination to create an overseas empire. The early years of Emperor Hirohito (who succeeded to the throne in 1926) saw a constitutional recession in which army leaders and extreme nationalists used the Emperor's traditional divinity to minimize the parliamentary liberalism encouraged during the Taisho era. The government was unable to prevent the occupation of Manchuria by the army in 1931 and political assassinations pushed successive cabinets to the Right until by 1936 those who believed in military expansion were effectively in control. To satisfy Japan's needs for food and raw materials, they sought to establish the so-called 'Greater East Asia Co-Prosperity Sphere'.

The Japanese also had a number of grievances against the West: they disliked the fact that, under American pressure, the British had terminated the Anglo-Japanese Alliance in 1921; they resented the prohibition on further immigration into the USA from 1924; and they were dissatisfied with the results of the Washington Conference and the London Naval Treaty (1930), which prevented Japan from achieving naval hegemony in her own waters. Combined with increasing American and British criticism of Japan's aggressive foreign policy, this encouraged a move towards Italy and Germany, which was formalized in 1936 when Japan joined the Anti-Comintern Pact and rescinded the Washington Naval Treaty.

In 1937 Japan invaded China, and during the next two years she occupied all the major ports and most of the larger cities, although she lacked the power to push the conquest home. It was at this point that the USA realized that the Japanese threat to world peace should be taken seriously. Because US materials were used in the war with China, the USA restricted exports of scrap iron and oil in 1940. This policy was strengthened after Japan joined the Tripartite Pact with Germany and Italy in September. The defeat of France in June 1940 provided Japan with the opportunity to establish military bases in French Indo-China, and this induced the USA, Britain and the Netherlands to place a total embargo on the sale of strategic materials in July 1941. This meant that Japan was at an important national crossroads as she had only 2 years' supply of oil and no alternative sources.

Japan had only two real choices: withdrawal from South China and Indo-China as the condition for any agreement with the USA to lift sanctions, or seizure of the remainder of South-East Asia in order to make her 'empire' self-sufficient. The first option was felt to involve a national loss of prestige. As the military and naval authorities virtually controlled the government (General Tojo, former war minister and leader of the military clique, became prime minister in October 1941), it was decided that war with the USA, Britain and the Netherlands was a price worth paying to acquire the resources of their wealthy colonial possessions. The decision was also influenced by the assessment that Russia was unlikely to intervene, that the Dutch colonies could expect no reinforcements, and that Britain had little to spare for the Far East (although there were signs of reinforcements from India and Australia). Most of all, however, Japanese thinking was influenced by what proved to be a correct belief in the fighting spirit of their men and by their ultimately wrong assessment of the Allied will to win. It was fully understood by those in authority that America's vast industrial capacity gave it a military potential that Japan could not hope to match in any long war. Therefore they concentrated on plans for a short war or, more realistically, for a brief period of conquest while Japan was strong and the Allies weak. This, it was expected, would give Japan time to assimilate and develop her new acquisitions behind a defensive perimeter that would be constructed many thousands of miles from the homeland. These calculations rested on the assumption that American public opinion would not relish the casualties that a long-range campaign across the Pacific would inevitably involve and that a compromise could be reached that would enable Japan to retain most of her gains.

Thus it was that on 7 December 1941 Japan declared war on the United States, the Netherlands and Britain. A surprise attack on the main US naval base at Pearl Harbor in Hawaii took place before the Japanese Ambassador in Washington was able to hand over the official notification. The element of surprise enabled the Japanese to eliminate the American battleships (though they missed the aircraft carriers, which were out of port) and they thereby secured immediate command of the sea. On the other hand this single act of 'treachery' united the American nation in a way that nothing else could have done and from that moment the United States became grimly determined to defeat Japan and her allies, Germany and Italy.

At approximately the same time as Japanese planes were leaving their carriers to bomb Pearl Harbor, Japanese forces began to land in Thailand and Malaya. Britain had made strong diplomatic efforts to preserve her traditional friendship with Thailand and had hoped that she would be able to maintain an armed neutrality if war broke out. With a strong Japanese army on the Indo-Chinese border, Britain did not expect active help from Thailand but thought she would oppose any attempt to cross her territory. This was, in fact, the position until just before the invasion, but then a Japanese ultimatum finally convinced a divided cabinet that the only alternative to co-operation would lead to a bloody defeat and the status of an occupied enemy.

The consequence of this last-minute decision to co-operate with Japan was that the landings were totally unopposed in Thailand and there were no casualties. The 5th Division and the HQ of the invasion force came ashore at Singora and Patani and, with a speed that was to mark all their future operations, were quickly *en route* for the Malayan border. One other consequence of the Thais' change of policy was that a relatively small group of Japanese infantry was enabled to cross the Kra Isthmus and capture the British airfield at Victoria Point in Lower Burma. Thus from the very beginning of the campaign a key point on the air route from India was knocked out and, in addition, Japan had acquired another airfield for her own use. This added considerably to the difficulties of the defenders of Malaya.

The Japanese plan was to put part of their 18th Division (known as Takumi Force) ashore at night near Kota Bharu. These beaches were well defended by infantry and artillery, and the RAF made a number of determined sorties from the local airfields. There was no Japanese air cover and although the RAF were only equipped with a few Hudsons and with ancient Wildebeestes they inflicted considerable damage, sinking one transport and damaging two others. However, RAF losses steadily grew and as these could not be immediately replaced their attacks became less effective. Sufficient Japanese then got ashore to push back the defenders and after the failure of a series of counter-attacks it became necessary for the now outnumbered British troops to withdraw to avoid encirclement. Only superficial efforts were made to destroy the three airfields in the area, partly due to an element of panic, and within a few days the enemy had them fully operational. Japanese casualties had amounted to only 179 killed and 314 wounded. With the benefit of hindsight it is now clear that part of the difficulty in opposing the landing at Kota Bharu was that the British Command was convinced that the main threat would come from the north. Thus many of its best troops were not available to fight the initial landings either in Malaya or in Thailand.

Japan's earlier acquisition of facilities in Indo-China was now destined to play a significant role in events. The Imperial Guards Division crossed the Thai border and after occupying Bangkok moved south by rail. On the way it secured a number of Thai airfields and these, supplemented by those already captured near Kota Bharu, provided valuable forward bases for planes flown in from Indo-China. Thus the combination of existing airfields in Indo-China and the co-operation of the Thais played a large part in getting the invasion off to a sound start and in ensuring early Japanese air superiority over northern Malaya. The bases in Indo-China were soon to make another vital contribution which had a direct impact on the subsequent war at sea.

Until the summer of 1941 the British government thought that there was little immediate chance of a war in the Far East. Consequently the Home Front, the Middle East and, after the German invasion, Russia were all given higher priorities than Malaya for most essential items. Winston Churchill was partly aware of the weaknesses there, but in the special circumstances of the time he felt that he would have to rely on the presence of the US battle fleet at Hawaii to act as a deterrent. Nevertheless the increasingly aggressive attitudes of successive Japanese governments convinced Churchill that something ought to be done and

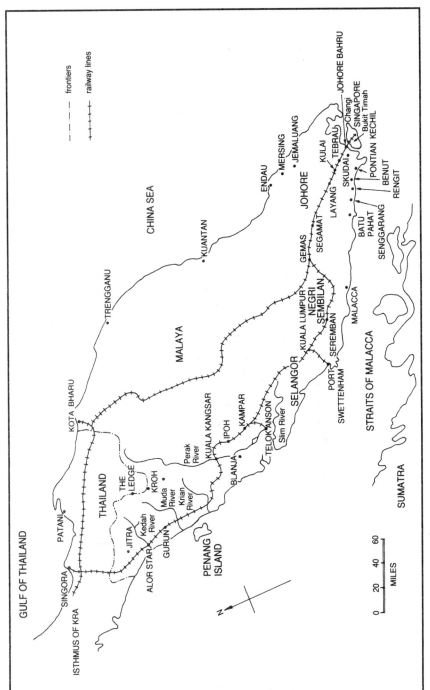

Map 1 : The Japanese Invasion of Malaya

37

he hit upon the idea of sending a small but powerful naval force to show the flag. The idea was consistently opposed by the Admiralty who wished to use the vessels as the nucleus of a much larger fleet that would be based in the Indian Ocean. However as this could not be expected until 1942 and as Churchill needed a gesture at once, he forced the Admiralty to accept his view. As a result *Prince of Wales*, *Repulse* and *Indomitable* were ordered to the East.

On 2 December 1941, the two battleships, *Prince of Wales* and *Repulse*, arrived at Singapore but the aircraft carrier *Indomitable* was delayed after running aground in Jamaica. The two capital ships were still lying in harbour when the Japanese attack came six days later, so their commander, Admiral Phillips, decided to make a surprise raid to try to catch the transports while they were still unloading. Without *Indomitable* Phillips had no air cover but he thought he would be in no danger while off the Malayan coast, where he expected RAF support. Just before he sailed it was realized that this cover would be difficult to guarantee owing to mounting losses of aircraft and the destruction of the northern airfields. Phillips was advised accordingly but, apparently having a low opinion of Japanese capacities, he decided to accept the additional risk.

All that night and the following day the ships made their way up the east coast of Malaya but when that evening they were spotted by Japanese reconnaissance planes Phillips turned round and headed back to Singapore at top speed. This would have got them back to safer waters by daylight but at about 1 a.m. a report was received that the Japanese were trying to land at Kuantan. The vessels were immediately diverted but when they arrived at 8 a.m. it proved to be a false alarm. Phillips then reset course for Singapore but was spotted two hours later. The returning flotilla was subsequently attacked by thirty-four bombers and fifty-one torpedo-carriers based in Saigon and both *Prince of Wales* and *Repulse* were quickly sunk. Fortunately their four escort destroyers were not damaged and they were able to save 2081 of the 2921 on board the two ships. This disaster was to give the Japanese total command of the seas round Malaya. Thus, after only a little over 48 hours of hostilities, the invaders had taken over southern Thailand, secured a landing in Malaya and obtained control of both the sea and the air. This had devastating consequences on morale, for the demonstration of how Japanese efficiency could triumph over British mismanagement suggested that further unpleasant shocks lay ahead.

3

The Malayan campaign

The Japanese landing

The Japanese campaign in Malaya planned for a general move down the peninsula until the prize of Singapore could be seized. This task was to be undertaken by the Japanese 25th Army, under General Yamashita.

At the end of the First World War the battleship was still regarded as the undisputed ruler of the seas. Thus if Britain wished to protect her interests in the Far East she needed a base, complete with all facilities, from which her fleet could operate in safety. The growth in the size and complexity of vessels meant that in 1920 the nearest place which satisfied these requirements was in Malta, so it was decided to construct a major dockyard at Singapore. At that time any possible threat would have been from the sea so a series of forts equipped with 15-inch and 9-inch guns were planned. The dockyard and the forts had been completed by the outbreak of the Second World War and these defences were to be completely successful in deterring an attack from the sea (see below, pp. 64–5). During the 1920s and 1930s it had been gradually appreciated that the rapid improvement of the aeroplane was causing a new situation to emerge. As a result, a series of airfields were constructed throughout Malaya so that offensive operations could be mounted against an enemy fleet or invasion force and also to provide an air defence in depth for the base at Singapore.

However, at a time when Britain was heavily engaged in actual warfare in other parts of the world, the potential threat to Malaya had necessarily to be given a lower priority. Consequently the army that had been gradually assembled in the Far East was largely made up of units and formations whose chief asset had been their availability. Moreover, while the army's original brief was merely to assist in the sea defences of Singapore its role subsequently increased to include the protection of the new RAF airfields in the peninsula as well. This inevitably meant that most of the available units had to be dispersed over the whole of Malaya. Once the Japanese had acquired bases in Indo-China, the strongest possible force was also required on the Thai border.

Lieutenant-General A. E. Percival, appointed as General Officer Commanding Malaya in May 1941, was the man who had to decide how best to counteract these potential threats. He regarded the threat from the north as the most serious and with the inadequate men and equipment at his disposal would have dearly loved to have been able to move into southern Thailand and oppose the Japanese if they attempted to land at Singora or Patani. Then, if this had failed, he would have had the consolation of being able to fall back on a natural defensive position – known as 'The Ledge' – which lay some 35 miles inside Thai territory.

Unfortunately, political considerations made this type of action extremely difficult. Britain was still hoping that the Thais would continue to resist Japanese pressure and was also aware of the likely effect on American opinion if she were the first to breach Thai neutrality. However, the military facts dictated that a British force would need at least 24 hours' notice if it were to forestall a Japanese landing on the Thai coast. Thus it appeared that the advantages and disadvantages of the proposed 'Operation Matador' were so finely balanced that it was eventually agreed that a final decision should be deferred. In the meanwhile the 11th Indian Division was ordered to make all the necessary arrangements for the move forward but told to act only on the direct instructions of the Commander-in-Chief, Far East, Sir Robert Brooke-Popham.

On 6 December 1941, two Japanese convoys were sighted by aircraft in a position that made it obvious that they were heading for southern Thailand. When Percival heard this news he anticipated that 'Matador' would be launched and he ordered the 11th Division to a high state of readiness. However, Brooke-Popham took the view that the convoys might have been about to change course for Bangkok and he decided to wait for confirmation. This was delayed by bad weather and did not come until the afternoon of the following day, by which time it was too late to forestall the Japanese landing. A great opportunity had, therefore, been missed and inexplicably, orders to Krohcol (which was made up of Federal Malay States' Volunteers) to occupy 'The Ledge' were delayed so long that the Japanese reached it first.

While the Commander-in-Chief was hesitating (perhaps for sound political reasons) to act, the 11th Division remained on standby for 48 hours in extremely wet weather. They were then ordered back to their original position at Jitra and began to re-establish themselves in what had become a deeply waterlogged defensive system. This was obviously going to take some time, so two units of Punjabis and Gurkhas were sent forward to delay the forthcoming attack. However, with the aid of their tanks the Japanese were able to drive straight through both of these formations and they were almost totally destroyed. The consequence was that the Japanese tanks came up against the main position far quicker than had been anticipated and this was in no state to resist a serious thrust. The tanks were halted but during the following night the Japanese infiltrated the defences and successive counter-attacks failed to dislodge them.

With the Japanese obviously preparing for a major offensive and with the 11th Division in disarray it was then decided to withdraw. It was thought that the defences might hold for a short time but the risk of the division being overwhelmed was regarded as being too great. The timing of the move was then influenced by the rapid advance of the Japanese force that had reached Kroh, via 'The Ledge', which was threatening to cut the division's communications with the south. Thus the retreat began at midnight on 12 December, and amidst great confusion and with immense losses of men, stores and equipment the 11th Division retired behind the Kedah River.

In many respects the battle for Malaya had already been lost. The ability of a small Japanese advance guard together with a company of tanks to drive a complete division from its long-prepared positions in less than a day caused great loss of confidence amongst the defenders. In addition, the 11th Division had been seriously weakened, so the situation on the western side of the peninsula was clearly grave and practically all of the troops that were then available in Malaya would have been needed to stabilize this front. While it was recognized that the main threat would have to come from this direction, General Percival was too concerned about the dangers of Japanese action elsewhere to agree to a concentration of his forces. What was still regarded as the overriding need to defend the airfields thus prevented the only realistic strategy from being adopted. The result was that formations such as the 9th Division, based in eastern Malaya, played no part in the early, decisive, fighting and the Japanese were able to deal with the British and Commonwealth units on a piecemeal basis.

The premature but incomplete demolition of the bridges over the Kedah River then gave the defenders further problems. A quantity of valuable vehicles and equipment had to be abandoned on the northern side and the Japanese had a weak point on which to concentrate. During the next day two battalions of the Gurkhas successfully fended off a series of minor probes but, in view of the disorganized state of most of the division, a second successive overnight withdrawal was arranged. This brought the troops back approximately 20 miles to Gurun where a combination of natural features meant that any further advance would have to be on a narrow front. No defences had been prepared at this point but it was expected that there would be at least some interval during which these could be improvised before an attack developed. However, the failure to complete the destruction of the bridges over the Kedah, plus the efficiency of the Japanese engineers, enabled enemy tanks as well as infantry to reach Gurun just as the last of the British units got into their positions (see Map 1 on p. 37).

These circumstances then led the commander of the 11th Division to suggest a major change of policy. Major-General Murray-Lyon's current experience of the Japanese Army and his direct knowledge of its capacity and tactics had led him to the belief that his men were too tired and inexperienced to continue with a series of frequent, short retreats. He recommended, therefore, that the whole of III Corps be withdrawn and regrouped with fresh units in an area to the south of Kuala Kangsar where they could not be outflanked by Japanese advancing from Grik. His corps commander, General Heath, agreed with this assessment but General Percival thought that such a long retreat would be damaging to both military and civilian morale and refused to give the necessary orders. It was for the same reason that Percival and, later, Major-General F. K. Simmons, Fortress Commander at Singapore, refused to allow the construction of defences in rearward areas. Events then took the course anticipated by Murray-Lyon. On 15 December the Japanese broke through the line at Gurun and the 11th Division was forced to undertake precisely the style of barely controlled withdrawal that their commander had been so anxious to avoid.

The rapid pull-back of the land forces from northern Malaya then led inevitably to a decision to abandon Penang. Few arrangements had been made in advance, so while some installations were destroyed many others, and vast stocks of material, were left undamaged. Of particular importance was the failure to sink or disable the large numbers of local craft that had been deserted by their crews, for these were to be of great help in enabling the Japanese to outflank the defences further down the coast.

Because the withdrawals were all under pressure the defenders had little opportunity to settle into new positions before they were again under attack. Thus only a day after the 11th Division had moved behind the Muda River it again withdrew – this time to a fresh site on the Krian River which appeared to offer a good obstacle against tanks. These defences were not, however, to be tested, for the imminent danger of being cut off by the further advance of the Japanese via the Grik road then forced a general move to positions behind the Perak River. This was completed by 23 December, on which date the airfield at Kuala Lumpur was evacuated by the RAF. Thereafter the

III Corps was to suffer even more from the Japanese domination of the skies.

The army's defence of northern Malaya had been complicated by the danger of being outflanked by Japanese troops moving over the mountains from the east. Once behind the Perak River this manoeuvre was no longer possible, so the tactics of the Japanese were changed. From this point onwards they aimed to supplement their major attacks down the trunk road with amphibious operations along the western coast. Until this stage the Imperial Guards Division had done little more than occupy southern Thailand and secure its airfields, but now these fresh troops were used to support the main thrust and also to take part in the seaborne operations. The Japanese plan had provided specialized landing craft which, after being landed at Singora, had been moved across the Kra Isthmus; the addition of the vessels acquired at Penang meant that these operations could now be on a much larger scale.

After a two-day lull the Imperial Guards Division came into the attack and forced the defenders back from Ipoh and Blanja into semi-prepared positions at Kampar, where they immediately came under pressure from the now rested 5th Division. This was successfully resisted but the situation had to be reviewed when a Japanese landing at Telok Anson could not be properly contained. Fears that this force might cut its communications then led to a further withdrawal and the defenders retired to the Slim River. The Japanese followed up with their usual speed and put in a major attack on 7 January. Partly through faulty dispositions but mainly because of the extreme fatigue of the defenders the Japanese tanks and infantry were able to force their way right through the centre of the position. Such, indeed, was the rapidity of their advance that they were able to seize the bridge over the river before it could be destroyed. In turn, this meant that the 11th Division was practically eliminated as a fighting formation for, apart from a large number of dead and wounded, its losses included over 3000 men whom the Japanese took prisoner.

The extent of the defeat at Slim River allied to a Japanese landing further down the coast at Port Swettenham ensured that a lengthy retreat would have to follow. In the first instance it was decided to fall back to Seremban, 30 miles to the south, and this left the way clear for the enemy to occupy Kuala Lumpur. The existence of extensive road networks in Selangor, Negri Sembilan and Malacca were thought to favour Japanese tanks and tactics so it was not considered possible to provide an effective defence in those states. Consequently the withdrawal was continued into northern Johore with the remnants of III Corps passing through Segamat on 12 January. In effect the Japanese had taken over all of northern and central Malaya in only five weeks. The following day the 53rd British Infantry Brigade – advance guard of the British 18th Division – including Lieutenant-Colonel Toosey, arrived in Singapore.

Toosey's war

Philip Toosey was on the bridge of *Mount Vernon* heading across the Atlantic when word was received that the Japanese had attacked Pearl Harbor and Malaya. Although it was clear that the American fleet had been taken by surprise and had suffered heavy losses, the immediate reaction was summed up by the captain's remark: 'You are all right now we are in it – we shall win the war.'[1]

A wave of optimism swept the ship, which was based partly on a real understanding of the industrial – hence military – potential of the United States and what was to be proved to be a false assessment of the capacities of the Japanese. Subsequent, almost immediate, news of the sinking of the *Repulse* and *Prince of Wales* was greeted with dismay and some degree of disbelief and reports of other Japanese successes were regarded with considerable scepticism.

These doubts and uncertainties were rapidly forgotten when *Mount Vernon* arrived at Cape Town a few days later. The warmth of the welcome was overwhelming – the local people just turned up at the port in their cars and took everyone home for meals and entertainment. After the rigours of wartime Britain and the confinement of the ship, South Africa seemed a different world. There was an abundance of everything and although the convoy was in harbour for only 2 full days many of the men, including Toosey, were given quite extensive sightseeing tours. Toosey also attended a briefing given by the South African prime minister on the progress of the war. General Smuts made it clear that the Japanese had achieved many initial victories and warned that many more defeats were to be expected. But he stressed that now that the United States had been forced to join Britain and Russia there could be only one end to the conflict.

It was with these thoughts very much in mind that Toosey resumed his journey up the eastern coast of Africa. This proceeded without incident until the ship reached a point somewhere off the coast of Madagascar. The vessels then stopped and, after a longboat from HMS *Exeter* had transferred the Commodore to another ship, *Mount Vernon* headed east at her maximum pace. It was then made known that orders had been received for the liner to make its way independently to Singapore while the remainder of the convoy – including its escorts – were to proceed to a port still to be decided in India.

It later transpired that the selection of *Mount Vernon* for this perilous voyage was due to her great speed and to the fact that she was carrying a complete brigade that was capable of operating as a separate fighting force. This meant, in practice, that the authorities in London were able to give their hard-pressed troops in Singapore and Malaya some immediate support without necessarily committing the whole of the 18th Division. As this division was one of the very few Allied units then actually at sea, the conflicting claims of India, Burma and Singapore needed to be carefully weighed. The independent dispatch of *Mount Vernon* thus appeared to be a sensible compromise which offered many advantages. Equally, however, it was an extremely dangerous tactic, for if the liner had been sighted by enemy forces her only weapon would have been her speed and a major disaster could easily have occurred.

The safest route lay to the south, but with the news from Malaya remaining consistently bad there was a desperate need for haste. Many risks, therefore, had to be balanced but in the event *Mount Vernon* successfully achieved a rapid and safe voyage. There was little that the troops could contribute at this stage but Brigadier Duke kept them busy with anti-aircraft, fire and boat drills. He also took over Toosey's miniature ranges and used them to provide practice in general manoeuvres, particularly concentrating on those concerned with retreat and withdrawal. These measures may have helped to occupy the mind and pass the time but when the ship made its first landfall with the islands of Java and Sumatra on either side everyone became extremely tense.

They passed through the Sundra Strait without incident but as they came out on the other side the captain's comment was not encouraging: 'Boy, did you hear that door clang behind us?'[2]

The remaining 24 hours of the trip were certainly the most hazardous of all but a combination of good luck and good timing, allied with heavy rain and low clouds, enabled *Mount Vernon* to reach Singapore without damage. A major air raid was in progress as she docked but the poor visibility kept her safe. Unloading began at once and within a very few hours all her troops were ashore and stores and equipment were being discharged at a tremendous rate. It was 13 January 1942. By nightfall the 53rd Brigade together with the 6th and 30th Anti-Aircraft Regiments and the 85th Anti-Tank Regiment were all securely established in their respective camps. Toosey and the 135th Field Artillery came ashore in a tropical deluge and were taken to a rubber plantation at Nee Soon between the port and the causeway linking Singapore to the mainland; they did not quite know whether to bless the storm that helped them to evade air attack or curse the rain which gave them such an uncomfortable introduction to the East.

After a miserable night, which he could do little to alleviate, Toosey received a visit from Brigadier Duke (Commanding Officer of the 53rd Brigade) and was instructed to attend a conference at the 28th Indian Brigade at 12 noon. This meeting resulted in an offer to supply his unit with its full quota of guns from the Singapore 'pool' but it was stated that only a limited number of towing vehicles could be provided. Suggestions were then made that the remainder of the 135th should be used as infantry but this idea so appalled Toosey that he made something of a fuss and was eventually able to secure a miscellaneous selection of gun-towers (including municipal dust-carts) that brought his regiment up to full strength.

Several days were then spent under conditions of great difficulty in adapting these vehicles and in preparing the guns for action. The weather had improved considerably but the 135th's situation in a damp, dull and green 'hide' was not helped by its closeness to Sembawang aerodrome – air raids on this major target meant that the regiment frequently received a large number of near misses.

While these essential tasks were being completed and the unit brought to fighting fitness Toosey received orders which attached his formation to the 11th Indian Division. The 135th was then given the job of supporting the 28th Indian Brigade whose function was to act on the mainland as 'flank guard' on the west coast of Johore. Toosey immediately arranged for himself and his three battery commanders to undertake a reconnaissance that was designed to familiarize them with the ground. To his surprise he found that there was little evidence of prepared defences so it was necessary to reconnoitre suitable gun positions. This was quickly and, in the circumstances, efficiently accomplished and time was found for ranges to be marked utilizing the milestones already in existence on the road.

Toosey's instructions were to deploy his batteries at various intervals along the coastal road which stretched back to Batu Pahat from Pontian Kechil. On 24 January he moved his headquarters to Pontian Kechil where the 11th Division had established its advance HQ the previous day and then sent one troop forward to occupy a position at Senggarang. Although the 1st Section arrived safely, the 2nd Section was ambushed on the outskirts of the village and most of its members were either killed or wounded:

> I [then] went up [towards] Senggarang myself to see what was going on and on the way three Japanese soldiers dashed across the road. I let them have the full contents of my tommy gun but unfortunately missed. This was a great pity; it was a simple crossing shot like at a hare.[3]

The road into Senggarang was found to be blocked and although an attack was mounted by one of the 135th's troops it could not be cleared.

The remainder of the unit then retired back to Rengit having suffered its first real casualties – one officer and one other rank had been killed, four other ranks were wounded while two more were missing. Toosey found this incident to be particularly distressing, for the officer concerned was Peter Bolt whom he knew well, as his home was at Hoylake on the Wirral; he had died on his 21st birthday.

Early next morning, 26 January, Colonel Toosey attended an emergency conference at Benut. This was addressed by General Key (Commander of the 11th Indian Division) who explained that the 15th Indian Brigade, together with a large number of wounded, had withdrawn from Batu Pahat to Senggarang. An enemy force, the same that had ambushed the 135th the previous day, was preventing any further retreat and although the able-bodied might be able to work their way back through the jungle this option was clearly not available to the sick and injured. It was decided, therefore, that an attempt should be made to force the road from the south, and a scratch unit under Major C. W. S. Banham – one of Toosey's battery commanders – was quickly assembled for this purpose.

The only troops that were immediately available consisted of five armoured cars of the 3rd Indian Cavalry, a section equipped with two guns from the 135th and 100 infantrymen of the Norfolk Regiment who had just arrived from Singapore that morning. The column quickly made its way from Benut to Rengit and then moved on towards the north. In a short distance it came under heavy fire and, without tanks, was not able to get through a series of road blocks which had been constructed from fallen trees and captured vehicles. The mission had to be abandoned but Major Banham, who was in a bren-gun carrier, decided to carry on and after a number of miraculous escapes eventually reached Senggarang without serious injury. He was then able to provide the 15th Indian Brigade with accurate information about the enemy's dispositions, which was later to be of considerable help in aiding some of the troops to slip past the Japanese and, although in a distressed condition, over 1200 were able to make their way back through the jungle to Benut. Another large part of the brigade missed its way and after coming up against an unfordable river was obliged to move towards the coast, which it reached at a point near Rengit. With the aid of a small boat a message was passed to HQ at Pontian Kechil and 2700 men were subsequently evacuated by sea to Singapore. The wounded could not, of course, be moved and had to be left under the protection of the Red Cross. However, the Japanese troops ignored this international symbol and many patients were killed where they lay. Their padré, Lieutenant Duckworth, who had stayed behind, did survive and he was later to become a great friend of Colonel Toosey after both had become POWs.[4]

While Major Banham was making his way through the Japanese road blocks to Senggarang, the remainder of his small column came under ever-increasing attack by superior forces. The two guns provided by the 135th were sited on either side of the road and under the direction of Lieutenant Raynor inflicted heavy casualties on the advancing enemy. However, as the action progressed the Japanese were able to work their way round to the rear and eventually the British troops were forced to disperse. The bulk of the men were then successful in finding a way back to Rengit through the jungle, but Lieutenant Raynor was killed at this stage and the two guns had, of course, to be abandoned.

Later on 26 January, Rengit itself was attacked. Toosey went forward with Brigadier Duke to investigate the situation, which proved to be so unfavourable that he was given immediate orders to prepare for a phased withdrawal back to Singapore. By the 28th this plan was in operation: one of the batteries was back on the island and Toosey's second-in-command was already selecting the most appropriate positions for the coming defence of Singapore itself. On the following day, when the remainder of the regiment were preparing to leave Pontian Kechil, a heavy attack suddenly developed. The guns of the 135th played a significant role in repulsing the enemy at this point but fear of being cut off from the rear then led to a series of retreats. By this time, Toosey and the Gurkhas with whom he was working had achieved some understanding of Japanese tactics, so together they devised a system which appeared to offer the best hope of slowing down the enemy and of making him pay the highest possible price for every advance.

A main feature of the Japanese invasion had been the rapidity of its operations. British troops attempting to disengage and regroup were barely able to break off contact and take up new positions before the enemy was on them again. Traditional delaying tactics such as the demolition of bridges, construction of road blocks and employment of rearguards did not seem to work. This was because the Japanese advance units were only lightly equipped and had the ability to move quickly through difficult country. Their instructions were to go round any strongpoints or batteries – leaving these to be dealt with by following troops – and to press forward by any means that came to hand. With the aid of almost total air superiority and the availability of abandoned supplies, these methods had worked well but they did mean that the forward formations were taking serious risks – it was Toosey's hope that the plan he had adopted would take full advantage of their vulnerability in becoming overstretched and temporarily outnumbered.

Following the loss of Pontian Kechil, the co-operation of the 135th and the 2/2 and 2/9 Gurkhas was put to the test. The positions they successively occupied had been previously selected but there had been no time to undertake physical preparations. So far as possible they were sited at the southern end of forest clearings so that when the Japanese emerged from the north, usually on bicycles, they presented an easy target for the regiment's 25-pounders. Then, once the initial thrust had been stopped, most of the guns were withdrawn to the next position with only one or two retained to deceive the enemy. These tactics proved to be quite successful in the circumstances, a large number of Japanese were killed and the pace of the advance was restricted to more manageable proportions. In addition, the reduction in the number of haphazard and unscheduled moves resulted in some limited relief for the already tired troops. Even so, they remained under constant stress, for the tactics employed by Toosey meant that as many as four moves a day were sometimes necessary.

While Toosey's tactics were enjoying some minor success, the cutting off of the 15th Indian Brigade and its loss as a fighting unit was now beginning to have serious consequences. Percival's plan for the defence of Johore had been overruled by Wavell, who had been placed in charge of all Allied forces in South-East Asia on 29 December 1941. His revised strategy made Westforce responsible for opposing the enemy's advance along both the coastal and central highways, while the smaller Eastforce was given the task of holding the lighter attacks which were anticipated from troops that had been landed at Endau on the east coast.

It is now generally agreed that Westforce's dual role imposed unnecessary strains without providing any compensatory benefits. Consequently it now appears that it would have been better to have had two separate commands, as Percival had originally intended, each with its own specific job to perform. This, in itself, was only a contributory factor to the rapid loss of Johore, but as it forced Percival to spend up to 18 hours a day in conferences and travel it was hardly conducive to the reaching of rational decisions.

A principal reason for the failure to delay the Japanese was certainly the faulty disposition of the available units. Thus, while those in the centre were able to hold the trunk road with some degree of comfort, insufficient troops were allocated to defend the coastal route. In the event, therefore, these forces proved to be far too weak to cope with the frontal attacks launched by the crack Imperial Guards Division and were in no position to deal with the continuing threat of amphibious landings in their rear.

The inevitable result of these arrangements was that the units protecting the west flank were always under attack by superior numbers. There was constant pressure for them to retire or to risk the danger of encirclement either via the jungle or from the sea. However, any retreat down the coastal highway meant that the whole central position on the trunk road would be undermined. Consequently decisions to withdraw were delayed until the last possible moment and sometimes, as in the case of the 15th Indian Brigade, the orders came too late and the entire formation was cut off. The remaining troops on the west coast, including the 135th and the Gurkhas, were not strong enough to do more than retire in a rapid though reasonably controlled manner. This, in turn, meant that the remaining troops of both Westforce and Eastforce were in danger of being isolated from Singapore, so it became necessary to organize a general retreat back to the island.

Once it was clear that the battle for Johore had been lost, the overriding priority was to evacuate the defenders in such a way that they would remain as fighting formations and be immediately available to play a full part in the forthcoming struggle for Singapore. The plan which was then put into operation was largely determined by the pattern of the road and rail networks that converged at a point just to the north of Johore Bahru, at the mainland end of the causeway. This lay-out made it essential to synchronize a withdrawal along each of the four routes – three roads and one railway track – which led to the south. For these tactics to succeed it was vital that the road junction at Skudai and the road-rail interchange at Tebrau be held until the last moment, for all of the retreating troops needed to pass through one or both of these strategically placed towns.

In the event the plan worked extremely well. The only blemish was the loss of the 22nd Brigade of the 9th Division, which was cut off at Layang while retiring down the railway and was subsequently destroyed while attempting to withdraw through the jungle. On the credit side, however, Eastforce was able to move back in such a controlled manner that it had time to organize an ambush on the road between Mersing and Jemaluang. This inflicted so many casualties that the Japanese 55th Regiment abandoned the pursuit and by the evening of 30 January the last of the 22nd Australian Brigade had crossed the causeway back into Singapore.

It was originally intended that the remaining units of Westforce would cross to the island on the night of the 31st, but increasing pressure from the Japanese 5th Division led to a change of plan. As a result, the withdrawal was timed so that the 8th Brigade and the 27th Australian Brigade broke contact at Kulai on the morning of the 30th and then followed the last of Eastforce back to Singapore. The remnants of the 11th Division continued to hold the road crossing at Skudai until all the retreating units had passed through, and then they too, accompanied by Toosey and the last battery of the 135th, retired across the causeway. The rearguard, provided by the Argylls, quickly followed and a naval demolition party then exploded a large charge which was designed to put the causeway out of action for as long as possible.

The attack on Singapore

The Island of Singapore on which Toosey now found himself has been said to resemble the Isle of Wight in both size and shape. It extends for 27 miles from east to west and has a depth of 13 miles from north to south. The Straits of Johore which divide the island from the mainland vary in width from a maximum of 5000 to a minimum of 600 yards. The causeway, which had provision for both road and rail traffic, crossed the water at one of the narrowest points.

Apart from a small group of low hills near the centre, the island is generally flat and during this period the rural areas were almost entirely covered with various kinds of plantation. Thus it was thought that any advantage which the Japanese may have possessed as 'jungle fighters' in parts of Malaya was not likely to be repeated in the more open ground on the island. On the other hand this type of terrain was more suitable for tanks, with which they were well equipped; the Japanese are thought to have landed 90 medium and 100 light tanks during the initial landing in Malaya.[5] The defenders faced a further problem in that the naval base was situated close to the causeway and so was a likely early target for any Japanese activity. The base was an important focus for both service personnel and civilian workers, but the vast majority of the local inhabitants lived in the city of Singapore. This was situated in the south-west at virtually the furthest distance from the causeway and in peacetime it had a population of about half a million. However the advance of the Japanese down the Malayan peninsular had led to a huge number of refugees moving into the city and within a month it had almost doubled in size.

The protection of the naval base was, of course, the prime concern of the British authorities. This was originally conceived in terms of an attack from the sea and a 20-mile stretch of permanent beach defences were constructed along the southern coast during the late 1930s. In 1938 it was decided to establish a number of north-facing positions in Johore but progress was only at an early stage when, following the fall of France, the Japanese acquired bases in Indo-China. It was then decided that the defence of Singapore would be best served by the holding of a line near the Thai-Malayan border and so the work in Johore came to a premature end.

Once it became clear that the Japanese could not be held in the far north, attempts were made to recommence the construction of the Johore defences. At the same time, consideration began to be given to ways in which the northern coastline of Singapore Island might be defended. Priority had, of necessity, to be given to the work in Johore and this, plus the difficulty of obtaining labour, meant that very little was actually achieved on the island itself until early in January 1942. By then the threat of a direct attack across the Straits of Johore was fully appreciated and great efforts were subsequently made to provide the maximum amount of labour and materials. Consequently considerable valuable work was accomplished in the 4 weeks which remained before the Japanese presence on the Malayan side of the straits made further construction impossible.

The earlier neglect of the northern coastline was compounded by natural factors. Much of this region consists of mangrove swamps and includes many tiny rivers and indentations from the sea, which meant that it was extremely difficult to build fixed fortifications. The water-table was too high for effective trenches to be dug and the waterlogged ground made land-mines unpredictable and unreliable. Nevertheless every effort was made at this late stage to repair previous omissions and although these were only partly successful in a physical sense, the plans which were prepared did help to make the most of the limited resources still available.

As a result of these preparations, decisions had been made for the allocation of the forces on the island and much progress had been made in such matters as the siting of gun positions, the locating of stores and arrangements for the setting-up of the appropriate administrative, communication and logistical networks. Thus as soon as Toosey and the remainder of the 135th had crossed the causeway they moved to pre-selected sites from where it was intended to support the 11th Division, which was to remain under the command of General Key. These forces, in fact, occupied the 'central' sector, just to the right of the causeway, while the 27th Australian Brigade covered the area immediately to their left and the 22nd Australian Brigade continued the cover along the coast to the west.

The batteries of the 135th were placed in rubber plantations, which were to provide such effective concealment that they were never located by the Japanese. Toosey established his HQ in the dockyard area close to that of the infantry and then selected points from where his observation posts (OPs) could provide the maximum amount of information without being too vulnerable to enemy fire. Forward positions were sited at the water's edge but the main OPs were placed in a water-tower and in an uncompleted block of flats which overlooked the causeway.

By 3 February all the preparations that could be made had been completed. By then the batteries were well dug in and efficiently organized and had registered all their likely targets. Toosey's command was then strengthened by the addition of the 21st Mountain Regiment. This included two batteries of light guns and four 6-inch howitzers and its OP was sited on a high hill which gave a magnificent view over the straits. Although this position was continually being shelled, Toosey decided to visit it at once. He found that, while the approach was extremely dangerous, the post itself was entirely safe as it was underneath a huge lump of granite. Toosey found that the personnel were all Sikhs, with the exception of one white officer, and that morale was rather low:

I asked them if they had done any firing and they said 'No' which seemed to me quite ridiculous so I pointed out a target to them – a large municipal building in the centre of Johore Bahru on the other side of the Straits and told them to have a go. They hit the roof with their third shell. The shell went through the roof and burst inside; there was a beautiful ring of smoke. This completely restored their morale and when I left they were roaring with laughter.[6]

The next few days were spent in making final preparations to resist the forthcoming attack. As usual this was not to be long delayed:

On the 5th of February the mass of Japanese artillery came into action. The Japanese said afterwards that it was the greatest concentration of fire ever laid on by the Japanese. Our guns replied with vigour. Outstanding in courage was Lieut. Colonel Philip Toosey, the commander of 135 Field Regiment. Whenever things were hottest he would be found, whether it was at an observation post, a section emplacement, or somewhere where his communications had been broken. He took no rest and his example was an inspiration to all ranks. Toosey was awarded the D.S.O. for his conspicuously gallant leadership. Wavell asked Key to send his congratulations to 135 Field Regiment.[7]

The Japanese barrage was followed by a series of minor probes designed to test the island's defences. One of these led the Australian artillery – on Toosey's left – to over-react, and all of their gun positions were revealed. This had the effect of concentrating the Japanese fire onto these sites and after a lengthy period of heavy shelling a number of the Australian gunners were found to have withdrawn. This, in turn, meant that the Australian infantry at this point received no cover when they were exposed to further, continuous, fire from the enemy and a number of units appear to have left their positions. According to the official British historian, a large proportion of these troops were absolutely raw and inexperienced and many had only just arrived in

Singapore. Their action was, therefore, understandable but it had the direct consequence of weakening the already well-extended Australian line.

An authoritative Australian account of these events stresses the severity of the Japanese barrage which, according to Lieutenant-Colonel Varley, was worse than anything he had experienced during the First World War in France.[8] The softness of the ground helped to keep casualties to what was considered an acceptable level but the continuous bombardment made it impossible for satisfactory communications to be maintained. This, it was thought, was the major reason for the Australian artillery's failure to respond to the Japanese landings and for the subsequent confusion amongst the defenders, which led to many unauthorized withdrawals.

The whole truth of this unfortunate episode will never be known but it is certain that, even before the enemy crossed the straits, contact between the Australians and the Indian troops on their right flank had already been lost. When General Key learned of this development on 8 February he instructed Toosey to give what support he could to his adjoining sector. This was not an easy task, for it meant that some of the guns of the 135th had to shoot over their 'left shoulders' but in spite of the difficulties a harassing fire was maintained. General Key also began the process of moving some of his 11th Division troops over to fill the gap but little actual movement was possible before the Japanese landed in strength on what had become a lightly defended part of the Australian front.

The following day saw the 135th engaged in heavy shelling on its predetermined targets, which included the straits and the gap which had been blown in the causeway:

> We sank a sampan trying to get across. We also spotted a Japanese Engineer reconnaissance party of 18 which was having a look at the gap in the Causeway to see how large it was. We had registered this gap as one of our targets and let them have a couple of rounds from the whole regiment. All but one disappeared and were never seen again: one single man was seen swimming back to Johore Bahru. However, such is the courage of the Japanese that very shortly afterwards a second reconnaissance party came out and they were dealt with also.[9]

However, it was not possible for the 135th to continue with these tactics, because they were quickly ordered to fall back to reserve positions. These sites did enable some of the original targets to be covered, but a second move then put most out of range. These withdrawals were necessary in order to avoid being cut off by the advancing enemy and were the price which had to be paid for the failure to hold the assault on the coast itself. Little blame should be attributed to the Australian troops for allowing this situation to develop, for it is quite clear (with the benefit of hindsight) that their units were not strong enough to prevent the Japanese from securing a footing.

In essence the problem was that, as General Percival could not be sure where the Japanese would attack, he felt obliged to disperse his troops along the entire coastline. In retrospect this can be seen to have been a mistake, particularly as Percival took this policy so far that he failed to retain sufficient units to act as an effective central reserve. This meant that he was unable to respond quickly enough to the initial landings. Percival did attempt to remedy this situation after the invasion had started but was frustrated by the speed of the enemy's movements and by difficulties of communication. The latter was also a fundamental cause of the loss of the vital Woodlands-Kranji area at the island end of the causeway, where the faulty tactics adopted by General Gordon Bennett were compounded by the lack of suitable intelligence at critical moments.

The successive withdrawals of the 135th meant that by 10 February the regiment was back in positions near Nee Soon. Toosey was then ordered to support an attack that was to be made by the 8th Indian Infantry Brigade. Their target was 'Hill 95', which overlooks the causeway. The action was completely successful. However, the infantry were forced to vacate the hill during the night and this left some of the batteries in danger of being cut off. The following day was spent in extracting the forward gunners from their exposed situation and this was accomplished only with considerable difficulty. At the same time the regiment was heavily engaged in responding to requests for support and a total of 7000 rounds were fired during the 24 hours. This already busy day was further complicated by a series of orders directing the 135th to new locations. As these had to be continually modified because of the confused nature of the fighting, it was not until late that night that all of the batteries were finally settled on fresh sites.

During the early part of 12 February an enemy attack on the road junction at Nee Soon was delayed with the aid of concentrated fire provided by the forward batteries of the 135th. However, the overall military picture was such that the defenders were soon under threat from Japanese forces working their way behind the flanks, and a general withdrawal again became necessary. The 135th were then allocated positions in what was to become the final perimeter around Singapore City, but because of the chaotic situation on the roads most of the batteries were not able to reach their destinations until well after dark. Thus the following morning the 135th was in a state of disarray and badly needed time for reorganization. Toosey jumped into this task with his customary enthusiasm so that by noon a number of guns were again in action. The regiment then received instructions to support the 8th Indian Brigade, so Toosey quickly established a forward HQ on the Serangoon Road near Woodleigh, only a couple of miles from the city.

Having successfully survived this crisis Toosey was summoned to Divisional HQ that same night. General Key informed him that he had been selected for evacuation so that his experience could be used elsewhere:

> I could not really believe my ears but being a Territorial I refused. I got a tremendous rocket and was told to do as I was told. However I was able to say that as a Territorial all orders were a subject of discussion. I pointed out that as a Gunner I had read the Manual of Artillery Training, Volume II, which says quite clearly that in any withdrawal the Commanding Officer leaves last.[10]

Toosey felt strongly that this was an ill-thought-out order, for he was concerned with the effect on his men if their Commanding Officer walked out on them. His refusal was eventually accepted and it was agreed that one of his battery commanders would go in his place. Major O. H. Daltry was then nominated and made his way to the docks. There he was badly wounded, losing an eye and a foot, and it was not possible for him to proceed.

With this distraction behind him Toosey returned to the task of maintaining the fighting efficiency of his troops and during the whole of 14 February his batteries were continually in action. By then his leadership was badly needed, for it was becoming clear that hostilities could only end in Japan's favour. Singapore was being constantly bombed and shelled – the latter being especially effective because of the use of an observation balloon – and civilian casualties were extremely high in the congested city area. Toosey saw this at first hand for his batteries lay close to coolie lines where thousands of Malay and Chinese refugees were living. Toosey was also aware of the problems being caused by broken water-mains and knew that a decision to destroy all intoxicants had already been made. As he understood that this was to avoid any possibility of a second 'Nanking Incident' (over 150,000 civilians had been killed by the Japanese forces which occupied the city of Nanking in 1937) he fully appreciated the gravity of the situation.[11]

It was against this background that Toosey was to experience the worse incident of his wartime career. This began when Battery Quarter Master Sergeant Cluff of 499 Battery reported to forward HQ with what amounted to an ultimatum from the Japanese Command. It appeared that Cluff had been captured with the 'B' Echelon of his unit which, for

Philip Toosey being congratulated by Alderman F. T. Richardson, Lord Mayor of Liverpool, after winning the King's Cup, 3 October 1935. Second right is Brigadier Servaes (then Major).

U.S. Transport *Mount Vernon* c. 1941.

SS *Sobiesky* photographed on a previous voyage during a visit to Dakar in Senegal.

Prisoners unloading attap for hut building.

A typical Thai 'pom-pom' river boat.

Water Transport on the River Kwae: Thai river craft at Banpong.

The river base at Thakanum.

The Wooden Bridge, the first bridge over the River Kwae, with the Steel Bridge in the background, c.1943.

The Steel Bridge over the River Kwae after its completion in May 1943.

The two bridges – the upper, the steel – taken late in 1943.

A Japanese group at Nong Pladuk, c.1944.

Korean guards at Nong Pladuk, c.1944.

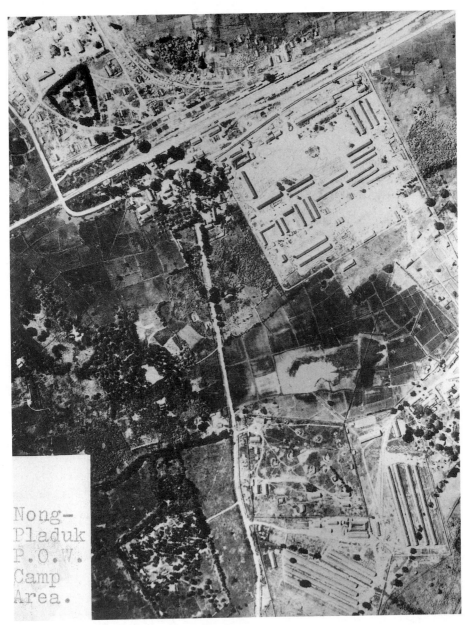

Nong-
Pladuk
P.O.W.
Camp
Area.

The POW Camp at Nong Pladuk, c.1944.

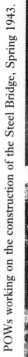

POWs working on the construction of the Steel Bridge, Spring 1943.

Japanese system of constructing wooden bridges.

Air attacks on the Kwae bridges: Bombs falling on the Steel Bridge.

The attack on 24 June 1945.

A ground view of the damage.
(taken by Col. Toosey's batman, A. E. Osborne)

An aerial view of the damage.

Locomotive C 5631, the first to travel the completed Kwae railway.

Locomotive C 5631 is now preserved at the Yasukuni Shrine, Tokyo, as a memorial to all who helped to build the Thai–Burma Railway.

Ren-ichi Sugano in 1942.

Yoshihiko Futamatsu in 1943.

Sugano and Futamatsu after the war.

Blasting through rock.

A cutting through rock at the 217km point.

Constructing the track: Surveying the route.

Moving rock by hand.

The viaduct at Wampo.

The joining of the tracks from Nong Pladuk and Burma at Konkuita on 17 October 1943.

The completed track. 'Hell fire Pass' at Kanyu.

Raised track through the tropical rain forest.

Mr Boon Pong.

Mr Lee Soon.

US Pilot Carl Fritsche.

David Boyle in 1982.

Teruo Saito in 1934.

Saito on horseback in 1939.

Saito at Toosey's grave in 1985.

Saito with Patrick Toosey (eldest son of Colonel Toosey) during his visit to Liverpool in 1985.

Colonel Toosey after the War: At the 1973 National Reunion of the FEPOW in London with Ted Coffey, Chairman of the London Branch, and Lady Toosey, centre.

Toosey talking with the Rt Rev. Stuart Blanch, Bishop of Liverpool, at the FEPOW Remembrance Parade, Liverpool, c.1970.

Heading the North West Region FEPOW at the 1964 Remembrance Parade, 1964. He was then President, National FEPOW Association. Front left is Steve Cairns (Parade Marshal, Manchester FEPOW), followed by Captain W. D. Harris (Bolton FEPOW). Behind Toosey, centre, Leslie Lever, Lord Mayor of Manchester. Front right, Major A. Burt-Briggs (Blackpool, FEPOW), followed by Jimmy Gardiner (Newcastle FEPOW).

some unknown reason, had never received orders to withdraw. After being tied up for the night Cluff was handed the ultimatum, marched at the point of a bayonet some way down the road, and then instructed to walk on and deliver the message.

The ultimatum consisted of a threat to kill the other ten prisoners and raze Singapore to the ground if the defenders did not surrender within 24 hours. Cluff was then dispatched to the Divisional HQ of the Royal Artillery, who questioned him and then sent the document on to Malaya Command. Toosey never learned of any further official action but he soon heard of the fate of the prisoners. Once the 24 hours had elapsed, all were tied to trees and shot or bayoneted according to rank.

This account was brought back by two survivors who arrived at separate times and who had no opportunity for collaboration. The first escaped unhurt, having worked loose his bindings, while the second (who arrived later) had been bayoneted and left for dead by the Japanese concerned.

Sunday 15 February began with the customary sound of heavy gunfire and bombing and, apart from the increasing signs of disintegration, there was no particular indication that the day was to mark the end of the fighting. So far as the 135th was concerned it was still business as usual and the batteries continued to provide support for the 8th Indian Brigade until the early afternoon. By then ammunition was beginning to run out and it proved to be impossible to obtain the supplies which had been anticipated. At the same time, rumours of an impending armistice began to circulate around the 11th Divisional HQ to which Toosey had moved his administration that morning. At 1500 hours it was confirmed that negotiations were taking place and half an hour later orders were received to destroy all guns, vehicles and technical equipment.

These instructions were immediately carried out to such good effect that a piece from one of the guns flew through Divisional HQ, narrowly missing Brigadier Rusher, commander of the Royal Artillery. The orders were, in fact, subsequently countermanded and the regiment was asked to resume firing. This was not, of course, possible so there was a period of consternation until the surrender order was confirmed. In the meanwhile Toosey took the precaution of withdrawing his forward HQ and all observation officers were pulled back. Thus when the cease-fire took place at 1830 hours the regiment was concentrated in a way which it was thought would best enable it to cope with the uncertain days which lay ahead.

Reflections on defeat

The responsibility for ending the struggle fell on General Percival and until the last minute he was undecided which course to adopt. He was under heavy pressure from both Churchill and Wavell and fully appreciated the need to 'buy time' so that defences elsewhere could be strengthened. He was also well aware of the likely consequences if the enemy launched a major attack which might reach the inner portions of Singapore City. His resolution to resist, irrespective of the consequences, was finally undermined by the opinions of Heath and Gordon Bennett and by a lack of knowledge of the Japanese Army's real strength.

Yamashita's diary underlines the last point very clearly:

My attack on Singapore was a bluff – a bluff that worked. I had 30,000 men and was outnumbered more than three to one. I knew that if I had to fight long for Singapore, I would be beaten. That is why the surrender had to be at once. I was very frightened all the time that the British would discover our numerical weakness and lack of supplies and force me into disastrous street fighting.[12]

While it is now certain that the Japanese were short of ammunition and water and that their troops were nearing exhaustion, there can be no doubt that the assault forestalled by the cease-fire would have gone ahead:

I had the pleasure of interrogating General Yamashita in private in October, 1945, the day before his trial. He told me then that had Percival not capitulated on the afternoon of February 15 he was intending to launch a final attack on Singapore City with three divisions. Had that attack gone in half a million citizens of Singapore City would have shared the fate of those of Nanking and Hangchow.[13]

Thus it would appear that Percival did make an accurate assessment of the situation and then made the correct choice. The question that concerned the many thousands who became prisoners as a result of his decision was rather how such an untenable position had been allowed to develop in the first place.

It could not be argued that Britain had no warning of Japanese intentions. As early as 1936 a translation of Ishimaru's *Japan Must Fight Britain* had appeared in English[14] and during the following year Major-General Dobbie (GOC Malaya at that time), aided by the then Lieutenant-Colonel Percival, had produced an almost exact prediction of the campaign subsequently followed by the Japanese in 1941. However, as Britain had originally envisaged, and prepared for, a direct, naval assault, plans for defence were based on the premise that a powerful fleet could be sent to relieve Singapore within a short period. The outbreak of the war in Europe and the fall of France in 1940 made this policy impracticable and it was decided to rely on air power. However, the demands of the home and Mediterranean fronts prevented any substantial reinforcements being sent to counter what was, after all, only a potential threat.

The net effect of these developments was that although the RAF had been given the prime responsibility for defence it had not been supplied with the equipment to cope with its task. The Conference of Commanders at their meeting in October 1940 had asked for 582 modern planes to be allocated for the defence of Malaya, but this had been reduced to 336 by the Chiefs of Staff in London. The diversion of aircraft, including 200 Hurricanes to Russia, in the period June–December 1941 meant that even this revised target had not been reached by the outbreak of war. In fact the RAF had only 158, mainly obsolescent, planes when the Japanese attack commenced and of the 110 of these that were based in northern Malaya only 50 were still serviceable by the evening of the first day. Thus, after the first few days the RAF was not able to provide much in the way of air cover except over Singapore itself. The RAF had expected to face unfavourable odds. What really caused consternation was the technical excellence of the Japanese pilots and the superior quality of their planes. Only the few Hurricanes which arrived towards the end of the fighting could approach the Zero in speed and overall performance, but by then they were too late to combat the overwhelming numbers and experience of the Japanese. At sea the early loss of its only two capital ships meant that, thereafter, the Royal Navy was permanently outnumbered and it could give little effective support to the ground forces. The Navy also suffered throughout the campaign from Japanese air supremacy and practically its only success was in protecting the convoys that brought reinforcements into Singapore.

In these circumstances the army was obliged to carry virtually the whole burden of the defence. The Japanese superiority in the air and at sea was mainly based upon overwhelming numbers (although the technical excellence of their aircraft came as an unwelcome surprise). This was not the case on land, for their 25th Army consisted of only three divisions (5th, 18th and Imperial Guards), with the 56th standing by in reserve in Japan. At first sight the Allied land forces commanded by Percival were quite impressive, but the reality was rather different. Although they numbered almost 140,000 at the outbreak of war, the majority were almost entirely without experience and many of the Australian and, particularly, the Indian troops were raw and had received very little training. In some cases they were scratch units that had never worked together before. They had the further disadvantage of being divided into four main groups (Australian, British, Indian and local volunteers) and in the time available these had not coalesced into a coherent fighting force. In addition, the defenders included large numbers of non-fighting personnel, such as administrators, technicians and ground crews (it was estimated that only half the troops were armed). Although substantial reinforcements arrived during the course of the battle, these too included a high proportion of untrained and non-combatant troops, so that the army under Percival was no nearer to becoming a cohesive and balanced whole. The invading Japanese Army, on the other hand, was a totally professional, integrated and balanced force made up of seasoned, battle-hardened veterans of the war with China. In practice, the Japanese used only 35,000 men during the campaign and the reserve was not needed.

Amongst the reinforcements which reached Percival was the British 18th Division. This had been at sea for 11 weeks, so was aptly described as 'fit but soft'. The 53rd Brigade, including Toosey, arrived on 13 January and were able to play a useful part in the fighting at a time when the issue was still in some doubt. The remainder of the division did not reach Singapore until 7 February and, while *en route*, serious consideration was given to the possibility of diverting it to Rangoon. In Alanbrooke's opinion the rejection of this proposal sealed the fate of Burma while making no real contribution to the survival of Singapore. Indeed the troops concerned paid a heavy price during their subsequent long years of captivity. A post-war view of these events can be seen from a letter to *The Times* which is reproduced in the Appendix on p. 209.

The army, lacking both sea and air support, was forced to rely almost entirely on its own resources and these, too, were woefully inadequate in many respects. The main deficiency was a complete lack of tanks during the whole of the fighting in Malaya. A light tank squadron did arrive from India with the 18th Division at the end of January 1942, but this was too small and ill-equipped to have any impact on the battle for Singapore. This meant, amongst other things, that the first time most of the Indian troops saw a tank it was a Japanese one that was attacking them. The tragedy was that, while the Far East was starved of tanks, large quantities were simultaneously being sent to Russia.[15] The British did have a number of bren-gun carriers which had the manoeuvrability of the tank but lacked sufficient fire power and armour to deter experienced opponents. They also employed some armoured cars but as these were confined to roads and tracks they were not effective in many areas.

On the credit side the quality and performance of the British artillery were recognized to be high. The difficulty here was that there were not enough anti-tank and anti-aircraft guns of the right types. The army was also well-equipped with motor vehicles and most units were completely mechanized. Unfortunately this meant that they tended to be confined to a road network which was not very extensive in parts of the peninsula. The availability of motor transport also had the effect of encouraging the carriage of excessive quantities of spares and stores. This was in marked contrast with the Japanese who travelled light and proved to be much more adept at improvisation and in living off the country. Even allowing for the inexperience of the Allied troops and for their lack of equipment, they should have been able to delay the Japanese for much longer. However, the requirements of the original strategy meant that the army could not concentrate its forces as the tactical situation demanded. According to General Heath, the requirement to defend the Malaya airfields 'disposed the Army in ridiculous fashion'. Had the RAF been fully equipped this might have been a price worth paying, but in the event the airfields were constructed for the use of the Japanese, and the army was fragmented to no useful purpose:

> The continual dispersion of the army garrison in order to defend airfields which could not be used was therefore not warranted. Percival continued to attempt to deny the Japanese the use of airfields instead of concentrating his forces to meet the main enemy thrust, which from the moment the Japanese had landed at Singora and Patani could clearly only be made down the western side of the peninsula.[16]

The Japanese campaign was aided by a series of meticulous schemes which were produced by a team led by Colonel Masanobu Tsuji, the Chief of Operations and Planning Staff of the 25th Army. These were based on impeccable intelligence reports and included the provision of detailed maps which enabled the smallest tracks to be utilized. The importance of maintaining supply routes was also recognized and, in order to deal with the problem of damaged bridges, local sawmills were clearly identified. The 15th Regiment of Engineers always kept twenty trucks loaded with heavy beams and planks and with the aid of the maps produced by Tsuji these were easily replenished during the course of each fresh attack.[17]

The work of their engineering regiment was another vital factor in the Japanese success. The speed with which obstacles were removed or circumvented prevented the Allied forces from enjoying any breathing space between engagements and, as a result, they were always kept 'off balance'. It was anticipated that the maintenance of supplies would also become more critical as lines of communication lengthened with every advance. Great efforts were, in fact, necessary to attempt to keep up with the demands for ammunition, but the task of providing fuel and food was considerably eased by what became known as 'Churchill's rations'.

This term was used by the Japanese to describe items of whatever description that had been abandoned by the retreating Allied forces. These included very large quantities of rifles, machine-guns, mortars and artillery which could not subsequently be replaced. Of even greater importance to the Japanese was that there 'was no necessity for us to transport even one bag of rice or tin of gasolene', so that the entire carrying capacity could be devoted to providing ammunition for the attack on Singapore Island.

However, it was the airfields that the Allies appeared to neglect most. Last-minute attempts at demolition proved to be so ineffective that the Japanese were able to repair them and have them ready for service in half a day. At Alor Star the Japanese were even more fortunate:

> We pushed forward with the advance party heading towards a large paved aerodrome which I had observed during my trip in the reconnaissance plane before the outbreak of hostilities and unexpectedly found that it was scarcely damaged. Here a gift of bombs piled high, and moreover in one of the buildings hot soup was arranged on a dining room table. Among the surrounding rubber-trees one thousand drums full of high-grade 92 octane petrol were piled up. About noon that day our planes successfully made their first landing at Alor Star. Completing their preparations that evening, one squadron of fighter planes and one squadron of light bombers pushed forward and carried further our brief attack over the heads of the retreating enemy, using the enemy's abandoned gasolene and bombs.[18]

The Japanese subsequently captured all four of the large airfields in Kedah Province. These were virtually undamaged and were much better than the bases which had been hurriedly built in southern Thailand. It was this factor which, according to Japanese sources, was decisive in enabling them to secure immediate air superiority.

The effectiveness of British demolition improved after the disastrous first days during which many major bridges were left in easily repairable conditions. Great emphasis was placed on the destruction of the railway system but in spite of heavy damage the Japanese engineers were able to make temporary, but adequate, repairs so that trains could reach Gemas by the end of January. Much traffic up to that point, and everything beyond, had to be carried by road in a region where many bridges were necessary and could not be easily bypassed. Most, though not all, were demolished but even so, only 3 days after the last British units had crossed the causeway on to the island, all the destroyed bridges up to the Johore Bridge had been repaired.

It was at the causeway itself that the deficiencies of some of the demolition work can be brought into clear focus. There had, of course, been plenty of time for this to be prepared and there were no shortages of suitable explosives at the adjacent naval base. Thus, as soon as the rearguard had crossed, the charge was detonated and water poured through a 70-foot gap. Unfortunately, at low tide the gap was, according to one source, only 4 feet deep and could be readily forded. Consequently it was repaired without difficulty or delay and Japanese troops found it a useful route which rapidly supplemented the assault craft and boats used in the initial landings. The limited extent of the damage to the causeway was confirmed by a visit by Toosey after the surrender. This was made while out on a working party at the invitation of a Japanese corporal who wished to show him their plan of attack. To Toosey's surprise the water was only 8 inches deep!

The tactics which the Japanese employed with such good effect in Malaya were based on the use of the 'hook'. Whenever they came up against a strong defensive position they always attempted to send a mobile force round the flank with the intention of blocking the defenders' supply routes. In the absence of air supplies, which would have enabled the position to be held, the only real option was to withdraw so as to be able to fight on another day. Time and time again Allied troops fought off frontal assaults only to be forced to retreat in order to save being cut off by enemy attacks on their rear. To a large extent this was due to the failure to destroy the small craft on the western coast, particularly at Penang. Under the umbrella of Japanese air power, which prevented British naval interference, these vessels could then deposit troops at any appropriate point and so the leap-frogging of our defences continued unabated.

The success of these manoeuvres meant that many units, including the Argylls, Leicesters and Ghurkas, were obliged to retreat in successive stages down the whole 350 miles from the Thai border:

> They were never allowed to contact the enemy seriously, but always –
> just as he advanced – withdrawn ten or fifteen miles by forced
> marches to yet another line. So that, for day after day and week after
> week, they marched, dug-in, waited sleeplessly at the alert, and then
> marched again.[19]

This experience, which was shared by all formations to a lesser extent, might have been worthwhile if the object had been to buy time so that the defenders could be concentrated in favourable positions on previously prepared defences. Unfortunately Percival's tactics prevented the concentration of units and he was against the building of fixed fortifications in rear areas on the grounds that it would affect morale. (This view was shared by Major-General Keith Simmons, Fortress Commander of Singapore Garrison.)

The really puzzling aspect of Percival's strategy is that it contradicted his stated aim of ensuring the security of the naval base:

It would appear that with this end in view he should have been only too anxious to have defences prepared in Johore so that the Japanese, if they were to advance into that State, could be brought to a halt out of artillery range of the naval base; such defences would also have covered the main reservoir at Gunong Pulai, on which Singapore Island depended for a large proportion of its water supply. Yet he refused to have any action taken though he knew that the northern coast of Singapore Island was not defended and was, in fact, unsuitable for defence.[20]

A number of other factors have also been suggested as root causes in the failure to halt the Japanese. These include the split in inter-service relationships, particularly between the army and the RAF; the lack of urgency and understanding shown by the civil administration – especially the role played by the governor, Sir Shenton-Thomas;[21] and Churchill's failure to appreciate the real nature of the Singapore 'fortress'. In addition, the British residents in Singapore were widely alleged to be passively, if not actively, antagonistic to the inflow of troops. This was particularly felt by the Australians and, even if this was not the universal experience, it certainly produced the wrong psychological atmosphere.

An even greater controversy concerned that symbol of British mismanagement, the supposedly incorrect siting of the coastal artillery. Typical of the many misunderstandings were the comments of a young Australian soldier:

> it had never been anticipated that an attack on Singapore Island could come from the North and consequently the big guns did not have a 180 degree traverse. The great guns were never fired in anger during the war with Japan: the Japanese were not told that they should have attacked the Island from the sea.[22]

Even Winston Churchill contributed to this 'myth' by stating: 'The fortress guns are sited for use against ships, and have mostly ammunition for that purpose only: many can only fire seawards.'[23] The truth was rather different. First, there were only five 15-inch, six 9-inch and twelve 6-inch guns. Secondly, they were designed purely to prevent an enemy attack from the sea and this is, in fact, what they achieved. However it is true that the 15-inch guns had no highly explosive shells and the 9-inch had only thirty rounds per gun. Orders for additional ammunition could not be filled in time, but attempts to widen the arc of fire of at least some of the guns were successful. As a result there is evidence that the armour-piercing shells that were fired did considerable damage to the Japanese in

Johore and that all of the ammunition was expended before the guns were spiked.

While it is quite certain that the heavy artillery could have inflicted further casualties on the enemy if it had been supplied with more suitable shells, this aspect, like the other factors considered above, and the errors in Percival's tactics, were not the fundamental cause of the loss of Singapore. The real blame lay with successive British governments who, throughout the inter-war period, were not prepared to pay the economic price to provide sufficient resources to build up a proper, balanced defence force on a sufficient scale.

The explanation for this policy is much simpler than might be expected:

> The idea of a direct attack on Malaya or the Dutch East Indies, still more on American possessions was implicitly rejected ... Even at that date [November 1941] few people were really prepared to believe that Japan would risk an open conflict with the United States, or, to speak more exactly, that she would dare to commit her main forces to an operation in the south, while the U.S. Pacific Fleet was still in being and able to act offensively against her.
>
> This supposition was, indeed, the basis of British policy in the Far East during this period; and it explains much that must otherwise appear complacent and over-confident in the attitude of the Cabinet and the Chiefs of Staff. They knew that the forces which they were sending to the Far East were inadequate; but they were unwilling to increase them to the detriment of other fronts, because they believed that our main defence (and the only deterrent that Japan would recognise) was to be found elsewhere – in American naval power.[24]

According to one major authority, vigorous action even after the outbreak of war might still have saved the island, but given the demands on the scarce resources then available it would be difficult to criticize the wartime leaders for omitting to give the Far East the highest possible priority. There was also the then unknown factor of the quality and dedication of the ordinary Japanese soldiers, and in retrospect they were seen to have exerted a major influence upon events:

> They are the bravest people I have ever met. In our armies, any of them, nearly every Japanese would have had a Congressional Medal or Victoria Cross. It is the fashion to dismiss their courage as fanaticism but this only begs the question. They believed in something, and they were willing to die for it, for any smallest detail that would help to achieve it. What else is bravery? They pressed home their attacks when no other troops in the world would have

done so, when all hope of success was gone; except that it never really is, for who can know what the enemy has suffered, what is his state of mind? The Japanese simply came on, using all their skill and rage, until they were stopped by death. In defence they held their ground with a furious tenacity that never faltered. They had to be killed, company by company, squad by squad, man by man, to the last.

By 1944 many scores of thousands of Allied soldiers had fallen wounded into enemy hands as prisoners, because our philosophy and our history have taught us to accept the idea of surrender. By 1944 the number of Japanese captured unwounded, in all theatres of war, probably did not total one hundred. On the Burma front it was about six.[25]

4

After the surrender

The initial confusion

The shock of surrender left Colonel Toosey and his troops dazed and numb. Like many other units their first need was for sleep and they then experienced the classic symptoms of all captured men:

Anger, disappointment, frustration, helplessness, hopelessness, shame, resignation or relief – whatever a man's feelings happen to be in the first few moments of becoming a POW, they are not likely to last long. Wonder about what lies ahead is likely to engender feelings of fear, especially if he is roughly treated on capture.[1]

The casualties experienced by the 135th during the campaign amounted to 118 officers and men, including those killed, missing and wounded. This was a very high proportion of its original complement of 372 but at least the regiment felt satisfied that it had acquitted itself well in very difficult circumstances. On the other hand there was a general feeling of apprehension. Following the attack and subsequent atrocities at the Princess Alexandra Hospital during the last days of the fighting there was a widespread knowledge of Japanese ruthlessness, and the fate of those men captured with BQMS Cluff was fresh in the memory. It was, therefore, with some trepidation that the first contact was made with the victorious Japanese but, when it happened, the main emotion was one of

amazement that they had won this first round. Little men in funny green uniforms all in rubber shoes and – with what appeared to us – somewhat obsolete weapons. We had waited in the curious silence of Singapore after the firing ceased for two days before any Japs appeared ...
Finally, a few soldiers turned up in our lines in their engine driver

hats or completely circular, miniature, pith helmets. One small Japanese private, with an outsize rifle and bayonet, searched me, found a compass which I had kept in the hope it might come in useful later on, took it, put it to his ear, shook it and handed it back to me saying 'No good'. It was a phrase we got to know well later on.[2]

One of the benefits of the cease-fire was that few Japanese troops were initially permitted to enter the city. Consequently only a small number of Allied servicemen came into contact with their captors at this stage and most were to have moved out before the main Japanese Army occupied Singapore. Some of the early arrivals proved to be fierce and arbitrary but Toosey's view was that, in general, these fighting troops behaved quite well. This was an opinion shared by many in spite of the fact that large numbers of POWs were obliged to part with their wrist-watches, rings and fountain-pens. Indeed, while it is widely accepted that the majority of the Japanese acted in a formal and correct manner, a few were positively affable.

The Japanese had already dealt harshly with any uncooperative members of the native community in Malaya so the reasonable treatment of Allied servicemen and European civilians came as a major relief. The Chinese had been singled out for special harassment in Ipoh and Kuala Lumpur and individual Japanese enthusiastically followed this example when suitable occasions arose.

The Japanese Army authorities in newly won Singapore were naturally concerned to secure their base and saw the elimination of any hostile elements as a highly desirable objective. However, the policy of indiscriminately rounding up and killing many thousands of Chinese was not only unnecessary, it was counter-productive. Indeed, once the news percolated to Tokyo a senior member of the *kempeitai* (secret police) was sent to investigate and he quickly realized the truth of the rumours and how these events were preventing any possibility of harmony with the local population. However Colonel Otani did not reach Singapore until 6 March 1942, by which date General Yamashita's orders had already been completed. He then introduced a more sensible regime but the damage could not be easily repaired and a mainly indifferent and apathetic population had already been partly converted to the Allied cause. Toosey's attention was drawn to these events when he, like other senior British officers, was forced to witness the execution of hundreds of Chinese civilians on the beach near Changi.

Official figures show that Allied losses during the campaign amounted to 138,708. These included British 38,496, Australian 18,490, Indian 67,340, and local volunteers 14,382. Over 130,000 of these men were captured, the vast majority at Singapore, and the Japanese were thereby landed with a problem which they neither anticipated nor wanted. The concept of surrender was so alien to the Japanese ethos that they may have been taken by surprise at the scale of the difficulty they had created for themselves. Alternatively they may well have been so little concerned for the welfare of any persons who had so dishonoured themselves by not fighting to the death that they were content to leave any decision to be dictated by events.

The presence of such a large body of prisoners was, of course, a great embarrassment and the Japanese were obliged to make immediate decisions. These resulted in the Allied forces being ordered to move out of Singapore City as quickly as possible – the white personnel being directed to the Changi area on the eastern tip of the island while the Indian troops were to move to the vicinity of Nee Soon. The Japanese instructions were issued on the day after the surrender via the British HQ and were quite arbitrary:

> By five o'clock tomorrow, the 17th, all British and Australian prisoners of war will be in the Changi area.[3]

The news was received with alarm and despondency, especially when it was learned that only a tiny amount of motor transport was to be made available. These arrangements were made with the specific intention of impressing the local population with the changed status of their former masters. By forcing the Allied troops to march out of the city into captivity, laden down with all the food and stores they could carry, the Japanese were to show the defeated defenders in the worst possible light. By then arranging for the Japanese victory parade to commence as the final remnants of the Allied Army moved out it was thought that the contrast would be even sharper.

The brief interval between the order being given and the commencement of the march marked a period of hectic activity. The military and civilian authorities were heavily engaged, under Japanese instruction, in a number of essential tasks. These included the burial of the dead, the demolition of unsafe buildings, the restoration of the water supply and – of special urgency – the movement of the sick and wounded. The Japanese insisted that the General Hospital be evacuated at once, yet there were still hundreds of stretcher cases in the cathedral and elsewhere. Civilian patients were therefore taken to the asylum and those military ones who could not be returned to their units were 'crammed into the Cricket Club, the Singapore Club and the Victoria Memorial Hall'.

In the brief time at their disposal, many individuals also took what advantage they could of the confused situation to forage for portable items such as food, tobacco, books and clothing, which it was anticipated would soon be in short supply. Articles of this kind could be acquired from the many deserted warehouses, shops and houses but this involved some element of risk. The Japanese were already attempting to end the massive looting being undertaken by the local population – especially at the docks – so military personnel tended to look for smaller, damaged, or unoccupied premises where they were less likely to be disturbed.

However, much depended on the circumstances in which an individual found himself. Many profited to the full from the buildings or homes in which they had been temporarily billeted. Thus, before his departure for Changi, Major Coombes and his fellow officers ransacked the house that had been serving as their headquarters and mess. Another group of officers were directed into Robinson's large store in the middle of the city where they slept on sofas in the furnishing department. The next morning they saw that a bookshop lay just across the square and a rapid sortie resulted in the acquisition of two volumes containing the works of Somerset Maugham and Rudyard Kipling. It was then noticed that the British dispensary was situated next door. A further visit was then made which happily coincided with one by a European employee. He was concerned only with locking up for the last time and gave the men everything they requested.

Of course such action was dangerous and could have resulted in severe, and unknown, punishments. On the other hand some sympathetic Japanese were prepared to allow small parties to leave their quarters and search for essential items.

At 10 a.m., whether fully prepared or not, the first of the troops fell in on parade and began their 15-mile march to Changi. A number of columns which had originated in various parts of the city gradually converged into a single large one:

> The column presented a pathetic sight. It was led by at least four files of Brigadiers and full Colonels, each of them laden with kit and carrying attaché cases and all manner of small baggage. Behind them followed a full company of officers and finally a long line of weary-looking soldiers who came from all parts of England.[4]

The march began with heads erect and arms swinging. There was also some singing over the early miles but then the men fell silent as the heat of the day and the weight of their baggage took their toll. At about 1 p.m. the 2000 or so civilians who had been assembled at the Cricket Club began their march into captivity. They were led by the Governor, wearing 'fresh white ducks', all the way to their first place of internment. This was near the Sea View Hotel and the 9-mile journey was a great trial to the mainly elderly people carrying heavy suitcases.

The Japanese did permit some motor transport to be used but the scale was very small. Thus virtually all of the troops, and most of the civilians, had to walk the full distance to their respective places of captivity. These weary miles were made the longer by the attitude of the local people. The crowds included large numbers of Malays and Indians but there was an almost complete absence of Chinese. While only a few were openly hostile, most waved Japanese flags and many

> looked at us as though drugged with disillusionment, their faces strained, bewildered, inquiring; a you-seem-to-have-let-us-down kind of look.[5]

In the country areas during the later stages of the march some local people did take pity on the near-exhausted troops and offered much-needed water. Even with this aid it still took the bulk of the men over 8 hours to complete their journey and it was past midnight when the last finally shuffled into their designated places.

Life in Changi

The area of Singapore to which the British and Australian troops had been ordered lay in the north-east corner of the island. This contained a substantial number of barracks and other buildings which had been specially constructed to house a large part of the peacetime garrison. The region also included a small settlement of Chinese and Indian shops, which together with a school, an open-air cinema and a police station made up the village of Changi. In the near vicinity lay Singapore's main prison, while a group of Malays lived in their *kampong* close to the sea on the east coast.

The barracks at Changi had been originally built to accommodate about 4000 men; by 20 February 1942 it was housing approximately 47,000 troops. During the campaign the military complex had been heavily bombed and shelled, so many of the buildings had been seriously damaged and further deterioration occurred during and after 7 February when the area was evacuated. Consequently the massive overcrowding was worsened by the lack of a water supply, a sewage system and an electricity network, all of which had been deliberately destroyed by our own engineers.

Toosey's regiment shared in the common experience, as a signaller recorded:

> We arrived at Changi at dusk on 17 February, 1942, after a very gruelling march of some fifteen miles during the hottest part of the day, and we were absolutely dead beat. We were too tired to eat the good meal prepared by the advance party, and we went to 'bed' and

slept soundly. The next day we went into Roberts Hospital and started cleaning the place out. The barracks were not too bad; I managed to scrounge a bed and make myself reasonably comfortable, but the worst trouble was water both for drinking and washing. For several days we washed in one of the malarial drains in, to say the least, very dubious water.[6]

The need to cater for the many wounded who were moved out of Singapore irrespective of their condition led to Roberts Barracks being converted into a hospital with over 3000 beds. In spite of an almost total absence of equipment, materials and drugs, the dedication of the surgeons, physicians and their staffs enabled the death rate to be limited to only two or three per day during the first 6 months. Most of this work was performed by members of the medical units but other personnel made substantial contributions to ancillary activities.

On 8 March the 135th Regiment was obliged to move out of Roberts Hospital in order to make room for more patients. The men then went under canvas on a site opposite the Post Office. This was not ideal in many respects but at least it kept the unit together and this was always Toosey's first priority. In addition to the 135th, Toosey was placed in charge of part of the 2nd Battalion Argyll and Sutherland Highlanders. This 'group within a group' or 'my own bunch' was then administered by Toosey with the aid of Major Peacock (one of his battery commanders), Captain Northcote (his regimental adjutant) and Captain H. S. Wood of the RASC.

The provision of water gradually improved although it was never plentiful until the number of troops had been greatly reduced. This was because the local wells were thought to be contaminated and the only supplies that could be used with safety had to be collected from some distance by a fatigue party pushing what had previously been a motorized water-tanker. In the early days this provided only sufficient for one water bottle per person per day, to suffice or   all purposes, although a limited amount of sea-bathing was permitted at that time.

For the first week or so the Japanese supplied no food of any description so all meals had to be provided from the limited quantities that had been brought in by the prisoners. A typical menu of this brief, initial period would be a half sausage for breakfast, two hard biscuits and a slice of sausage meat for lunch and a half mess-tin of stew in the evening. These meals had the virtue of being in the English style but the run-down in stocks was so rapid that there was great relief when the first Japanese rations arrived:

The news flashed quickly round the camp and everyone rushed to the gun-park where the consignment had been laid out. There were mountains of bulging sacks from each of which seeped a desultory trickle of rice, alive with weevils. We picked up handfuls of the small dirty-grey granules and let them run slowly through our fingers. The rice smelled musty, as though it had been stored for years in the dark and damp. It was strongly impregnated with lime and had, we later heard, been intended for digging back into the ground as fertilizer.[7]

The Japanese also supplied irregular quantities of vegetable matter. This included sweet potatoes and pumpkins, the leaves and tops of various plants and a long, woody, root which Toosey described as a kind of Chinese radish. All of these items, like the rice, were in successive stages of decay but, fortunately, the rice was delivered complete with its husk. This added considerably to its value as a foodstuff, although it did nothing to make it more palatable. This was the really crucial aspect, for the basic diet remained completely dependent upon rice. In the course of time the cooks acquired considerable expertise and were able to present the rice in a wide variety of ways. By roasting and grinding the granules a type of porridge could be created and ground rice could also be used both for producing a form of 'shortbread cake' and as the basis of rissoles. Rations were progressively increased from 5 to 8 to 10 ounces per day but irrespective of how much was consumed it never seemed to satisfy the appetite. Thus the lack of suitable food dominated all aspects of life in Changi and prisoners lived from one meal to another:

We awoke hungry, thinking greedily of breakfast, which was served as late as half past ten, to shorten the period between that meal and tiffin – a hollow mockery of a meal, consisting mainly of unsweetened tea, which only increased our unsatisfied and famished appetites. During the long afternoon, we thought only of supper, talked about it, discussed it, enquired about it, anticipated and finally consumed it, only to find that after the last crumb had disappeared from our plates, leaving them as bare as a puppy's dish, we were still capable of doing more than justice to a ten-course meal, and so to bed still hungry, we gloated as we fell asleep thinking of breakfast. In inverse proportion, the less we ate, the more we thought.[8]

In addition to the entire absence of most commodities previously regarded as essential and the need to adopt a new life-style, large numbers of mosquitoes, flies, scorpions and centipedes made life even more miserable.

In these difficult circumstances the British military authorities considered that the most sensible policy was to maintain the command structure and normal system of discipline. This desire was assisted by the Japanese decision to work through the senior officers who received their directions at what became a daily conference with their captors. In turn it was arranged that whenever work-parties were required the men would be supervised by their own officers. While this system placed a heavy responsibility upon the junior officers it did provide them with a positive role and it was anticipated that the Japanese would adhere to the many international agreements that the officers themselves would not be required to work. These arrangements were beneficial to the Japanese, for the self-regulation of the prisoners greatly reduced the effort which direct control would have involved; they were also valuable to the troops in Changi for they limited the points of contact and possible controversy to a bare minimum. Apart from several parades and reviews which were arranged by the Japanese for visiting generals, the troops saw very little of their captors or the Indian renegade troops (largely Sikhs and Hindus) which they employed as guards.

The British and Australian decision to co-operate with the Japanese meant that heavy pressure was placed on their senior administrators to ensure that this mutually advantageous relationship was not disturbed. To this end a strict routine was imposed and everyone was kept busy even if this meant undertaking unnecessary jobs. These tactics also involved the maintenance of all the trappings of military discipline and, on occasion, the punishment of those who offended against the official regulations.

This policy may fairly be described as a successful one and the prisoners were never allowed to degenerate into a disorganized rabble as had been feared. However, there is no doubt that some individuals, including many of the Australians, felt that too much emphasis was placed on superficial and irrelevant matters. Thus, in the opinion of Russell Braddon:

> Changi was phoney not because of the mass of men in it but because of the official attitude behind its administration. The Command determined to maintain full military discipline and establishments, regardless of circumstances or psychology, waiting upon the day when Malaya would be invaded by a British force. Accordingly, two principles seemed to guide every decision. One, to retain full divisional and regimental staffs pottering round achieving nothing useful at all in divisional and regimental offices; two, to preserve the Officers-Other Rank distinction by as many tactless and unnecessary orders as could be devised.[9]

Braddon none the less found that there was a credit side to the policy followed by the Allied administration. The absence of the Japanese was a considerable compensation and he was pleased to receive a shirt, shorts and a pair of boots, which restored him to a respectable appearance.

In the course of time a series of other improvements helped to raise the general condition of life in Changi. In June 1942, the Japanese began to pay small amounts as 'amenity grants'. These were very tiny, amounting to only twenty-five cents per day to officers, fifteen cents to NCOs and ten cents to privates. In September that year officers began to receive increased pay at rates between 10 and 30 dollars per month depending upon rank. This was of particular value in enabling hospital and company mess funds to be established to purchase small quantities of food to supplement the official rations; individuals were able to utilize the balance to purchase the few 'luxuries' that became available when the Japanese permitted a canteen to be set up within the camp.

The poorness of the diet even when supplemented by the canteen and by the few items brought in from outside via the black market meant that most people quickly became lethargic. Nevertheless it was necessary for a great deal of work to be undertaken. In the early days considerable efforts were required to improve the facilities in the camp. In addition a constant supply of labour was needed each day to collect both water and fuel, while many men were employed in various aspects of cooking, cleaning and maintenance. The provision of sanitary facilities was another major task and special squads were formed who were responsible for the drilling of boreholes and the hygiene of latrines. By and large the troops welcomed the opportunity of passing the time in some meaningful way and even the task of wiring the perimeter was attacked with a degree of enthusiasm.

There was a general acceptance of what was essential and while work in the cookhouse was always regarded with favour the need to wash the dirty linen from the hospital was not in dispute. Any resentment related entirely to the value which the individual placed on the work that was performed. Much displeasure was felt at the endless sweeping of already clean paths and at the constant parades and roll-calls, whereas activities such as gardening, which were not only pleasant in themselves but offered potential rewards in the future, attracted many volunteers. Crops such as sweet potatoes, tapioca, papaya and pineapple grew well and were ultimately to make a helpful contribution to the overall diet of the camp. Unfortunately the unpredictable movements ordered by the Japanese meant that those who originated such projects were rarely able to reap the benefits of their work.

Once the initial period was over the cases of wounded began to be supplemented and then overtaken by the number of men who were admitted because of disease. The most widespread illness was dysentery and over a third of the inhabitants of Changi were to suffer from this complaint during their first year. Over 200 prisoners died from dysentery during the period February–August 1942, while a further 50 died from beri-beri. Malaria, dengue fever and various skin diseases were also common but seldom fatal at this stage. Diphtheria was much more serious and resulted in at least 60 deaths. However a total death toll of about 400 during the first six months was really a remarkable achievement and extremely low when compared with what was to follow in Thailand.

A major reaction to the problems of life in Changi was the development of a whole range of leisure activities. These included all the usual outdoor games, with soccer and cricket proving the most popular. Indoor games such as Bingo and cards enjoyed long spells of popularity, while talks of every kind always attracted large audiences. Academic lectures, indeed, were considered to be so valuable that a series of 'university' courses were given official support. Not surprisingly, there was little interest in sex. The emotional strain to which most had been subjected and the poor state of health caused by the lack of food seems to have reduced any sexual urge and there are no reports of any homosexual activity.

The construction of a permanent outdoor stage facilitated regular entertainments by the concert parties which spontaneously sprang up. This theatre was subsequently fitted with all the customary equipment, including lighting, so that a wide variety of plays and revues could be presented in a professional manner. Amongst the producers of these quite substantial shows was Major Osmond Daltry – the officer of the 135th Regiment who had been badly wounded while attempting to escape from Singapore after Toosey had refused to leave. The presence of numerous talented musicians, both amateur and professional, provided a further important dimension to recreation.

Sunday was used as a day of rest whenever the situation permitted. Reading always occupied an important section of the day, and evening concerts provided a useful highspot, but it was the availability of church services which marked the Sabbath in a special way. In the beginning there were no churches so the congregation stood in the open on Temple Hill. These were inter-denominational meetings but it was not long before each group constructed its own building and was able to make provision for its own separate services.

The spiritual uplift received from the presence of the church plus the range of other interests from which individuals chose to help pass their time could not disguise the fact that boredom was an ever-present factor. Thus, when working parties were called for to undertake various tasks in Singapore, there were always plenty of volunteers. The work was mainly to help load and unload ships and generally to clean up the mess on the docks. These tasks provided enormous scope for the acquisition of all those items which were not available in the camp, and in spite of heavy punishments for those who were caught, prisoners quickly became expert at opening cases and removing part of the contents. This was, in many ways, the easy part. The difficulty was to avoid being caught in possession of these 'stolen' goods or even those which were legitimately purchased from local people in the city.

One solution was to eat and drink as much as possible on the spot. However, sometimes this policy was taken to extremes:

> Came the unprecedented day when in Go-down 2 we found a mixed cargo. For eight riotous hours, as we worked under the justifiably suspicious eyes of our guards, we ate chocolates and cough jubes, drank bay rum, cough mixture, cod-liver oil and essence of vanilla – in equal and indiscriminate quantities; applied hair tonic to the hair, face cream to the face and iodex to almost everything; mixed handfuls of sugar with handfuls of herrings in tomato sauce and devoured the resulting mess and sold lipsticks by the dozen to the Chinese outside the back door.[10]

The real problem was, of course, to retain some of these items for future personal consumption or to help friends who were not able to take advantage of these opportunities. The prisoners were liable to search at any time but the two periods of serious danger were while waiting for transport at the end of the day and on arrival back at camp. Many brave men were caught and punished but this did not stop the others from devising and attempting numerous ingenious schemes to deceive their guards. Toosey gave these efforts whatever support he could, but always on the understanding that a proportion of the proceeds would go to Roberts Hospital.

Thus in spite of Japanese efforts a useful quantity of food and other goods filtered back into Changi and did something to alleviate the harsh conditions and shortages. The Japanese authorities must have been aware of this traffic but could not afford to forgo the use of this enormous pool of labour. The scale of damage to be cleared and the extent of the stores which needed to be sorted and loaded meant that they required the maximum amount of assistance. They also appreciated that local workers, who would have to be paid, would be no more reliable than the troops. They decided, therefore, to continue to utilize their prisoners but whenever possible limited the scope for pilferage by employing them to move non-edible commodities and munitions. Prisoners were also allocated to tasks such as the construction of the Shinto Shrine, named Shonan Jinjya, which was to commemorate those Japanese who were killed in the battle for Singapore.

The scale of these activities then convinced the Japanese that daily working parties, which spent much of their time travelling from Changi, could not cope within the period they had allocated. The decision was thus made to establish a number of temporary camps near to the work-sites which meant that a substantial number of prisoners were moved outside Changi. In the case of the 135th, orders to move were received at the beginning of May. Their destination was the site of the ex-RAF HQ in the vicinity of Bukit Timah, about 22 miles from Changi.

The move to Bukit Timah

When Toosey arrived at Bukit Timah the camp was already in existence and was under the control of Brigadier W. L. Duke of the 53rd Infantry Brigade, 18th Division, whom he knew very well. Toosey acted as second-in-command until the middle of June when Brigadier Duke, like all other officers over the rank of Lieutenant-Colonel, was moved to Japan. The administration which Toosey then established included his former team but was strengthened by the addition of Lieutenant-Colonel Robertson of the Australian Army and Lieutenant-Colonel Mapey of the Cambridgeshire Regiment. Personnel in the camp at that time amounted to about 3000 men and included 800 Australians, 500 of the '135 Group' and a number of Suffolks, Norfolks and RASC of the 18th Division. The facility

> consisted of wooden huts with atap roofs which had been seriously damaged during the battle. The Camp site itself was a good one. All the buildings were damaged, there was no electric light and no water supply, and the whole area was filthy with the aftermath of a battlefield which included many dead British and Japanese troops, in most cases only partially buried. By the time I took over the Camp, thanks to the efforts of Brigadier Duke it was very clean, makeshift water and electrical supplies had been arranged and living conditions were generally reasonable.[11]

The troops were required to work from 8 a.m. to 7 p.m. with one day off per week. Their task consisted of helping in the construction of the Shinto Shrine, which was to be built on an island in the middle of the Mac Ritchie Reservoir. This was located on the Bukit Timah golf-course near to the camp, so little time was lost in travelling to the site. Toosey's original 'group' was mainly concerned with building the elaborate system of roads which led to the shrine; they also helped in the construction of a number of small bridges:

The Japanese methods of constructing roads, or for that matter anything they built, were extremely primitive. They had no machinery except three old concrete mixers and a very few trucks. All work was done by spades and chunkels [a kind of pick-axe or hoe], and wicker baskets were used to carry earth and turf from one place to another. The work was very boring and monotonous but we soon got used to it. It rained often and we usually got soaked at least once a day.[12]

It was at this time that Toosey began his long apprenticeship into an understanding of the Japanese mentality. For the first time he was brought into direct contact with an alien administration and obliged to come to terms with it. Fortunately the Bukit Timah camp was controlled by an engineering unit which had fought in the Malaya campaign and its commanding officer, Lieutenant Matsuzawa, was a reasonable man whose prime aim was to complete his task with a minimum of aggravation. Consequently Toosey always looked back at Bukit Timah as the best of his camps, but this did not mean that there were no difficulties.

A major lesson which had to be learned was that the Japanese system of punishment for even the slightest infringement of discipline was immediate and physical. This usually took the form of severe beatings with whatever was to hand and that was normally the end of the matter. There was, however, one serious incident which instilled a fresh wariness into the minds of all concerned:

A party of the 135th were digging earth and loading it on to trucks and one of the British drivers had a slight dispute with a guard who alleged he had threatened him. The driver was taken along to the officer in charge named Aoki and another officer ... who was supposed to be the Welfare Officer. They set upon him, knocked him on the ground, then one held him while the other kicked in the face and body and eventually knocked him unconscious. He was later taken to the hospital with a leg and two ribs broken and other injuries. Meanwhile the working party, because they had witnessed the 'humiliation of a Japanese soldier', were stood to attention for six and a half hours in the blazing sun, being beaten and kicked if they dared to move an inch. Several fainted and were pulled to their feet again and beaten. When they were eventually released they were too stiff to move and it took some time before they were well enough to stagger back to camp.[13]

To troops accustomed to British Army regulations, where it was a crime for an officer or NCO to strike a man, it was, perhaps, small consolation to know that the Japanese were equally hard on their own subordinates. From Toosey's point of view these Japanese tactics had to be resisted whenever they occurred but his main problem was with renegade Sikh soldiers after they had replaced the Japanese as guards. On one occasion Toosey found that two of his young officers were tied up in front of the guardhouse and were being well and truly beaten up. By being 'extremely rude to the Sikhs' (and at great personal risk) Toosey managed to get them away, but thereafter he was always very cautious in his dealings with these former members of the Indian Army.

Apart from the difficulties experienced with the Japanese and the Sikh guards, other aspects of life at Bukit Timah were relatively good. The food showed considerable improvement over Changi and regular, if small, supplies of meat, vegetables and rice were received every day. The arrival of Red Cross parcels was an added bonus. This was also true of the canteen where extra quantities of food, soap and tobacco were made available. These supplies were obtained by Captain Northcote who was permitted to visit Singapore once a week and were paid for by the wage of ten cents received by each man for his day's work.

The combination of a reasonable diet and a not excessive level of work enabled a satisfactory standard of health to be achieved. On arrival at Bukit Timah many of the troops were badly undernourished and a large number of men were suffering from deficiency diseases including pellegra and mild beri-beri. The improvement in conditions restored many to moderate health; the few who did not respond were subsequently returned to Roberts Hospital in Changi.

The general boredom was relieved as far as possible by a continuation of the lectures and classes started at Changi. The formation of a concert party and the establishment of a library with the aid of books 'borrowed' from surrounding houses also helped, while the ability to move freely round the camp area gave at least a superficial feeling of freedom. News of the 'Selerang Incident' caused many to further count their blessings. This began on 30 August when all the troops remaining in Changi were ordered by the Japanese to sign a form which declared:

> I, the undersigned, hereby solemnly swear on my honour that I will not, under any circumstances, attempt escape.[14]

Although it was pointed out by Lieutenant-Colonel E. B. Holmes of the Manchester Regiment (who had succeeded General Percival as officer in charge) that this was against British military law, the Japanese insisted. Further refusal was followed by every prisoner being ordered to move on to the square at Selerang Barracks. This measured only 250 × 150 yards, yet 15,000 officers and men were soon packed into this tiny space and the surrounding buildings. The Japanese permitted only the smallest of rations, there were only three points from which water could be obtained and the sanitary facilities were totally inadequate for the numbers involved. Consequently the centre of the parade ground was cut up and a series of trenches, 8 feet deep, were dug to act as latrines. Thus negotiations with Major-General Fukuei were pressed forward with great urgency but found little response. Indeed on 2 September Fukuei ordered the execution of four men who had attempted to escape during the early weeks of captivity. He also insisted that a number of senior officers, including the Bishop of Singapore, should witness the event and this further heightened the tension. Fukuei was subsequently charged as a war criminal and after being found guilty was executed on the same spot in 1946.

In this situation Lieutenant-Colonel Holmes decided to recommend that each man should sign under duress. So far as the British were concerned this meant that their declaration had no force in law. The Japanese clearly understood this point but chose to ignore it, probably because they were glad to end an impasse which was threatening to become a major embarrassment.

News of the incident at Selerang was closely followed at Bukit Timah and the other work camps and great relief was felt when, on 5 September, the troops were able to return to their normal quarters. The example set at Changi was quickly followed at Bukit Timah and everyone signed without further difficulty. Nevertheless this period of unpleasantness created a general air of uncertainty and it was with mixed feelings that the members of the 135th heard that they were soon to move to 'a much better area somewhere in the north'. This information was not unexpected, for the work was obviously coming to an end. Few wished to return to Changi, so the possibility that their new destination might offer some advantages helped to overcome the reluctance to leave what many had come to regard as home. It was in these circumstances of doubt and hope that Toosey prepared to lead his men into the unknown.

The uncertainty felt by Colonel Toosey and his regiment when instructions were received to prepare to leave Bukit Timah on 22 October was partly caused by their ignorance of external events. Once Singapore had surrendered, communications with the outside world had virtually ceased and it took some time to establish reliable fresh links. The Japanese attempted to fill the gap by publishing a version of the *Singapore Times* in English. This was known as the *Syonan Times* and although deliberately designed to dispense their propaganda it could not avoid providing a general outline of the progress of the war.

A number of radios were gradually constructed and then operated clandestinely within Changi. Not all of these worked very well and it proved difficult, at first, to make regular contact with the nearest station of New Delhi. At a later stage only a single, efficient, set would be used so as to reduce the risk of discovery. Periodic news bulletins would then be issued and passed by word of mouth through the camp. But this lay in the future and for a time fact and rumour were frequently so deeply intermixed that most listeners tended to choose the version that suited them best.

A radio was operated at Bukit Timah and this provided a reasonable amount of accurate information. The broadcasts from New Delhi were not, at this time, specifically directed to the prisoners. Thus they were obliged to glean items of particular interest from, to them, a whole range of irrelevant material. In any case the authorities in India had little real knowledge of Japanese plans so their broadcasts could shed no light on the 135th's ultimate destination.

In the absence of solid news there was, of course, considerable conjecture. It was thought that the Japanese did not like having a large body of prisoners near their major base. The likely prospect of a shortage of food in the future was also put forward as a probable motive. These criteria were then both met by the suggestion that the troops were to be relocated in the Cameron Highlands in northern Malaya where they could fend for themselves in a strategically unimportant backwater. Others felt that Indo-China or Thailand, where food was plentiful, would offer more suitable sites. It was even rumoured that the troops were required to help build a railway in Burma, but this was generally dismissed as being yet another example of someone's over-fertile imagination!

5

Background to the Thai–Burma railway

The progress of the war

The Japanese decision to use their vast reservoir of POWs to help establish a link between the rail networks of Thailand and Burma was based on a range of circumstances of which the captured troops had little knowledge. A major factor was the very extent of Japanese success, for while the Japanese 25th Army was fighting its way down the Malayan Peninsula towards Singapore, its 15th Army was already preparing for the conquest of Burma. The last-minute agreement with the Thai government (see above, p. 35) enabled elements of this second force to enter Bangkok on 8 December 1941, and within a few days they were in complete control of the entire communications network. The 15th Army was made up of the 33rd and 55th Divisions which, under the command of Lieutenant-General Iida, had a strength of 35,440 officers and men. During the initial stages of its operations the 15th Army was reinforced by the Imperial Guards Division but within a brief period this was moved to the south to aid in the Malayan campaign. It did, however, retain the powerful support of the 10th Air Brigade which quickly achieved a strength of 200 aircraft and was to play a key role in the forthcoming battles.

The 15th Army occupied Victoria Point in the Kra Isthmus on 11 December but it was not until 19 January 1942 that Tavoy – much further to the north – was captured. This had the effect of bypassing the British garrison at Mergui which had to be withdrawn. These events placed the Japanese in control of the southern coastline of Tenasserim but the absence of roads prevented any further advance into Burma along this route. However, these operations did provide the Japanese with the three airfields constructed by the British at Victoria Point, Mergui and Tavoy, and these were to be of great value in covering the subsequent advance route to Rangoon.

The region between Thailand and Burma is extremely mountainous and experiences one of the heaviest rainfalls in the world. Large areas are covered in such dense jungle that communications between the two countries were possible only through a few small tracks. The British Command had no direct knowledge of Japanese intentions but thought that the most likely route would be from Chiengmai (which was connected to Bangkok by rail) via tracks which led to Toungoo in the Shan States (See Map 2 on p. 87). In the event the Japanese chose to direct their main thrust over the Kawkareik Pass which meant that troops and supplies could be transported by the Thai railway to Phitsanulok. From there a minor road ran towards Raheng and a trail then continued the route over the Dawna Range and entered Burma at Kawkareik. Further small roads and tracks reached into the coastal zone while others supplied inland links with the north.

When war broke out Burma had few military resources at her disposal and the demands of Malaya and Singapore meant that few reinforcements could be secured. Thus when the Japanese invasion began on 20 January 1942 and overwhelmed a small detachment near the Kawkareik Pass only the equivalent of two weak divisions were available to oppose their advance. The bulk of these Burmese and Indian troops were, at best, semi-trained and lacked the support of adequate ancillary units. They were also very short of air cover, although the RAF's thirty planes and a squadron of the American Volunteer Group did a great deal with their limited resources. The consequence was that the enemy's progress could not be halted and Moulmein was lost on 31 January. Worse was to follow. The tactic of an orderly withdrawal to a fresh defensive position behind the Sittang River went badly wrong when, in confused circumstances, the only bridge was destroyed with many troops still on the wrong side of the water.

This event devastated the 17th Indian Division and even the landing of the 7th Armoured Brigade at Rangoon on 23 February and the movement of Chinese forces into central Burma were not sufficient to offset its loss. Thus the failure on the Sittang

> was the decisive battle of the first campaign. After it, however gallantly our troops fought, there was little hope of holding Rangoon. And when Rangoon went as it did on the 9th March, the whole army in Burma was cut off from the outside world almost as effectively as had been the two brigades on the east bank of the Sittang.[1]

In retrospect it can be seen that the possession of Rangoon was the key to the whole campaign. The difficulties of maintaining supplies via the tortuous route from Thailand meant that the Japanese could not keep more than two divisions in the field. On the other hand Rangoon's port capacity provided the Allied forces with the potential to supply far more troops than were actually available. It is against this background that the decision not to divert the 18th Division from Singapore should be judged. The level of forces involved was such that one additional division could have made a great difference to the outcome. Moreover, had the 18th Division landed it might well have encouraged the Australian government to permit its 7th Division, then on its way home from the Middle East, to be diverted to Rangoon. This could, in fact, have arrived on 27 February and further reinforcements of both British and Indian troops were scheduled to follow on 2 and 8 March. There would have been no special problem in reaching Rangoon at this time – American and British fighter pilots had inflicted so many casualties on the Japanese that after 26 February they made no further daylight raids on the city.

However, following the bombing of Darwin the Australian population was apprehensive that a Japanese invasion was about to take place. Thus the Australian government felt obliged to repatriate the 7th Division in order to support civilian morale. In the event, as neither the 18th nor the 7th Division were diverted, the Japanese were able to seize Rangoon and with the aid of its facilities to introduce much larger forces. This meant that by April 1942 the Japanese had not only occupied Malaya and Singapore but had also secured the Philippines and the Dutch East Indies. The conquest of Burma had nearly been completed and a number of Pacific islands had been taken with a view to creating a defensive wall around what the Japanese referred to as the 'Greater East Asia Co-Prosperity Sphere'.

The ease with which these vast areas had been seized led the Japanese planners to consider a further extension of their widespread perimeter. Their strategy envisaged the capture of Samoa, Fiji and New Caledonia in order to cut the communications between the United States and Australia, and of Midway Island (where there were air bases protecting Hawaii) so as to plug the gap in Japan's outer defences. Above all it aimed to bring the remnants of the US fleet to battle while the Imperial Navy retained its numerical superiority.

The final plan included an attack on the Aleutian Islands and the capture of the vital base of Port Moresby in Australian New Guinea only 150 kilometres from Australia. It was the latter which began a series of events which was to involve nearly 200 Japanese ships over an area of many thousands of miles. The invasion force, which included three carriers and six cruisers, left the main Japanese base at Rabaul on New Britain on 4 May. The Americans, who had broken the Japanese fleet code were already in position with two large carriers and seven cruisers. In the ensuing Battle of the Coral Sea, US planes sank or immobilized all three Japanese carriers for the loss of one carrier. This American success thus prevented a direct seaborne attack on Port Moresby and effectively checked the Japanese naval offensive southwards towards Australia. Tactically it was a prelude for the decisive victory of Midway Island 4 weeks later, when good intelligence work enabled the Americans to anticipate Japanese plans and to strike early at the Imperial Fleet, losing only one carrier to the Japanese four.

The net result of these events was that Japan had lost the mastery of the seas which she had secured at Pearl Harbor and, with it, the power to wage an aggressive war. In the words of the official historian:

Japan, by reaching for the shadow of further conquests, lost the bone of naval supremacy, without which she could not hold the vast area she had already won.[2]

Thus within 6 months of the beginning of the conflict which she had initiated, Japan could no longer hope to end the war on favourable terms. This was recognized by the highest authorities in Tokyo and the policy which was then adopted was purely intended to reduce the extent and humiliation of her inevitable defeat. Such a strategy required a stubborn defence, so that the price to be paid for successive advances would lead the United States and her allies to settle for something less than 'unconditional surrender' (this term was not used until the Casablanca Conference in January 1943). These tactics demanded that the outer perimeter be held for as long as possible and that subsequent defensive positions be kept at the greatest feasible distance from the homeland.

As part of Japan's new strategy it was decided to give the Imperial Army a larger role in strengthening Japan's outer defensive wall. To this end substantial forces were landed at Buna on the north-eastern side of Australian New Guinea towards the end of July 1942. This was an easy task, for Japanese air bases in the Solomon Islands still gave them con··· over the Bismarck Sea and the coast was virtually undefended. Once ashore the troops began a rapid movement towards Port Moresby. This was eventually stopped by Australian ground forces with the assistance of Allied bombers, which effectively closed down the enemy's precarious supply routes. During the next 6 months substantial numbers of American and Australian troops were deployed and gradually pushed their opponents back to Buna. Throughout this period the Japanese received little in the way of additional support, and in January 1943 their resistance was finally terminated. This surprising failure to provide adequate reinforcements was partly due to Allied air superiority. However, another major factor was the higher priority given to resisting an attack by a substantial force of US Marines on Guadalcanal, two weeks

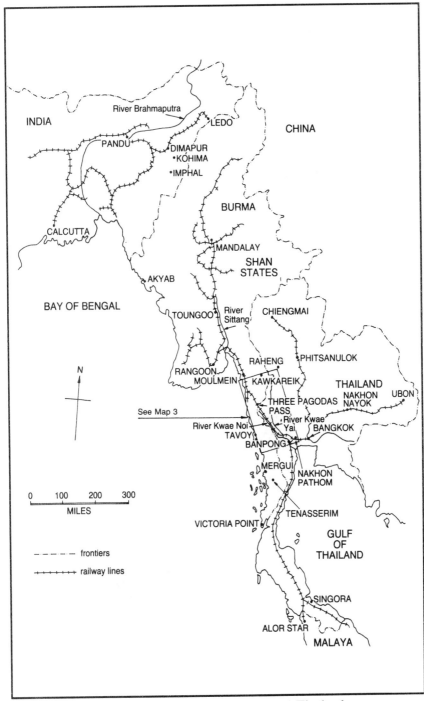

Map 2: Strategic Map of Burma and Thailand

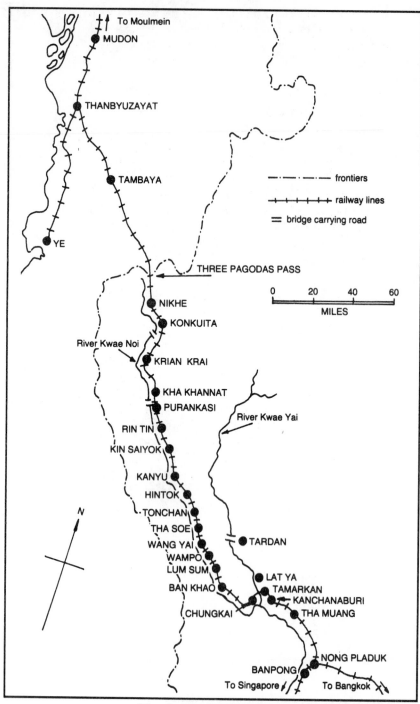

Map 3: The POW Railway

after the landings at Buna. The few Japanese on the island were mainly construction workers engaged in building an airstrip and they fled into the jungle after offering very little resistance. The Marines quickly occupied the half-finished airfield and within a few days had made it fully operational.

As the Americans were determined to hold on to their early gains, the conflict turned upon the ability of each side to strengthen and supply their fighting troops. After 5 months of fighting it was clear that it would not be possible to eject the Marines from Guadalcanal. Increasingly heavy losses of planes and ships convinced the Japanese High Command that their surviving units should be evacuated. This was completed during the first week of February 1943. While this prevented a complete disaster, the Japanese had lost at least 30,000 men and had failed to hold Guadalcanal. Twenty-three of their naval vessels had been sunk and of even greater importance to the Japanese was the loss of so many of their trained pilots, for this elite body of men could never be replaced during wartime conditions.

In retrospect the failure of the overland attack on Port Moresby and the loss of Guadalcanal can be seen as a real watershed in the progress of the war. It is clear that these successes were made possible by a build-up in Allied power.

This then enabled the Allied – essentially American – forces to secure a number of further gains. Japanese attempts to reinforce their positions on the northern coast of New Guinea and to regain the initiative over the Solomon Sea led to heavy losses of ships and aircraft. The failure of these tactics led Admiral Yamamoto Isoroku to undertake a morale-raising tour of the forward bases. His intentions quickly became known to American intelligence and on 18 April 1943 his flight was shot down. Yamamoto, as the commander-in-chief of Japan's combined fleet and as the man responsible for the success at Pearl Harbor, held a unique position in the esteem of Japanese public opinion and his death was a massive blow to the nation's self-confidence.

The ending of Yamamoto's attempts to secure air superiority in the South Pacific left the way clear for further American advances. By September 1943 all of New Georgia and many of its adjacent islands had been captured. The increasing command of both air and sea meant that those strongholds which remained in Japanese hands could be effectively isolated by the acquisition of bases on nearby sites. These events in the Solomons were paralleled by an equally successful campaign to remove the Japanese from those parts of the Aleutian Islands which they had occupied in June 1942. Though not important in itself this minor victory was to have useful consequences for the Allied cause. The loss of their bases in the Aleutians encouraged the Japanese to believe that an attack on their homeland might come from that direction. They were obliged, therefore, to use vast quantities of fuel oil and merchant shipping to develop the defences of the Kurile Islands and these expenditures fell precisely in Japan's area of greatest weakness.

These events were complemented by developments in Burma. The Japanese had completed their occupation of this vast country by 20 May 1942, and this was followed by a period of inactivity on land while both sides reassessed the situation during the monsoon period. At first the Japanese organized many air attacks on targets in India but in the autumn most of their planes had to be transferred to the south-western Pacific and Allied air superiority was never again to be seriously challenged. Long-range raids, particularly on Rangoon, were gradually built up and Bangkok was attacked for the first time during November 1942.

During this period the British Army in India was totally reorganized and greatly strengthened. This encouraged planning to commence for the reconquest of Burma, but shortages of landing craft ruled out a direct attack on Rangoon, and Chinese reluctance to co-operate until the Allies had complete control of the Bay of Bengal prevented an attack across the Indian frontier. However, it was possible to undertake two limited offences. The first was aimed at the seizure of Akyab, but failed to achieve its objectives. The other initiative was undertaken by the 'Chindits', a group of guerrilla-style fighters led by Brigadier Wingate. The use of long-range penetration groups to be supplied by air on this scale was a new concept which needed to be proved under combat conditions. Accordingly 3000 troops spent several months in Burma harassing the Japanese from behind their own lines. The ease with which the 'Chindits' had operated convinced the Japanese military command that a more positive policy was required. This was ultimately to lead to the Japanese decision to attack Imphal in 1944.

The need for a rail link with Burma

These developments in the Pacific and in Burma had the effect of placing maximum strain in two areas where Japan was at her weakest.

The first of these lay in the mercantile marine, for Japan commenced the war with only 6 million tons of ocean-going vessels. In 1941, the last year of peace, these ships were able to carry only 65 per cent of Japanese imports. It was, therefore, quite obvious that it would be an extremely difficult task to continue the work of transporting essential raw materials and food as well as having to cope with the fresh demand to carry and supply an increasing number of overseas forces. Japan's other great weakness was her chronic shortage of oil. This was, indeed, a major factor in encouraging her entry into the war, for it was anticipated that the seizure of the supplies from the Dutch East Indies would enable her to become virtually self-sufficient (see above, p. 34). The Japanese calculations were based on two separate premises. One was that production in the captured oilfields would be maintained at high level; this was largely achieved. The other was that it would be possible to transport the fuel to Japan or to where it was required; this could not be accomplished on the necessary scale. Two special factors contributed to this failure. The first was a relative shortage of oil tankers. The second was a sharp increase in Japanese casualties as the American offensive gained strength and tankers became a 'priority target'. In these circumstances every possibility of saving shipping space received careful scrutiny and amongst the projects was one to supply the Japanese forces in Burma by rail.

The existing line of communication with Burma lay through the China Sea, around the Malay Peninsula and then up the Malacca Strait to Rangoon. It was calculated that a saving of 1200 miles could be made if Rangoon could be replaced by Bangkok as the shipping terminus. However, there was no link between the Thai rail network and the Burmese railway system, and the extreme nature of the terrain and rainfall made a viable road connection quite impractical.

It quickly became obvious that the only way in which Bangkok's situation and facilities could be utilized was if a rail link could be established between the port and the area of operations in Burma. This possibility had already been considered in the 1920s and 1930s. However, all indications were that such a connection would be excessively expensive to build and maintain and could not be justified by the potential traffic. As a result the proposals were shelved and all trade between Bangkok and Rangoon continued to be carried by sea.

As part of its pre-war planning, the *Daihon'ei* (HQ of the Imperial Japanese Army) had initiated a feasibility study of this subject. This was undertaken during 1939 and 1940 by a civilian consultant named Kuwabara, who concluded that a

> route closely following the river Kwae Noi as far as the Three Pagodas Pass and thence down to Thanbyuzayat could be built by two railway regiments in about a year [See map 2 on p. 87].[3]

The conquest of Burma and the hope that it could form the base for an invasion of India then led to a re-examination of supply routes. The increasing shortage of merchant shipping and the vulnerability of the Rangoon service to attack were fully appreciated and led to a fresh look at Kuwabara's report. Japanese engineers agreed that his plans could be implemented but thought it would take five or six years to complete the project because Japan's engineering resources were already fully stretched and the proposed work lay in an area where little local labour was available. It was at this point that a number of separate, but related, decisions were made which ultimately resulted in the use of the vast numbers of prisoners who had been captured in early stages of the war.

Japan had ratified the Hague Convention of 1907 but not the more liberal Geneva Convention of 1929. She was, therefore, committed to the principle that POWs must not be required to undertake work that was useful to their captors. Nevertheless, in April 1942, when Japan had acquired almost 300,000 prisoners of various types, it was decided that all military personnel be made to earn their keep. The vast majority of these captives were on Singapore Island. It was the existence of this huge pool of labour which convinced the Japanese authorities that the building of a rail link to Burma was a viable proposition.

Preparations for constructing the railway

As early as March 1942, the commander of the Southern Field Railway Group in Saigon had ordered that the preliminary preparations for the construction of the railway be commenced as soon as possible. The formal decision to proceed was not taken by the *Daihon'ei* until 20 June and did not officially reach Saigon until late in August. This ordered that work should begin in the following November, but as operations were already well advanced it can be seen that this instruction was a mere formality.

The preliminary arrangements which were initially authorized at a local level fell into a number of distinct categories. A 'right of way' had to be negotiated with Thai landowners and this could be finalized only after agreement was reached between the Japanese and Thai governments. The terms which were eventually agreed provided for the Thais to contribute the necessary land and to help build a road that was to run parallel to the railway track. They were also to supply certain quantities of material.

The physical preparations which then followed required the presence of both skilled and unskilled labour. Tangible evidence of the decision to use prisoners of war came on 24 June 1942, when Major R. S. Sykes RASC with 600 British POWs from Changi arrived at Nong Pladuk to begin the construction of base workshops and stores (see Map 3 on p. 88). A few days later they were joined by a further 600 men under the control of Major W. E. Gill RA, who, as the senior officer, took command on 2 July. This 'mainland party' was then built up to a total strength of 3000 as additional parties arrived later in July and August. This was not, in fact, the earliest use of the pool of prisoner labour, for, in May 1942, 3000 Australians under Brigadier A. L. Varley had already been sent to help repair the former British airfields in lower Burma. This group, usually referred to as 'A' Force, was moved to Thanbyuzayat during the following September where it formed the nucleus of what became known as No. 3 Thai POW Branch. This eventually achieved a strength of nearly 10,000 (including many Dutchmen) and, with the aid of 'No. 5 Branch', which arrived in January 1943, was made responsible for the building of the track toward the Burma border at the Three Pagodas Pass.

The Japanese allocated 12,000 of their own personnel to deal with the technical aspects of the construction and to control the unskilled labour which was to be supplied by their prisoners (some reports suggest this figure should be 15,000). These were organized into two railway regiments, a supply depot (later split into two parts) and a number of ancillary engineering and building units. The 5th Regiment, raised in 1938, spent three years in China before moving to Saigon just before the invasion of Malaya. It was then made responsible for operating the line down the west coast of the peninsula to the south and so played an important role in maintaining the supplies that enabled Singapore to be captured. Once this campaign was over it was moved to Burma to take control of the railway between Rangoon and Mandalay. Then, in September 1942, it was ordered to Thanbyuzayat at the northern terminus of the proposed new line.

The previous history of the 9th Railway Regiment was very similar. It was formed in Japan in 1940 and proceeded to Haiphong in French Indo-China during October 1941. Then, after the opening of the fighting in Malaya, it moved down the peninsula and operated the east coast railway as it came into Japanese hands. After the surrender of Singapore the regiment was ordered to Burma where it was engaged in the repair and operation of the lines to the north of Mandalay. In August 1942 it was moved to Banpong in southern Thailand in order to establish its HQ close to where the track to Burma was to commence.

It is at this point that the career of Yoshihiko Futamatsu should be outlined. In pre-war days he had been employed as an engineer for what is now Japan's National Railway but in 1941 he was seconded to the army to act as a civilian engineering consultant. In October that year he left Japan with Renichi Sugano. Both landed in Malaya with the invasion force and Futamatsu then worked with the 4th Special Railway Bridging Group while Sugano was attached to the 9th Railway Regiment. The latter had the task of making temporary repairs to the bridges and other railway installations which had been damaged in the fighting. They normally operated alongside, or just behind, the attacking infantry, while the 'Special Group' followed up to construct more permanent structures.

These activities inevitably overlapped on many occasions and Futamatsu and Sugano became firm friends. However, once the campaign was over their paths parted, so that while Futamatsu joined the staff of the Southern Field Railway Group, then based at Singapore, Sugano was sent to Burma with the 9th Railway Regiment. Futamatsu was then employed in preparing the contingent plans for the proposed rail link and in June 1942 was appointed to the HQ of the 9th Railway Regiment which was just beginning its move from Burma to Banpong. There he was given the responsibility for surveying the route and after this had been completed was placed in charge of bridge design and of all technical aspects of the construction as far as the Burma border. Thus when the remainder of the 9th Regiment returned to Thailand Futamatsu was able to resume his friendship with Sugano. By then Sugano had been promoted to command the 1st Battalion of this unit and had achieved the rank of major. As Futamatsu (although a civilian) also rose to the status of a major there were no barriers to their continued association, which was to last for the remainder of hostilities and on through the post-war era to the 1990s.

Planning the route

Futamatsu's instructions were to implement the recommendations of Kuwabara's pre-war feasibility study. This required the construction of a track through flat country to Kanchanaburi. It was then to follow the valley of the Kwae Noi and cross the frontier at the Three Pagodas Pass. This meant that a major bridge would have to be constructed across the Kwae Yai at its confluence with the Kwae Noi.

This route was chosen primarily on logistical grounds. Kanchanaburi was already an established river port with direct access to the Gulf of Siam via the Kwae Yai (also known as the Mae Khlaung). It also had the advantage of being connected with Banpong, and thence with Bangkok, by a modern road suitable for motor traffic. As Kanchanaburi was the chief marketing centre of the province, rice, vegetables and fruit were always in plentiful supply there, so it might reasonably be expected that food as well as materials and other supplies could be readily transported up the Kwae Noi.

Consideration of any alternative route was not within Futamatsu's brief, although this did not preclude his making marginal changes where he thought these were necessary. Thus, as it was not possible to cross the Kwae Yai at Kanchanaburi because of the swampiness of the west bank, it was decided to site the bridge at the village of Tamarkan, some 3 miles further up the river. The channel at this point varies from 100 to 500 yards (according to the season), so moderately-sized barges could readily bring heavy equipment and stores. The only difficulty was that the level of the river fell dramatically in the dry season, so navigation on any scale was possible only from June to December. Many commodities could of course be stockpiled, but the twin problems of the transportation and storage of food could not so easily be overcome and were to be major factors in the ensuing tragedy.

Futamatsu has been greatly criticized for not attempting any fundamental realignment of the route. Typical of the many prisoners who thought that the Japanese had made a major error was Captain Verne Toose, an Australian who was a distant relative of Philip Toosey:

> Due to an incredible error by a Japanese engineer the railroad crossed the River in its present position instead of further north at a point opposite Laddya (Lat Ya) where the hill was known as Chong Kai.
>
> Subsequently all maps and aerial surveys were mislabelled and the small hill across the river from Kanchanaburi was called Chung Kai (correct name is Khao Poon) and the bridge was built there, causing many miles of track to be built in almost impossible terrain. This delayed completion and no doubt caused many lives to be unnecessarily wasted.[4]

Captain Toose's conclusions can be criticized on a number of counts. Both the Japanese and the prisoners appear to have been confused about the correct Thai names for various places but this does not seem to have been a factor in the siting of the main bridge at Tamarkan. Any assessment of Toose's ideas requires an understanding of the two possibilities which lay within the general outline of the southern route. There can be no dispute about the first section, which ran from Nong Pladuk to Kanchanaburi, or in respect of the path which took the track from Wang Yai to the north. It is the choice of the route from Kanchanaburi to Wang Yai that requires further explanation.

Fatamatsu's decision to cross the Kwae Yai at Tamarkan and then follow the valley of the Kwae Noi through very difficult country to Wang Yai, involved a massive cutting through solid rock at Chungkai and a double viaduct round the rock face at Wampo. Captain Toose has pointed out that an easier option would have been to take the route from Kanchanaburi to Tardan and thence to Wang Yai (the real village Tardan lies further to the north and the site referred to by the Japanese by this name was really Ban Tha Manao). This would have had the advantage of reducing the overall distance by up to 20 kilometres as well as traversing flatter land and crossing the Kwae Yai at a more convenient place. This was, in fact, the direction taken by an existing path, which it had already been agreed would be upgraded by the Thai government to make a motor road.

However, at the time that Futamatsu had to make his final decision little progress had been made on the construction of the motor road[5] so the comparative ease of this route was not appreciated. In addition there were no detailed maps of the region which he could consult. Thus Futamatsu made his decision in ignorance of the relative merits of the two routes but, in retrospect, he thinks that even had he known all the facts he would still have made the same choice.

Futamatsu's conviction that he made the correct choice is based on the value he attached to the Kwae Noi as a means of transport. The need for speed meant that the Japanese were obliged to construct the railway simultaneously at many points and the river provided the only crtain way of moving large quantities of construction material and supplies. On the alternative route the Kwae Yai could have been utilized for part of the way but the section between Tardan and Wang Yai required that the motor road be fully operational before construction there could have been remotely viable.

Whether Futamatsu's decision was right or wrong, there can be no doubt that the Japanese subsequently did utilize the Kwae Noi as their main channel of communication. Large quantities of bamboo were obtained from the upper reaches of the river and then floated down in vast rafts to supply building materials to the many camps situated close to its banks. Heavy items were brought in directly from Bangkok via the sea and the Kwae Yai (the Mae Khlaung), while many other supplies were brought in through Kanchanaburi. Then when the newly constructed track from Nong Pladuk became operational in January 1943 Kanchanaburi quickly became established as the principal base for the entire railway project.

Futamatsu's position did not include responsibility for the acquisition of materials and equipment. Nevertheless, the necessity to use items and expertise available either locally or within the South-East Asian area imposed severe limitations on the kind of railway that could be envisaged. Futamatsu also had to take account of the lack of certain skills within the railway regiments and the absence of detailed maps of the whole area. Thus the route contained no tunnels – deep cuttings were employed instead – and only one large-scale bridge (at Tamarkan). The rail gauge was fixed at 1 metre, with a 200-metre minimum radius of curvature and a maximum gradient of 2.5 per cent. (In the area of the Three Pagodas Pass some gradients reached 2.9 per cent and two locomotives were necessary at these points.) It was anticipated that these plans would produce a track capable of carrying 3000 tons per day.

Modifications to the plan

Those engaged in planning the rail link with Burma knew sufficient of the global situation to understand its crucial significance to the war effort. They were, therefore, determined that it would be completed as quickly as possible, irrespective of cost or inconvenience to themselves or others. The overall plan had, of course, been approved by the *Daihon'ei* which had also allocated the military units and agreed to the use of POW labour. However, no other provisions had been made by the authorities in Tokyo. The enormous problems which remained were to be solved in whatever manner seemed appropriate by the Southern Army Railway Corps.

The major difficulties that could be anticipated were in respect of the materials and equipment required for the construction and the subsequent need for locomotives and rolling stock to operate the finished line. The desperate shortage of shipping meant that as little as possible was to be imported and local sources could provide only inferior substitutes. This meant that many compromises had to be made. The lack of heavy equipment and excavating machinery could be offset by the use of massive amounts of labour utilizing primitive hand tools and there was no shortage of stone and gravel. Large quantities of timber were also readily available, so that bamboo was used extensively in the construction of buildings and hardwood was specified for the making of sleepers. In addition, all but 8 of the 688 bridges on the line were built of timber. Somewhat surprisingly, hardwood was seldom employed for this task, its strength and durability being sacrificed for the speed with which the local softwoods could be cut and fabricated.

The Japanese were also able to fit out what has been described as 'the best equipped workshop in South-East Asia'.[6] This was sited at Nong Pladuk and was a completely independent unit which, if fully staffed, had sufficient capacity to deal with the entire requirements of the line. Its facilities included three forges, three engine shops, a foundry, three power stations, a sawmill, a water conduit and an installation for the refining of crude oil. Practically all of the items to equip this unit were obtained from the Malayan tin mines, while most of the balance was secured from railway workshops in Kuala Lumpur, Java and Sumatra. Only a few of the more specialized pieces of machinery had to be brought in from Japan.

This was the case for many other materials. However, there was no indigenous manufacture of rails in the area so the Japanese attempted to deal with this problem by dismantling a number of non-essential branch lines in Burma and Malaya. The rails obtained in this way varied from 30-foot lengths at 60 pounds per yard from the Malayan railway to the 30- or 39-foot lengths at 60 to 75 pounds per yard from the track that was dismantled in Burma.[7] Some reports also mention the use of rails that had been manufactured in Germany but their immediate origin is not known. These 'second-hand' rails may have been supplemented by new ones taken from stores in Singapore and elsewhere but a shortage still remained and had to be made up by supplies from Japan. This was also true of locomotives and rolling stock. A limited amount of bridging material was also brought in from Japan though the spans for use over the Kwae Yai were to come from Java. The ultimate consequence of these constraints was that the resulting track was far less solid than had been intended. Combined with the use of inferior or incorrect fuels, this prevented many of the locomotives from achieving their designed performances and reduced the potential carrying power of the railway to 1000 tons per day even before it was operational. This was accepted as being the best that could be managed in the circumstances.

6

Building the bridges

Toosey's arrival at the bridge camp

Once it had been decided to construct the major bridge across the Kwae Yai at Tamarkan the Japanese ordered the erection of a camp to house the personnel who were to complete the project. It was at this clearing in the jungle that Colonel Toosey arrived on 26 October 1942 (see above, p. 7).

On the following day Lieutenant Kosakata, the commander of the camp, accepted that Toosey was now the senior POW officer and outlined the work which was to be undertaken:

> Our job was to make a wooden and a concrete bridge across the river, and to construct about two kilometres of railway embankment on either side of this bridge, this work to take nine months to a year.[1]

Although he did not know that the decision to use POW labour for military purposes had been taken in Tokyo by the highest authorities, Toosey was well aware that the work he was being ordered to perform was illegal (see above, p. 8). He protested on many occasions to this effect, but was always told that the international conventions (to which Japan was party) did not matter, for 'Japan was going to win the war and we can do as we like'.[2]

Toosey, in fact, quickly realized that he had no real option in this matter and accepted that the vital question was not whether the troops were to perform the tasks laid down, but how many were to die in the process. Toosey's decision to comply with the inevitable brought him into direct contact with Kosakata who, he came to the conclusion, was rather stupid and awkward but not really dangerous. The other two members of the Japanese administration were more helpful. The first of these was Sergeant-Major Saito who was the senior NCO on the site.

99

Toosey found him to be very strict but he was always regarded as being honest and just in his dealings with the prisoners. The second key figure was RQMS Murakami, for his responsibilities included the acquisition of the food ration and, later, of items for the canteen. In Toosey's opinion this NCO performed these tasks with considerable competence and he usually succeeded in obtaining a satisfactory share of whatever was available.

The working arrangements which Toosey developed with Saito showed that the Japanese sergeant-major was a practical soldier who knew how to handle troops. Toosey's respect for this man's character and capacity was, however, tempered by a degree of curiosity as to why such an experienced campaigner should be languishing in charge of prisoners instead of pursuing a more exacting role on the battlefields. At the time Toosey came to the conclusion that Saito had been wounded or ill and that his appointment to Tamarkan was to give him a period of recuperation. This was partly true but the real reason was more complicated. In 1930, when Saito was 20, he was conscripted into the army and joined the 10th Battalion of the 10th Division of Horse. During the next decade he saw several periods of active service in Manchuria and China but had been moved to Hanoi just before the start of the war with the West. His unit crossed into Thailand early in 1942 but within a short time all of its horses had died from the excessive heat. The battalion was then disbanded and its personnel were reallocated to other formations. Because of traditional antagonisms between different branches of the army it was thought to be inappropriate to post Saito, a long-standing sergeant-major of the cavalry, to serve with the infantry, so the excuse of ill-health was used to find him a niche elsewhere.

On Toosey's second day in Tamarkan a further party of men arrived from Singapore. Additional small groups continued to swell their numbers so that by November the total had risen to 1600. All of these were British but in February 1943 1000 Dutch troops joined the camp from Java and these, too, came under Toosey's control. The administration of such a substantial body of men was a heavy burden for Toosey. His prime responsibility was to produce sufficient fit men to meet the Japanese daily schedule of work, but in order to do this he was obliged to organize virtually every aspect of the camp's life and routine. To help in this massive task Toosey gradually recruited a team of individuals who, over time, were welded into a compact command structure. These included Major R. G. Lees of the 2nd Gordon Highlanders, who as his second-in-command became his 'right-hand man' for the next three years, and Captain David Boyle, who acted as camp adjutant and as official interpreter (see above, p. 8). He was assisted in these duties by Captain H. S. Wood of the RASC, while Captain M. P. Northcote of

Toosey's own regiment took charge of the canteen. Toosey also selected Regimental Sergeant-Major Coles of the 135th to act as the camp sergeant-major. The group was later joined by Colonel Scheyerer and his adjutant, Lieutenant de Grijs, who were appointed to represent the Dutch POWs after their arrival.

These arrangements enabled Toosey to delegate much of his authority so that he could devote himself to those things he felt he could do best. Regular 'management' meetings of his HQ Group were held every day, but once decisions had been made Toosey had the faith to leave his team to get on with their respective jobs. In practice, therefore, he was able to spend most of his time moving round the camp and work sites so that he could see everything that was taking place. He also attached great importance to being seen by the troops and keeping them as well informed as possible. Thus as soon as he had received his orders from Kosakata he called a full parade and explained the situation. He told them that good discipline was essential and would be enforced and that if they worked cheerfully he would do his best to obtain fair treatment and the best food that was available.

This style of leadership was well received for a variety of reasons. Though not regarded by his contemporaries as a master of administrative detail, Toosey had a remarkable capacity for remembering names and faces. This facility was supported by a tremendous and infectious enthusiasm. However, it was his ability to present a jaunty air of complete unconcern irrespective of the circumstances which endeared him to his men – many of whom appeared to have thought of him as a kind of eccentric English gentleman of the old school. The fact that he was always prepared to take their part against the Japanese was subsequently to confirm the widely held opinion that he was indeed a man worthy of command.

The bridges

The Japanese engineers gave their highest priority to the construction of the temporary wooden bridge, for until this could be completed little work could be undertaken on the far bank. Lieutenant Yoshida of 7 Company had made a geological survey of the proposed crossing sites in July 1942, and plans for the building of the timber structure were then prepared. During the following month, 6 Company of the 3rd Battalion of the 9th Railway Regiment was given the task of completing this project and even before the prisoners were involved they had secured much of the material and commenced the actual construction. However, it was the arrival of Toosey and large quantities of unskilled labour that permitted real progress to be made, for every pile had to be moved and riven into the river-bed by manpower alone:

> We started work the day after we arrived, carrying huge baulks of timber. It was the heaviest work I have ever known; the Japs drove us on and by nightfall I was so tired and sore that I could not eat my dinner and just crawled on to the bed and fell asleep. The next day was spent carrying stretchers of earth, also heavy work and incredibly monotonous. The hours were 8.30 am until 7.30 pm with an hour for lunch.[3]

All of this work was supervised by Japanese engineers who lived close by in a similar but more lavishly constructed camp. Their method of operation was to divide the prisoners into parties of about fifty men and then allocate each group to tasks such as the moving of timber, the pile-driving of foundations in the river and the digging and carriage of earth to form the embankment for the track. After the first few days a task system was evolved so that each party was given a particular amount to do during the day. In theory when this had been completed the POWs should have been free to return to the camp, but the Japanese frequently found additional tasks to employ those who had finished early.

Colonel Toosey complained vigorously when this happened and tried to explain that such tactics removed any incentive for the troops to do their best. He also pointed out repeatedly that this very heavy work could not be sustained for long on a diet which consisted mainly of rice and vegetables with only minute quantities of meat, salt, sugar and oil. He then proposed that if the Japanese really wished the work to be kept to schedule they must increase the rations, arrange regular hours and allow one day off each week. With the aid of Sergeant-Major Saito, these suggestions were gradually adopted, although the improvement to the food supply proved to be minimal and spasmodic. However, as these measures led to an immediate decrease in the men reporting sick and thus an increase in the number available for work the Japanese authorities did attempt to keep to their side of this arrangement.

The construction of the wooden bridge was undertaken with considerable energy and was virtually finished in December 1942, when much of it was swept away by especially severe floods. It was then quickly rebuilt, for most of the materials could be re-used and the labour and expertise were readily available. Thus it finally came into operation during the following month and was then used by light trains, pulled by diesel locomotives, until the main bridge was finished.

Throughout this period, work on what the engineers referred to as the 'Mekuron permanent bridge' was also proceeding at a great pace. (In all western accounts it is called the steel bridge.) Like the temporary structure, this had been planned after Lieutenant Yoshida's survey but its final form could not be arranged until suitable materials could be found. After an extensive search throughout the occupied territories a number of steel spans were discovered amongst the railway stores in Java. The plan was to place the eleven 20-metre trusses on to concrete abutments supported by concrete piers built on the 'well-sinking' principle. This would give an effective length of 238 metres, which was enough to cross the Kwae Yai at its normal level but not sufficient to cater for the additional width that followed the rainy season. A further nineteen 5-metre wooden spans were, therefore, incorporated into the design and these were to be placed at the northern end of the site where the channel was very shallow.[4]

The major engineering difficulty in such a construction is the building of the piers. The technique that was adopted by the Japanese in charge – H. Nishijima and Ko Sato – was the standard method used wherever the water is very deep and the bottom is not too hard. In this particular case the bed-rock (described by Futamatsu as 'slate') lay beneath 2 or 3 metres of softish over-burden and was always under a minimum of several metres of fast-flowing water. Thus it was very suitable for the well-sinking system, even though little modern machinery was available; on the Kwae Yai human muscle could always have been used as a substitute.

The building of a pier commenced with the erection of a temporary circular coffer dam which was filled with earth. A concrete ring, prefabricated at the side of the river from local gravel and sand, was then placed within the dam and as the earth was removed from the centre its weight would help it to sink. The provision of sharp bottom edges and of additional weights would further help the ring to settle and when it reached an appropriate level a second ring would be slotted on to its upper surface. The gradual accumulation of weight as successive rings were fitted would then slowly force the whole structure down into the strata but an essential element in this process was the removal of first the earth, and then the over-burden from within the pier.

The normal procedure would have been to use some form of mechanical device to cut into the river-bed and then raise the debris to some point outside the pier. The absence of virtually every type of modern machinery meant that even this task had to be undertaken by hand – a particularly difficult and dangerous occupation. Private Robert Hislop of the 2/80 Anti-Tank Regiment recalls:

About four of us used to do this work. We used to wear a very old-fashioned diving helmet which was fitted with an air pipe which in turn was fitted to an old-time air pump. We used to have to get inside these concrete pillars and go down to the bed of the river and keep removing the river-bed from under the concrete so that the pillars would sink. This was quite unpleasant as it was quite dark and we had to keep our bodies upright because if you bent over water was liable to get inside the helmet. I cannot remember how long we used to be under water before we came up for a spell, but it certainly seemed a hell of a long time.[5]

Private Hislop received extra rations while engaged on this special task but he thought that the real reward was that he was out of sight of the Japanese for brief periods: Yoshihiko Futamatsu has confirmed that POWs were employed in this manner but was sure that this practice ended as soon as a Gatmel digging machine became available in December 1942.

The erection of the concrete piers was undertaken simultaneously with the building of the approach works. These, too, were completed almost entirely by hand and required an immense amount of labour. In its later stages the need to synchronize the construction of the embankment so that the track could be laid as soon as the spans were fitted to the bridge meant a period of extra hard work. For a short time the troops from Tamarkan were obliged to work 18 hours a day. The result of these efforts was that everything was ready once the bridge was finished and it became fully operational in May 1943. The track was then diverted from the original wooden bridge and this was allowed to fall into disrepair.

Life at Tamarkan

In many respects Tamarkan was not typical of the camps which the Japanese established for the building of the railway. The construction of the bridges was such a substantial task that it required a large number of men to be employed over a relatively long period. This degree of permanency was a major factor in helping Colonel Toosey to create an organizational structure that was not possible elsewhere. In addition, the camp enjoyed excellent communications with the remainder of the country. The existing path to Kanchanaburi was improved to an acceptable standard within a few weeks, and by January 1943 the railway track from Banpong had also become operational as far as Tamarkan. The bridge camp was therefore able to avoid the worst of the difficulties, particularly the extreme shortages of food that camps further to the north were obliged to endure. Each mile up the Kwae Noi made the river shallower and less dependable, while the road constructed by the Thai authorities made only slow progress and was always liable to be washed away during the rainy season. Thus with all its problems the camp at Tamarkan had much to commend it and, under Toosey, was regarded by many as the best on the line.

When Toosey and his party arrived at Tamarkan a number of buildings had already been constructed by earlier arrivals with some guidance from the local Thais (see above, p. 8). One of the first men to arrive with Major Roberts's party was Private Hislop, who remembers that at that stage the only shelter was provided by six tents or tent flies:

> The day after we arrived we were taken to the River. All along the River Bank were rafts upon rafts of bamboo and great logs. All of this bamboo had to be got out of the river and carried to camp. This bamboo was to be used to build the huts for Tamarkan camp. The logs, which were about one and a half times the length of a Telegraph Pole, also had to be taken from the River and stacked – they were to be used for building the first bridge. Removing the bamboo and logs was no easy task as the banks of the river were very steep. This type of work went on for a few weeks. Several long huts were then built which we were able to move into – more troops then arrived – I think that about this time Colonel Toosey took over the camp.[6]

The accommodation constructed by Major Roberts's men was insufficient to house the substantial numbers brought by Toosey, which he quickly learned were rapidly to increase. He therefore saw the extension of the camp as his first priority and the building of additional huts was commenced immediately. These were to follow the traditional design using local materials:

> We slept six and a half to a bay, which gave us about 18 inches each, on bamboo slats raised about two feet off the ground. The roof was thatched with atap, which is made from the leaves of a certain variety of palm. The whole building was made of bamboo and lashed with a kind of raffia; there was not a nail used at all in its construction.[7]

Toosey planned to dig extra drainage ditches and extend existing latrines and other basic facilities as soon as everyone had a roof over his head. Unfortunately these arrangements were interrupted before they could be fully activated, for on the day after his arrival the Japanese began to make heavy demands for labour. As these rapidly increased, the number of men available for camp improvements quickly declined, and much of the task had to be completed by troops who had already undertaken a full day's work on official projects. At a later stage the Japanese insisted on using so many prisoners that too few able-bodied men were left to organize the essential services of the camp. In these circumstances the only way that fuel could be gathered, food prepared

105

and the fragile buildings maintained was by the employment of every individual – including officers – who even the Japanese accepted were too ill to be useful to them.

The basic food supplied by the Japanese consisted of broken rice, some green vegetables and a kind of long radish which Toosey likened to 'eating small bits of wood'. The only other items provided officially were in such small quantities that they could only be distributed as part of the daily stew. Saito permitted the purchase of a cow every 10 days and this meat also helped to flavour the mixture. Trading of personal possessions and of tools and materials stolen from the site helped to supplement this very inadequate diet. The most prized acquisitions from the local population were duck eggs, which were purchased in thousands, for these contained the nutrients which saved many lives. At first these were secured by a variety of unofficial means but after the Japanese gave their approval for the opening of a canteen in December 1942, eggs, fruit and Thai tobacco could all be legally acquired.

The money used in the canteen was a special Japanese currency issued generally in Thailand and used for the payment of POWs' wages. The amount earned by each individual was very tiny – a full week's employment would buy only three duck eggs – and was paid only to those actually at work. Officers' pay was much more substantial (see above, p. 75) but part was stopped for 'board and lodgings' and a further portion was banked for use after the war. Even so, officers did receive considerably larger amounts than the other ranks, so Toosey felt quite justified in deducting 30 or 40 per cent to help those who were sick and not able to earn. As all wages were paid through Toosey's administration, this was an easy matter to arrange and was never disputed by the officers involved. Some of this new paper money was used by those brave enough to buy items outside the camp where prices were much lower than in the canteen. Toosey did not attempt to prevent this illegal activity, but exacted a 10 per cent toll on all black market transactions. This was also used to aid the hospital and, in return, he always did his best to support those who were unfortunate enough to be caught by the Japanese.

The availability of regular supplies of even poor-quality rations, plus the opportunity to supplement this diet from the canteen and elsewhere, prevented the absolute hunger and malnutrition experienced in other camps. The health of the prisoners was also assisted by the abundance of beautiful, cold, clear water which could easily be pumped by hand from a conveniently placed well within the camp. The site itself was a good one that was quick to drain, while the closeness of the river meant that it was usually possible to enjoy a bath of sorts. Swimming in the Kwae Noi was subsequently forbidden after an outbreak of cholera further upstream, but Tamarkan remained remarkably healthy. Toosey placed great emphasis on the need for cleanliness and hygiene and in spite of the lack of mosquito nets, or even blankets, malaria was kept under control. Other common illnesses included those caused by vitamin deficiency, tropical ulcers and dysentery – the latter being vigorously fought by an anti-fly campaign and the sterilization of all cooking and eating utensils. Another aspect of this policy was Toosey's refusal to allow the growth of beards in case they housed lice. Part of one of the huts was screened off and designated as the 'hospital' and with the aid of drugs from Singapore only nine deaths occurred during the whole 10-month period that the bridges were under construction.

This comparatively idyllic situation was not, of course, the whole picture. In a situation where several thousand men were being pressed to perform uncongenial tasks by members of an alien culture, incidents were to be expected. Some of these involved disputes between the prisoners themselves or were concerned with physical problems. In these cases Toosey would quickly attempt to get to the root of the difficulty and dispose of it as rapidly as possible. These tactics have led to some suggestions that he sometimes acted in an arbitrary manner. If this is true it was from the best of motives, for he early realized that he must give the Japanese authorities no opportunity to intervene. Many of the incidents specifically involved Japanese engineers or Korean guards who undertook much of the routine supervision. The daily contact between the working troops and their masters produced constant friction. Most of the incidents were quickly over:

> Among both engineers and guards savagery alternated with outbursts of good temper, rather like children. Some we got to know well as characters. Most of them had nicknames and very descriptive they were: 'Undertaker', 'Mad Mongrel', 'Efficiency' and 'Hank the Yank'. Our captors were so different from ourselves that at worst we looked on them as wild animals rather than human beings, and at other times they were ridiculously funny.[8]

The engineers do not appear to have been personally vindictive. This was not true of the Koreans, many of whom were only too pleased to use any pretext either at work or within the camp as an excuse to beat a man up.

Anything which appeared to be restricting progress on the site was liable to lead to instant punishment irrespective of the merits of a particular case. The Japanese code of discipline was extremely harsh:

> Their discipline was immediate, physical and severe. Face-slapping, blows with anything available – rifle, shovel or lump of

wood, standing to attention for hours on end in the sun, sometimes holding heavy weights over our heads, sometimes solitary confinements in tiny cells of earth and bamboo for weeks at a time. It was often difficult to know what we had done wrong.[9]

In these instances there was little Toosey could do but protest after the event. This he invariably did, for from the very beginning he made a rigid rule that he would make an official complaint in respect of every illegal action. His insistence on this policy was to bring much verbal and some physical abuse upon himself and his interpreter, but in the long term its nuisance value undoubtedly helped to limit the more vicious attacks on the labour force.

To counteract the danger of incidents Toosey insisted on maintaining a strict control over the men in his charge. In extreme instances – for example, where an individual had stolen a blanket from a hospital patient – this involved his own brand of physical punishment which was administered by the regimental sergeant-major. His real aim, however, was to promote a degree of self-discipline and this was largely achieved because of the respect he gained from his ability to stand up to the common enemy. Even the few Australians under his command seem to have accepted his authority without too much difficulty, although they had a reputation for doing things in their own way. By and large the Australian troops were larger and fitter than their British counterparts so Toosey always called upon them when he needed volunteers to carry the heavy sacks of rice from the transport into the store – a task that was beyond the capabilities of the majority of the British prisoners. Some, though not all, of the Dutch also responded to Toosey's style of leadership and he found their specialized knowledge of tropical conditions a very useful asset.

A particular problem which was to create difficulties in a number of the camps along the line concerned the role and status of the officers. At Tamarkan, unlike many other establishments, a serious attempt was made to ensure equality of sacrifice. Thus Toosey would not permit a separate Officers' Mess, as he believed that this would undermine the unity he was so anxious to promote. As part of this policy Toosey arranged for the officers to sleep in the same huts as the men. This not only aided communication and understanding but also demonstrated that the officers were indeed sharing in the hardships being endured by the other ranks. A further aspect of Toosey's tactics was his insistence that his officers should go out with the working parties so that they could be on the spot to intervene in case of trouble. This decision was, however, to have unfortunate consequences with the Japanese.

At first the Japanese were quite content to allow the officers who accompanied the working parties to act purely as supervisors. This attitude then gradually changed and the officers were pressed to take an active part in the labour itself. A number of minor incidents followed and these culminated in the camp commandant ordering Lieutenant Bridge to get into a cutting and work with his men. This he refused to do and resisted when Lieutenant Kosakata attempted to push him into the ditch. After a brief struggle Lieutenant Bridge was overpowered and was subsequently confined in the guardroom. Toosey immediately complained but was told that in future all officers must act as labourers in exactly the same way as the men. He then received a direct order to this effect, so decided to call a meeting and consult with the officers themselves.

At this conference Colonel Toosey expressed his personal opinion that the officers had no real option and would have to work as instructed. He did feel that he would be able to persuade the Japanese to accept the principle that officers should go out only with their own particular unit and would not be obliged to form separate 'officers only' parties. In this event they would be able to continue to act as a buffer between the engineers and their men even though they were to undertake physical labour for the first time. He went on to suggest that there were only two alternatives:

> Either you are going to work and we will try to get the best terms we can or you are not going to work and you are going to stand there if necessary until they shoot you.[10]

Toosey then told the meeting that he was prepared to be guided by their view – 'If you refuse I will stand and get shot with you.'[11]

The result of this consultation was a unanimous decision to work on the best terms that could be secured. When this news was given to the Japanese they agreed to release Lieutenant Bridge from the guardroom and on the following day the officers went out with their men. They went fully prepared for physical labour and a few were, in fact, engaged in manual tasks. However, once Lieutenant Kosakata had made his point he lost interest in the matter and at a later stage prevented officers from working. In the meanwhile they continued to accompany the parties to the sites but gradually resumed a purely supervisory role.

The resolving of this major dispute at an early stage in the building of the bridges did much to enhance Toosey's authority with both the Japanese and the prisoners. His stronger position then helped him to restrict the arbitrary actions of some of the Japanese and Koreans. Thus an attack on Major Roberts was ultimately settled by an apology from the soldier concerned in spite of the fact that the British officer had retaliated. Toosey's special situation was not affected when Lieutenant

Takasaki took over from Kosakata on 30 December 1942, although a serious incident took place the next evening. This involved a number of soldiers of the Highland regiments who, after celebrating Hogmanay, were alleged to have pushed a Korean guard out of their way when returning to their huts. Toosey was woken by Takasaki and the entire camp was eventually called on parade and instructed to stand to attention until the culprits confessed. After a while 4 men came forward and said that they were responsible. Toosey doubted their story and when the parade had been dismissed was able to convince Takasaki that they had acted from the highest motives. Consequently their punishment was relatively light – 12 hours in the sun standing in front of the guardroom.

At a later stage an assault on David Boyle, the camp's official interpreter, confirmed Toosey's status. A misunderstanding with a Korean guard led to Boyle being struck with a rifle and suffering a broken arm and crushed ribs. Toosey refused to allow Boyle to return to his duties, which might well have involved him in serious injury. Boyle's absence had the effect of totally disrupting the organization of the working parties so after failing to persuade Toosey to change his mind, the Japanese gave the Korean a severe beating. It was agreed at this point that the 'key people' must not be treated in this way and that Boyle, although still in considerable pain, should resume his duties. Thereafter the Koreans, at least, tended to confine themselves to verbal abuse.

These advances did not mean an end to Japanese brutality, but they did help to establish a restraining influence. Officers may have been given rather more favourable treatment but were still liable to suffer on occasions. Thus Lieutenant May, of the 80th Anti-Tank Regiment, was struck by a Japanese sergeant while out on a working party. He fought back and after knocking the NCO down was dragged back into the camp. Although he had not started the fight, Lieutenant May was subsequently sentenced to 28 days' solitary confinement, which he had to serve in a tiny room only 6 feet square on a diet of rice and water – a very light punishment by contemporary standards.

Some incidents were much more serious and in these cases there was always the danger that the *kempeitai* would become involved. This body of security police – the Japanese equivalent of the Gestapo – were completely ruthless and feared as much by their own nationals as by the prisoners. They employed very refined methods of torture to gain information, although this did not always obtain the right answers. In one such incident a Corporal Lawson was caught stealing Japanese tools and selling them to the local population to raise funds for the hospital. He was subsequently interviewed by the *kempeitai* and after hearing a long series of groans and screams Toosey was finally given permission to enter the room where he was being questioned:

> There was Corporal Lawson standing completely naked, facing the Japanese Officer, who had a drawn sword on the table, and his back was raw with weals from a whip, from his neck to his heels. I asked what the trouble was and he said: 'Well Sir, I have told these little brutes the truth and they won't believe me and I am not going to lie to please them.' I said: 'Now Lawson, don't be a fool, do you know what they want you to say?' and he said: 'Yes Sir', I said: 'Well say it, and if your conscience is in any way hurt, I will take full responsibility when we get home.'[12]

As soon as Lawson told them what they thought were the real facts his punishment stopped and he was sentenced to a long term of imprisonment. Lawson lived through this and survived the war; the incident taught Toosey that torture does not always produce the truth – merely what the other side wishes to hear. Although extremely serious, this incident, and others like it, were completely overshadowed by the events which followed attempts to escape.

Tamarkan was not a POW camp in the accepted sense. It did have a perimeter fence and ditch but it was comparatively easy for prisoners to evade these obstacles and slip out during the hours of darkness. Although many took advantage of this fact to visit local people in order to trade, few were tempted to try to escape altogether. The great distance from the nearest Allied centres in China and India would have been a formidable problem in any event. When the lack of equipment and supplies, plus the hostility and fear of the native populations were added, the feat became a near impossibility and there are no records of any successful escapes through the tropical rain forest.

In spite of the obvious hazards, a number of individuals decided that they would take their chance while they were still reasonably fit. When Toosey heard of these plans he thought he would go with the party but was eventually dissuaded by the argument that his departure would lower the morale of those who remained behind.

Consequently the group that left on 28 January 1943 was made up of just two officers and four other ranks. Toosey arranged for their absence from roll-calls to be concealed for a period of 48 hours. When it was discovered the *kempeitai* were quickly notified. The men who slept in close proximity to the absentees were questioned and, partly as a gesture to these feared interrogators, Sergeant-Major Saito kept Toosey standing at attention for 12 hours in front of the guardroom. This symbolic punishment for Saito's 'loss of face' probably saved Toosey from more serious attention elsewhere.

After leaving the camp the escape party quickly split into two sections, which then went their own separate ways. The group containing the four other ranks was soon caught and within 10 days they had been brought back to Tamarkan. Toosey's attempts to intercede on their behalf proved to be useless and 2 days later they were taken away by truck. According to the subsequent check on this vehicle's milometer it travelled into the jungle for a distance of only 4 miles and then returned without the British prisoners. The local Thais later reported that they had been shot, but the Japanese refused to confirm this at the time.

The other group consisted of Captain E. G. Pomeroy of the 2/12th Frontier Force Rifles of the Indian Army and Lieutenant Howard of the 80th Anti-Tank Regiment RA. Details of their journey and recapture were learned from Pomeroy's diary, which was afterwards stolen from the Japanese Office at Tamarkan:

> It was a very tragic document. In the early stages they talked of the joy of being free again, hearing the jungle cock crowing, and so on and so forth. Their route was close to the river because that was the only place they could get water. Gradually their move was shortened each day. They caught malaria and in the end they were handed over to the Japanese for a pretty large sum of money by the Thais.[13]

Pomeroy and Howard were returned to Tamarkan under escort on 20 February 1943. In spite of repeated requests, Toosey was not allowed to speak to them and three days later they were driven away and not seen again. During this period they endured severe interrogation by *kempeitai* and were then sentenced to death. Both Saito and G. P. Adams, a POW who later wrote an account of Tamarkan, understood that Lieutenant Takasaki made such a strong recommendation for a reprieve that he was subsequently reprimanded. Toosey was never convinced that this was the case and Takasaki was executed as a war criminal for this offence at the end of hostilities.

The news of Pomeroy and Howard's fate was not revealed until after the war but both local Thais and Korean guards provided eye-witness accounts at the time. These sources agreed that Pomeroy and Howard were required to dig their own graves before being beheaded by ceremonial sword. These details led to great consternation in Tamarkan and in Toosey's view it was foolish of the Japanese to have brought their captives back to the camp. However, they undoubtedly felt that they were obliged to demonstrate the futility of attempts to escape and, in fact, very few further ventures of this kind were to be undertaken anywhere in Thailand.[14]

7

The completion of the railway

Construction of the Line

The completion of the 'permanent bridge' at Tamarkan removed a major obstacle and the track could then be pushed to the north at a great pace. However, even before the railway was able to cross the Kwae Yai at this point, a considerable amount of preparatory work had already been accomplished. This had started with the establishment of a series of camps along virtually the whole of the proposed route (see Map 3, p. 88). These had then formed the focal points for the build-up of materials and supplies which were scheduled to be delivered while the river was at a high level. The rapid increase in the numbers of both POW and civilian labour meant that the work of clearing the jungle, levelling the ground and building embankments and bridges could be pressed forward and the combination of cool, dry weather and the presence of adequate water in the Kwae Noi meant that substantial progress had been made by February 1943.

This favourable situation, plus the worsening of the military position, then encouraged the Japanese to advance the target date for the completion of the railway from November to August 1943. Unfortunately this decision was made just when the increasing heat and the fall in the water level were making the conditions of work much more difficult. Nevertheless the route was completed along level ground and through a large cutting which had to be blasted through a high ridge near the base camp at Chungkai, so that by the beginning of April the track was finished as far as the 87-kilometre mark at Ban Khao.

The constructors then had to face the formidable task of taking the rails through the narrow gorge which the Kwae Noi had cut through the high plateau at Wampo. As there was no possibility of a detour, a ledge had to be hacked out over the river for a distance of over 400 yards. At some points gaps needed to be filled in along the cliff face and these

113

required massive timbers up to 60 feet in length to be fixed into the rocks at ground level.

By an enormous effort and with an absolute disregard of the welfare of their workforce, the Japanese were able to finish this task as planned:

> Three weeks ago there was nothing there at all: now there is not only this vast bridge but steam engines limping slowly over it. The two thousand pre-dynastic slaves of Wam Po had built the entire thing in 17 days! We would have liked to, but couldn't, deny the stupendous achievement: and it was characteristically Japanese, not only because it was a crazy wooden bridge that nevertheless functioned, but because no other nation of the world in 1943 would have bashed and bullied, and sweated and slaved prisoners to such fantastic lengths for such an object.[1]

Thus by early May major obstacles at Tamarkan, Chungkai and Wampo had all been overcome and the railway was operational as far as Tha Soe approximately 130 kilometres from Nong Pladuk. However, the deterioration in the weather was causing considerable slippage to the revised programme so in an attempt to counteract this slowdown the Japanese arranged for further large numbers of men to be moved to the area. This resulted in over 61,000 Allied prisoners and a quarter of a million Asians being employed on the project and in a decision to speed up the whole process of construction.

The correctly called 'Speedo' period which followed saw the Japanese utilize every form of brutality in a desperate attempt to achieve their aims. These tactics led to grave hardships and heavy casualties but were not sufficient to offset the difficulties induced by the onset of the rainy season:

> In 1943 the monsoon proper broke on the 22nd of May and for the next sixteen days the driving rain lashed the railway trace almost without pause. The Kwae Noi rose in flood and swamped several of the jungle camps completely, every unmade road and jungle track became a watercourse and a layer of thick glutinous mud lay on the surface of even the higher camps.[2]

In addition to the immense problems caused by the incessant rain, the route above Tha Soe presented its own set of natural hazards. For the next 50 kilometres the terrain was extremely harsh and required the construction of a large number of cuttings and bridges. One of the former, at Kanyu, was 600 yards long and involved the removal of such massive quantities of rock that it became known as 'Hellfire Pass' and caused many deaths. Some of the bridges were also very substantial – over the length of the railway, sixty-three measured more than 50 metres and many of these bigger structures were to be found in the Tha Soe to Rin Tin sector. Of particular note was the high bridge at Hintok which was a quarter of a mile long and 80 feet high. Although, like all others on the line, it was designed in accordance with the American Merriman-Wiggin standard practice for timber bridges, it was to collapse three times during the course of its construction.

By any normal standard the appalling conditions should have prevented any form of work being undertaken during the monsoon period, but the determination of the Japanese and their total indifference to the suffering of others did enable some limited progress to be maintained. At first this was very slow and the rails did not reach Tonchan (139 kilometres) until the end of June. As the weather gradually eased, the rate of construction slowly improved and Kin Saiyok (172 kilometres) was reached on 30 July. This meant that light traffic drawn by diesel Plorries fitted with special steel wheels could use the line to this point, but the rails needed to be properly gauged before they were suitable for steam locomotives. A further improvement in conditions and the terrain then permitted the track-layers to make more rapid progress. This party of what became specialists was made up, for much of the route, by members of the 9th Battalion of the Northumberland Fusiliers. Their expertise and the increasingly favourable situation then allowed them to lay up to 3 kilometres a day and the track became operational as far as Dha Khanun, otherwise known as Takanun, (218 kilometres) in September. The final sector to the north of Konkuita (262 kilometres) could then be finalized with relative ease and the line from Nong Pladuk was joined with the track built from Burma on 17 October 1943.

Tamarkan's new function

Once the steel bridge was completed, the majority of the fit men were quickly deployed to working camps further up the line. Colonel Toosey fully expected to move with them but, in the event, the Japanese ordered him to stay behind and organize Tamarkan as a base hospital. Once it was clear that this decision could not be reversed Toosey put all his energy into the task of securing the maximum quantity of men and resources that would enable him to cope with his new responsibilities. These efforts were redoubled when, towards the end of April, parties of up to 250 men arrived on successive nights. These were *en route* to the neighbouring camp at Chungkai, which was also being turned into a base hospital. Although each group stayed for only one night this was sufficient for Toosey to understand the deplorable condition of many of the individuals being evacuated from the north and the need to make adequate preparations for their reception.

115

Unfortunately, Toosey was not able to arrange for any structural alterations within the site, so the huts previously used for working troops were merely redesignated as hospital wards. Toosey was also unsuccessful in persuading the Japanese to supply more than negligible quantities of drugs, and as the items brought by his party from Singapore were virtually exhausted by this time he could see that a serious shortage would quickly arise. He foresaw a similar situation in the case of food, for he knew that the ration scale for the sick was considerably less than the already inadequate levels allocated to the fit.[3]

When these unpalatable facts were added to the knowledge that the sick would receive no pay to supplement their rations and that the proportion of men working would be too small to make a significant contribution to Tamarkan's amenity funds, Toosey viewed the future with great apprehension. His misgivings were soon to be fully justified:

> Parties of approximately 100 arrived nightly and the Camp reached its maximum strength [of 3000] by July. The sick were in an appalling condition, approximately 75 per cent of the parties were stretcher cases and men frequently arrived dead. They were brought in cattle trucks ... the load being between 30 and 40 per truck. No arrangements had been made for feeding or treatment on the journey by the Japanese. On one occasion a party of 60, mostly stretcher cases, were dumped off a train in a paddy field some 2 miles from the Camp in the pouring rain at 0300 hrs. They were left without a Guard and a search party had to go out from the Camp to locate them. It is impossible to describe adequately the condition of these men. As a typical example I can remember one man who was so thin that he could be lifted easily in one arm. His hair was growing down his back and was full of maggots; his clothing consisted of a ragged pair of shorts soaked with dysentery excreta; he was lousy and covered with flies all the time. He was so weak that he was unable to lift his head to brush away the flies which were clustered on his eyes and on the sore places of his body. I forced the Japanese Staff to come and look at these parties, which could be smelt for some hundreds of yards, but with the exception of the Camp Comdt. they showed no signs of sympathy, and sometimes merely laughed.[4]

As Toosey was responsible for coping with these individuals he carried an almost intolerable burden. Fortunately his load was to be shared, and considerably lightened, by the team he gradually recruited to perform specific tasks. As a result of his representations Toosey was ultimately allowed to retain Captains Boyle and Wood, who continued with their previous jobs as interpreter and quarter master respectively, and six other ranks to provide an ongoing administration. He was also able to obtain forty members from various units to act as cooks while five doctors and forty-five medical orderlies were transferred to Tamarkan from other camps. In addition Toosey was fortunate to be able to obtain the services of Captain Chaplain J. Carel Hamel of Semarang, Java, who was a member of the armed forces of the Netherlands East Indies. Throughout the period that Tamarkan was used as a base hospital, Hamel was the only padre in the camp and as the Japanese consistently refused to provide other clergymen he was kept constantly busy caring for the sick and seeing to the burial of the dead. The high esteem in which he came to be regarded has been summarized by one of his colleagues:

> His untiring work and fine example were an inspiration and solace to men of many diverse nationalities and creeds.[5]

It was, however, the arrival of the medical personnel which led Toosey to believe that it would be possible to provide some real help to the patients that were expected at any moment. Dr. Arthur Moon of the Australian Army Medical Corps recalls:

> I was sent down from Hintock camp, joining Major N. C. Lendon, R. A. M. C., and Captain Ross, R. A. M. C., at Tarsao [Tha Soe] arriving at Tamarkan in the evening of 1st May, 1943. The original medical staff consisted of six medical officers drawn from the various jungle camps, one Dental Officer [Captain Diggle, A. D. C.] and a party of fifty medical orderlies under the charge of R. Q. M. S. Hanlan from Nong Pladuk. We were warmly welcomed by Colonel Toosey and his staff, were fed, had time for a quick look round the empty camp and then bedded down in one of the large huts. My immediate reaction was a feeling of relief on having arrived at a clean, well established camp, under the command of a friendly and energetic British officer.
>
> The following morning I was appointed by Colonel Toosey as Senior Medical Officer [SMO] and immediately became involved in detailed planning for the arrival of the sick ... The first batch of 117 patients arrived the following day, by which time plans had been made for their reception, classification, and allocation to appropriate wards according to diseases, such as dysentery, malaria, malnutrition, skin infection and injuries.[6]

Toosey's judgement in selecting Dr Moon to be SMO was quickly vindicated: he rapidly earned a fine reputation as an excellent surgeon and as a man who would spare no effort to aid those in his care. This was just as well, for the number of patients rose at an alarming pace and a highly organized administrative structure became necessary. Extra assistance was secured by the employment of those convalescing at a stage in their recovery when they were well enough to undertake minor tasks though not sufficiently advanced to be sent back to the working camps in the north. These included men who also had other responsibilities as hut commanders, hut sergeant-majors and messing NCOs. This process was greatly aided by Toosey's extremely retentive memory. Thus when he came across William Naylor during one of his regular visits to the wards he recognized him as a gunner from the 135th Field Regiment who possessed considerable clerical ability. Consequently when Naylor was discharged he immediately became a member of Toosey's team at camp HQ. In a similar way Toosey recalled that Captain Blackater had previously been a poultry farmer. As a result when permission had been obtained to start a duck and pig farm he was the man chosen to be placed in charge.

Even when particular skills were not required Toosey apparently had the knack of selecting the right individual for the job. In the case of Len Baynes this meant that he was given the responsibility for planning the cemetery and of seeing that sufficient graves were available to meet the demand. Needless to say Toosey's judgement was soon vindicated and the later work of the War Graves Commission greatly eased. This task brought Baynes into close contact with Padre Hamel:

> One of the most lovable and tolerant men I have known. His English
> was quite good and he conducted every service, whatever the
> denomination. Many of the Dutch were Roman Catholics, and
> 'Dominee', as he was called, had acquired a Catholic service book,
> and meticulously carried out every jot and tittle of their ritual although
> some of it was against the teaching of his own church. He told me that
> he was not really allowed to bury them, but that as it seemed to make
> the other surviving Catholics happy, he hoped the Pope would forgive
> him if he ever found out.[7]

Thus a dual system of control, which involved both medical and non-medical staff having direct access to Toosey, gradually emerged and this proved to be a highly successful and harmonious arrangement.

Everyone was found a place within this structure where he could make his own individual contribution. Toosey saw this as a major part of the rehabilitation process, for even taking a minor part in a programme of fly-swatting made people feel that they were improving their situation and, in a way, controlling their own destiny. Captain Burton of the Royal Norfolk Regiment experienced this system at first hand. Although barely able to walk and in only the early stages of recovery he was still pressed into service as a 'book reader' and subsequently spent many hours detailing the exploits of Hercule Poirot in Agatha Christie's *Murder on the Blue Train* to listeners frequently in great pain. Burton was also aware of the terrible dilemma which faced the medical staff on many occasions: with a limited quantity of drugs the policy which had to be adopted was to give them to the patients who stood the best chance of pulling through – they could not be 'wasted' on those who seemed certain to die.

In spite of its very obvious limitations, Tamarkan was soon regarded as the best organized and best administered POW camp on the railway. One consequence of this was that the Japanese took very little interest in the running of the camp and regarded it as a necessary evil where men who could no longer make a contribution to the building of the railway could be conveniently dumped and forgotten. The low status with which Tamarkan was then perceived can be judged by the appointment of Sergeant Hosomi as its man in charge. Although he subsequently showed his good intentions on many occasions, his inferior rank prevented him from achieving very much with the Japanese hierarchy. He was also unable to maintain any effective control over the Korean guards and it was only by constant pressure and complaint that Toosey was able to bring to an end a series of incidents involving brutality and stupidity.

The other side to Japanese indifference was that it allowed Toosey and his team to arrange matters in what they felt were the most convenient and efficient ways. Thus the organization which then developed was a pragmatic one designed to minimize the lack of suitable buildings and adequate staff and to help overcome the initial shortages of drugs and food. A major aspect of this policy was that everyone was expected to provide the maximum effort that his particular circumstances permitted. The tremendous success of these tactics was largely due to the example set by Philip Toosey.

Toosey's special role

Many independent sources stress the beneficial impact which Toosey exerted on the lives of all who came to Tamarkan. This began with their arrival, for irrespective of the time or of the state of the weather he always made it his business to meet every party. He tried to welcome every individual personally, helped to carry the stretcher cases and ensured that everyone was given a cup of tea before being allocated to a place in an appropriate hut. Then, before the hour was out, a hot meal of some kind was invariably provided. The net effect of these activities was that each person felt that he had entered a new world, far superior to the one he had just left, and for the first time in a long period enjoyed the belief that someone was really interested in his welfare.

Typical of many accounts of this reception is that provided by Len

Baynes, then a sergeant in the Cambridgeshire Regiment, who arrived on 11 May 1943:

Colonel Toosey told us to sit on our kits while he spoke to us. 'This is Tamarkan camp', he told us, 'and it's about the cleanest in Thailand: I'm going to rely on you to help me keep it this way.' This was the first and only time that I was welcomed to a camp, but then Toosey was a quite exceptional officer ...

After our pep talk we were allocated a space each in a nice clean hut, and at five o'clock given our first meal. As soon as we had eaten we were called out again and taken down to the river to wash. The Colonel had no intention of letting us remain in our dirt any longer than was necessary.

When I got the chance to look around, I had to admit that it really was clean and tidy. Colonel Toosey proved to be the best officer I was to find running a camp.[8]

Captain Burton reports a similar experience though, as he was desperately ill, the circumstances were a little different:

The journey on the stretcher was only a short one. We came to a camp and I was taken into a long, low atap hut and placed near the end. There were a few lights and in this semi-darkness I could see a small group who seemed in charge of everything that was going on. Their obvious chief was a sunburnt, fair-haired man clad only in white shorts. When he came nearer I could see that he was quite good-looking.

He introduced himself as the C. O. of this camp – Tamarkan Bridge, which was a fairly well organised hospital camp. Like all the other hospitals for prisoners-of-war it was fantastically short of necessary medical equipment and supplies. So to achieve any degree of organization called for superhuman ingenuity and improvisation.

The C. O. spoke kindly to me, assured me that I was out of danger and would soon be on my feet again. It was probably a formality, for the doctor had yet to examine me: but it was tremendously encouraging.[9]

Walter Kirley, an Australian infantry man, has also spoken of how Toosey made him feel happy and welcome at Tamarkan. Captain Blackater of the Indian Army initially found the bridge camp attractive purely as a reaction to the appalling conditions at Tha Soe:

But Tamarkan was good for another reason. During the summer and autumn of 1943 its British Commandant was Lt. Col. P. J. D. Toosey, 135 Fd. Reg., R. A. He showed what could be done when a Camp

Commandant stood up to the Japanese. And not in that alone. He moved freely through the camp and hospital, he spoke to the men, he was their friend and they knew it. He maintained discipline, too, and that on occasion with a strong hand ...

Colonel Toosey and [Captain] Boyle met every party of sick who arrived from up country, whether they came by day or by night. A long time later the Colonel said to me, 'I shall never forget the look on those men's faces when they arrived at Tamarkan.' I knew what he meant.

On arrival we all received a mug of hot tea, a smoke, and – perhaps the greatest blessing of all – a cake of soap. Within an hour we had a hot meal.[10]

Toosey's concern did not end with his reception for the new intake of patients. He made it his business to get to know as many of the troops as possible and took a keen interest in all aspects of the camp's activities. A considerable amount of time had to be spent smoothing out difficulties as they arose with the Japanese and the Korean guards, but much more was occupied in regular tours of inspection and in attempting to improve the physical conditions in which all were obliged to live. However, it was his desire to keep an eye on the welfare of his men – both staff and patients – which provided a never-ending task but one which, ultimately, was extremely rewarding both for them and himself.

These tactics enabled him to be aware of the particular pressures experienced by many individuals and, in turn, allowed him to provide the help or solace that was within his power. An example of his practical concern can be seen through the case of George Downes of the 18th Division's Royal Engineers:

I was the second person to have a leg amputated in Tamarkan in September, 1943, by Major Moon. Brigadier Toosey (Colonel as he was then), the Camp Commandant, visited the ulcer ward every day, a great figure, immaculate in uniform. As he walked down the hut this particular day he asked when I could get on my crutches. I told him that I would be allowed to the following day, so he invited me to his office for a cup of coffee at 5 p.m. But on that day I got a dose of malaria and I told the Colonel's batman to let him know that I wouldn't be able to come. But at 5 p.m. along came the Colonel to the hut with a tin plate and a cup of coffee in his hands. He sat down on my bamboo-slatted, sack-covered bed and said: 'As you couldn't come to see me, I thought I would visit you.' And I dined on the fried egg, sweet potatoes, ersatz coffee he had brought me, with a Nippon cigarette to follow.[11]

Even when former patients had fully recovered and were ready to be redeployed in the working camps, Toosey still attempted to soften the blow of their departure. All prisoners are agreed that a major factor in their survival was the comradeship provided by their friends. Toosey fully appreciated this fact and always did his best to keep units, smaller groups and even friends together. One instance where Toosey intervened directly involved a junior officer of the Royal Norfolk Regiment. D. G. Horner was placed on a draft for the north but wished to remain at Tamarkan until his friend, Robert Cole, who was suffering from scarlet fever, could recover. Unfortunately he could not find a volunteer to take his place so became resigned to going on alone. At this stage Toosey learned of his difficulty and, without being asked, ordered another officer to go in his place. The effect of his instruction on the officer concerned is not recorded but it certainly made Lieutenant Horner very content and demonstrated that this part of the army's administration still retained a human face.[12]

Colonel Toosey possessed another characteristic which greatly endeared him to those who worked with him and especially to those who served under him. This was his readiness to take off his shirt and lend a hand whenever help was needed. One, relatively minor, incident shows this very clearly. On this occasion the pigs for the 'farm' arrived unexpectedly before their pens had been constructed. A large working party had to be organized at once and both Toosey and David Boyle joined in and did not stop until the building had been completed after dark.

A more serious event occurred soon afterwards. This involved a great storm with exceptionally high winds which caused the hut containing the ulcer patients to collapse. No one was killed, but as this accident took place in the dark this could not be finally established until the following morning:

> I suppose ... these storms are apt to frighten people when they are sick, I know I was – perhaps not afraid but a little bit concerned that night because that hut of probably 200 badly or very ill ulcer patients were soaked to the skin for a matter of hours and if you can imagine being soaked to the skin from 10 o'clock at night to 4 or 5 in the morning on probably empty stomachs and a very sore leg, it is not the best of circumstances, I am afraid, to give a great deal of confidence. Anyway, within a very short time of the hut blowing down Colonel Toosey, Captain Boyle, Major Moon and Carel Hamel, were walking amongst us up and down the hut, talking to everyone, hurricane lamp in one hand and a word of friendship and hope and it is something I will never forget.

Colonel Toosey was a man amongst men: a man who not only showed his bravery in combat conditions but on a night like this that I can remember very vividly, Colonel Toosey showed he was a man, a Christian, and a friend to us all.[13]

One man who worked very closely with Colonel Toosey during this period was W. M. Naylor. His role as chief clerk made him a key member of the team and put him in an excellent position to assess the character and motivation of his Commanding Officer:

He was a man of great energy and also a man who was very fit. I think he had very high standards and a need for discipline. He was not a strict disciplinarian, but he believed that if one maintained good discipline then this was good for morale. He was particularly concerned about personal hygiene – and the need to keep flies down. A lot of the diseases we have talked about were fly-borne diseases. So things like latrines and rubbish or dirt or tidiness he was hot on. He used to do regular inspections of the huts we were working in. He was particularly concerned about hygiene in the kitchens and he was a stickler for that sort of thing ...

He had a way of making the men feel things would improve: that he was there to do what he could to make things improve. He gave pep talks which were pep talks ...

He was a good speaker and he was convincing. He was just a very good natural leader of men. We saw the results of what he did. He was always on the spot if anything went wrong. He was ready to intervene with the Japanese if it was necessary, and he was determined to get everyone as fit as possible and get them to look after themselves. He had got ... a charisma which made people feel confidence in him.

I don't know that he had any extraordinary qualities in that he was extraordinarily gifted in any way. He was a man who obviously cared for his troops. He would always put himself out to do anything for the troops and, unlike many of the other officers, he was concerned about other people more than for himself.[14]

It should not be thought that Toosey was anxious solely for the physical welfare of those in his charge. He fully understood the need to cater for the 'whole' man and strongly encouraged a wide range of sporting and cultural activities. Although these were obviously constrained by the circumstances, it was possible to arrange many events. Games were permitted in the afternoon and baseball became particularly popular. A stage was also available and the concert parties which gradually emerged provided a large number of successful shows which helped everyone to forget their immediate problems. Many of the prisoners also found solace in the pursuit of various types of arts and crafts. In an effort to give further stimulation to these therapeutic pastimes Toosey suggested that an exhibition of work should be held. This duly took place on 9 September when an astonishing array of paintings, engravings, woodcuts and models were put on display. The colonel then held a special ceremony at which a number of prizes were awarded – somewhat surprisingly the majority of these went to the Dutch prisoners who formed a small minority in the camp. These activities and amenities

> played an important part in maintaining the morale of the troops and the rehabilitation of convalescents. As camp conditions improved football, soft-baseball, volley ball and badminton were played regularly on the weekly *yasumi* or rest day. Concerts, lectures, discussions, bridge and chess tournaments, arts and crafts exhibitions and music of all sorts, from a 'squeeze box', violin and banjo. These amenities did not come as gifts from our captors but were hard-won from them by the sustained efforts of Colonel Toosey and his staff.[15]

Morale was also raised by the increasingly better news provided by the radio which, in spite of the enormous risks involved, continued to supply a welcome link with the outside world. The fall of Italy on 9 September was rightly regarded as a significant step towards ultimate freedom for the prisoners but it had no impact on the practical difficulties faced by those in charge of administration of the many railway camps including Tamarkan.

Tamarkan and the 'V' scheme

The tremendous efforts made by Colonel Toosey and his team to establish Tamarkan as a viable base hospital were threatened from the outset by two major factors outside their control. The first of these was the supply of food, for the Japanese policy of reducing the rations of those who were sick pressed very heavily in a camp where only 400 out of 3000 were classified as workers. As the full issue itself was woefully inadequate, it will be appreciated that food quickly became very scarce. This gloomy picture was made worse by the fact that no pay was received for the patients and although Toosey deducted two-thirds from those earning full salaries he could do little to supplement the rations for any but the severely ill. A great deal of local food was available outside the camp, so items purchased and bartered from the Thais helped to overcome the shortages in the early months. Then, as the last remnants of hoarded cash and prized possessions were exhausted, the situation became really critical.

These circumstances made it extremely difficult to provide proper care for the sick and their chances of recovery were further reduced by the failure of the Japanese to provide more than a token quantity of drugs and medical equipment. The first issue to what was to become a substantial hospital catering for large numbers of seriously ill patients consisted of only a few dozen iodine crystals, three bandages and five aspirin tablets.

These twin deficiencies of food and medicine had the inevitable consequence of raising the death rate and an early peak was reached on 18 June when six men were buried. As the grim average of deaths gradually rose both Toosey and Moon experienced a degree of despair as they felt the situation slipping outside their control. It was under these dire conditions that Toosey was approached by an NCO he did not recognise. This individual, whom Toosey was later to identify as Corporal R. C. H. Johnson, told him that he was acting as an interpreter for a party of Japanese who were visiting Tamarkan from the nearby camp at Chungkai. He went on to inform him that Chungkai was in receipt of considerable help from the local community and that he was prepared to establish contact with his friends so that Tamarkan could also benefit.

When Toosey asked how he might follow this up, his visitor suggested that he should write down his name, rank and number on a piece of paper which he said he would give to a man named Boon Pong who owned a store in Kanchanaburi. Then, when Toosey was next allowed to accompany the ration truck into the town, he was to make himself known to this gentleman in as inconspicuous a manner as possible.

This development placed Toosey in an quandary, for while he was desperate to secure aid he was well aware that he might be walking into a trap which could have dangerous consequences. His confidence was further eroded by the fact that Johnson, an Anglo-Thai, looked very Japanese to Toosey's suspicious eye and, in the short term, there was no way of confirming his identity with the authorities in Chungkai. However, such was the need that, after discussing the matter at great length with Dr Moon, Toosey decided to take a chance.

In the event these arrangements were quite genuine and worked perfectly. Thus on his next trip to Kanchanaburi Toosey was able to encourage his guards to enter Boon Pong's establishment. Its proprietor quickly appreciated the situation and proved to be very hospitable. Then, while the Japanese were enjoying a quiet drink, Toosey was able to make arrangements for cash and drugs to be delivered to the bridge camp. These were to be mixed in with the vegetables which Boon Pong normally supplied in huge baskets and, unless there was a special search, it seemed unlikely that they would be detected. He was also able to make provisional plans for ongoing supplies. As part of these arrangements, Toosey subsequently sent Boon Pong the following letter for onward transmission:

> There are 1730 sick men in this camp; 28 have died during the last month. We have no money and the men do not receive pay.
> We are urgently in need of money for food and medicines. The amount of money required by this camp is $4,000 per month. We should be very grateful for any help. This camp has no connection with Chungkai Hospital Camp.[16]

The items promised by Boon Pong duly arrived at Tamarkan and proved to be the first of many such deliveries. A simple but effective system was quickly devised so that messages were transmitted via the ration truck on its regular trips into Kanchanaburi. Toosey travelled with the vehicle on most of the early visits to Boon Pong's store but when the Japanese showed some suspicion he took the driver into his confidence. Thereafter Corporal Locke undertook responsibility for these transactions and small quantities of drugs and bank notes were smuggled into camp on virtually all of his return journeys. Although the self-imposed rule of 'little and often' was carefully adhered to, the quantities of cash and medicine received in Tamarkan rose rapidly. Thus in the period June–November 1943 (after which the camp lost its status as a base hospital), the value of these items amounted to 42,105 ticals (approximately £3500).

The provision of this outside support was to exert an immediate and beneficial influence on the lives of all who lived at Tamarkan:

> In July a noticeable improvement came about in the camp. Colonel Toosey had made contact with the so-called, and very secret, 'V' Organization and money began coming into the camp for the supply of extra food and drugs for the sick. It is impossible to describe the life-saving effect of this. It permitted the purchase of suitable food and essential drugs such as emetine, sulphonamide, chloroform, codoform, dressings, etc. This also raised the morale of all the troops in the camp.[17]

The value of the additional food and drugs can be seen in the official statistics, which indicate that while an average of four men were dying each day in August this had been reduced to only one per week in October. Major causes of death included dysentery, malaria, beri-beri, heart failure and diphtheria. No cases of cholera occurred at Tamarkan but ninety-one serious operations (including nineteen amputations) and seventy-four of lesser importance were carried out, in spite of the fact that the Japanese had originally intended that all surgical work should be undertaken by Kanchanaburi hospital camp. A total of 208 prisoners died during Tamarkan's era as a base hospital but, as the following incident demonstrates, the situation could easily have been considerably worse:

> I was now in the dysentery ward, and the officers were in a section by themselves. I was holding my own with a daily score of seven which just would not reduce, but it looked as if both Pearson and Hirsch would go. I watched them lose ground with alarming rapidity and then emetine arrived. It was miraculous! After the first injection they slept, after the second their score fell rapidly, their pains ceased, and, as the abbreviated course continued, they lived.[18]

It was the evidenced provided by literally dozens of cases like these which convinced Toosey and his staff that they must continue to accept whatever risks were necessary in order to maintain the supplies of medicine and money. There can be no doubt that the contact with Boon Pong, the smuggling of items into the camp and the purchase of extra food all involved tremendous risks which could have had disastrous consequences. There was also the difficulty of assimilating the relatively substantial sums of money that were brought into the camp. All expenditure for the canteen and for additional local foodstuffs had to be recorded and it was feared that the Japanese would notice any discrepancy between Tamarkan's official income and the amount it spent. Accordingly Captain Hannah of the RASC, who prepared the accounts, is reported to have resorted to every trick in his financial armoury in a successful attempt to conceal the truth.

A further pitfall which had to be considered concerned the possession of notes of large denominations. Those issued by the Japanese seldom exceeded 20 ticals, so if prisoners were found in possession of any of greater value they were inevitably judged to have acquired them illegally. Unfortunately it was difficult to smuggle or handle a large sum in small notes, so there was always the tendency to reduce this risk by introducing another. After several near-misses this fact became fully appreciated by the 'V' organization and Toosey was able to avoid this particular danger. However, two of his colleagues at another camp were not to be so lucky and escaped severe punishment only by a combination of sound tactics, good fortune and extreme bravery.

This particular incident concerned Lieutenant-Colonel A. E. Knights, who first received aid from the 'V' organization when he was the comandant at Tha Soe. This assistance included many 1000 tical notes, but as the Japanese also provided these in their pay to the camp this

127

caused no special difficulties at the time. However, when Knights was moved to Tha Muang the Japanese no longer issued notes of large denomination, so those supplied from outside became an increasingly serious hazard. Knights therefore discussed the situation with Lieutenant-Colonel Lilley who was acting as a kind of 'treasurer' for the camp and they decided that the notes should be changed in the neighbouring village. This task was undertaken by Private Letts, a Thai-speaking member of the Malayan Volunteers, and was duly completed without difficulty.

At a later stage, when both Knights and Lilley had been moved to the officers' camp at Kanchanaburi, the Japanese arrested Private Letts on another matter and under interrogation he admitted changing notes for an officer whom he identified as Colonel Lilley. Lilley was then pulled in and questioned by the *kempeitai*. He vigorously denied the charge and was released but was re-arrested the following day after the Japanese had received confirmation from a Thai that he had changed notes for Letts at Tha Muang.

During the interval between the two interrogations Knights and Lilley were able to discuss the situation and agree on the strategy to be adopted. As a result, and only after heavy pressure, Lilley 'confessed' that notes had been changed and that Knights alone had been responsible. Knights was then sent for and immediately admitted that he had given Letts the money. He told the *kempeitai* that he had accumulated the 1000 tical notes at Tha Soe by making deductions from the officers' pay. When his interrogators made enquiries they found that this could have been possible and Knights omitted to inform them that he had spent the cash on the purchase of additional food. They also found that Knights had been specifically forbidden to continue with this practice. This gave Knights the opportunity to admit that he had disobeyed Japanese orders but by claiming that this was in the interest of the many sick in his camp he was able to divert the charge to a much lesser one. This satisfied the *kempeitai* that they had cleared up the matter and, although Knights was guilty in a technical sense, they were eventually convinced of his good faith and he was discharged.[19]

Had these tactics not been successful it is likely that both Lilley and Knights would have been subjected to such severe torture that they would ultimately have revealed the source of their money. The trail back via Boon Pong to the 'V' organization in Bangkok would then have been open and it seems certain that all of the participants, including Toosey, would have suffered severely. In his opinion it was only Knights's bravery that saved the entire scheme from 'desperate trouble'.[20]

The development of the 'V' scheme

The crucial importance of Colonel Knights's astute manoeuvre and bravery can only be appreciated by an understanding of the scale and scope of the effort made by the individuals and groups known collectively as the 'V' Scheme. The leadership and administrative skills of Colonel Toosey and his fellow camp commandants and the devotion of Dr Moon and many other medical officers along the line would have been much less effective without the support they received from external sources. Few of the recipients of this help knew much of the existence of the supplies that frequently meant the difference between their living and dying, and even the most senior officers were only aware of their immediate contacts.

However, most POWs did feel that the local population were generally sympathetic to their plight. This was not surprising, for while Britain and Thailand had enjoyed good relations for many years there was an almost universal distrust of Japanese intentions. Thus when the terrible conditions under which the railway was being built became known a genuine desire to help quickly emerged. But few Thais were prepared to give active, as distinct from passive, support to any attempts to alleviate conditions in the camps. The initiative was taken by a number of British civilians who had been interned in Bangkok after the outbreak of the war. Although their captivity was arranged by the Thais and conditions were relatively good, their freedom of movement was greatly restricted so their efforts required the co-operation of many other individuals. Friends amongst the local community in Bangkok proved to be very helpful and a number of Europeans whose neutral status gave them a degree of independence were also ready to lend a hand. However, the dangers of disclosure in the highly charged atmosphere of a city under stress meant that all moves required considerable caution, so progress was slow and some activities were organized in ignorance of parallel developments arranged by different groups.

The earliest recorded contact came at Banpong in September 1942 when Lance-Corporal R. G. Payton RASC was surreptitiously handed a note by a Chinese while engaged on a ration lorry detail. On his return to Nong Pladuk, Payton passed the letter to Major R. S. Sykes, his commanding officer. The messaged stated that a number of civilian internees in Bangkok had heard rumours about the adverse conditions under which prisoners were working and wished to know if they were true and, if so, what help was required. It was signed with the single letter 'V'.

After due consultation with his senior colleagues, including Captains C. E. Escritt, K. A. Bailey and P. E. Priggs (all of the 54th Infantry

129

Brigade Group Company, RASC), and with Lieutenant-Colonel W. E. Gill, the camp commandant at Nong Pladuk, and Major Davidson of the 4th Gurkha Rifles, Sykes decided to risk the possibility that the note had been planted by the *kempeitai*. He then produced a detailed account of conditions in Nong Pladuk and of the camps to the north. He also provided a résumé of recent Japanese troop movements. Both of these items were passed on to his Chinese contact when Corporal Payton next visited Banpong for rations. It might be thought that the sending of what would have been regarded as military intelligence was a foolish action since it would have ensured a death sentence had it been discovered. This is undoubtedly true, but Sykes's descriptions of the camps were so comprehensive and so unfavourable to the Japanese that he took the view that his offence already carried a capital sentence so there was nothing more to lose!

The successful delivery of Sykes's reply established a firm line of communication and thereafter a monthly contact was maintained. Sykes subsequently felt that Corporal Payton should not be exposed to such great risks, so had himself appointed as 'camp buying officer' and personally carried all messages. The rewards for his efforts came in the form of small packets of drugs, especially emetine, which were highly concentrated and could be easily concealed. In addition, 250–400 ticals pert month were supplied and these were used to purchase bulkier items, including medicines, in Banpong.

This level of assistance, although extremely valuable, proved to be insufficient as the number of those who were sick gradually increased. It was therefore decided to seek a substantial loan and this resulted in 12,000 ticals being made available against Sykes's personal guarantee. As the largest note then being issued was only of 20 ticals, this amount was too bulky to be brought in via the normal channels. Accordingly it was packed into small bags of tapioca flour and transported by a 'middle-aged Thai woman' from Bangkok and left in the market at Banpong. These bags were then collected by Major Sykes and, after being safely transferred to the camp, the money was dispersed within the cook-house premises.

The first contact between Nong Pladuk and the embryonic 'V' organization was the work of Mr K G Gairdner of the Siam Architects Imports Company with the aid of Mr E P Heath of the Borneo Company. Like other civilians of the warring nations these two Britons were interned at Vejiravudh College in Bangkok soon after the commencement of hostilities. However, as Mrs Gairdner was a Thai citizen she retained her freedom of movement and it was through her contacts that news was received of the difficulties being experienced by the prisoners employed on the railway project. Mr Gairdner decided to investigate these rumours and with the help of a Chinese employee, Mr K. S. Hong, was then able to establish the link with Major Sykes at Nong Pladuk. The 'middle-aged Thai woman' referred to previously was, of course, his wife – Milly Gairdner – and it was her bravery that did so much to bring into being what subsequently became known as the 'V' Scheme.

The early assistance was, therefore, the joint work of Heath and Gairdner, but after December 1942 they separated their activities and both subsequently created their own organizations. The reason for this split was that with the impetuosity of youth, Mr Heath wished to expand the operation whereas Mr Gairdner thought it advisable to keep the scheme on a much smaller and personal basis. The group under Gairdner continued its association with Nong Pladuk, but the new section under Heath and his friend R. D. Hempson of the Anglo-Siam Corporation, attempted to cater for a much wider range of the railway camps. Unfortunately, both retained the use of 'V' as their *nom de plume* so some misunderstanding has arisen as to precisely what each party actually accomplished.

It was Mr Gairdner who received Sykes's request for a large loan early in 1943. This was arranged by a Mr S. Brighouse in the first instance, but was later taken up by J. Knudtzon, Ina Jorgensen and Mr J. Gairdner. It is understood that further assistance was provided to Nong Pladuk until October 1943, when a change in the ration collection point led to contact being lost. Although this was re-established under different circumstances in June 1944, it is certain that this section of the 'V' organization played a smaller role than the complementary group under Heath. Nevertheless it made an enormous contribution to the welfare of a large number of prisoners who all owe a huge debt to the bravery and enterprise of Mr Gairdner, his wife, Milly (who delivered the loan to Banpong), and his Chinese messenger, Mr K. S. Hong.

Messrs Heath and Hempson of course had full knowledge of the original arrangements and were aware of their subsequent progress. However, when Peter Heath ended his part in this operation, Mr Gairdner was led to believe that he played no further role in the provision of aid to the prisoners. This was achieved so completely that the two former collaborators did not speak for the remainder of the war. When it was over and the truth was revealed Gairdner apologized, saying that he thought that Heath had opted out.

The true facts were very different. Heath and Hempson aimed at responding to all requests for help, and during the remaining two and a half years of the war they provided assistance to a value of 306,243 ticals. Of this sum, 30,327 ticals were contributed as a free gift from various sources while the remaining 275,916 ticals were borrowed on the strength of IOUs that guaranteed repayment in sterling at rates which meant that this was the equivalent of nearly £20,000. The raising of these very large amounts in wartime Bangkok where no one knew from day to day where the allegiance of their friends really lay was a very hazardous activity. Yet this was only the beginning of the many dangers which threatened the existence of the project. Once the money was collected it had to be transported to camps that were frequently in restricted or inaccessible areas. Some, of course, was used for the purchase of specialized drugs and food-items which were even more difficult to handle and move to where they were most needed. And all these matters had to be arranged in absolute secrecy by organizers whose own freedom of action was permanently constrained.

In spite of all these problems, substantial assistance was provided to the prisoners based at Chungkai, Tamarkan, Kanchanaburi No. 3 hospital camp, Tonchan, Tha Soe and Nakhom Pathom. All of these lie in the southern part of Thailand and it was not possible to maintain regular supplies to camps further to the north. The only help which could be offered to the northern camps came in response to a request made by Captain G. E. Angier in March 1943. As a result, a number of sums were sent to permit the stocking-up of essential items before units were actually moved. Commanders who benefited in this way included Lieutenant-Colonel L. Morrison (1st Leicestershire Regiment), Lieutenant-Colonel A. A. Johnson (5th Battalion, the Suffolk Regiment) and Lieutenant-Colonel J. H. Stitt (2nd Battalion, the Gordon Highlanders). In October 1943, the sum of 10,000 ticals was sent to the camp then established at the 212-kilometre mark but this was a rare and difficult event so it was fortunate that the completion of the railway reduced the need to assist the distant working camps.

Although Messrs Heath and Hempson were the prime movers in this enterprise, they were obliged to rely very heavily on the abilities and goodwill of a number of key personnel for the successful operation of their scheme. Mme Millet, wife of the French military attaché in Bangkok, was a most enthusiastic supporter and became responsible for all bulk purchases of medicines. She was also active in the raising of large sums of money, while her husband made a special and risky trip to Saigon in an attempt to hand over a list of 5000 POW names. Mme Millet, like both Heath and Hempson, was awarded an OBE after the war in recognition of her efforts. Another important contribution was made by Mrs Mary L. Clark, of the Churches of Christ Mission, who was instrumental in helping to provide assistance at Nakhon Pathom.[21] This camp, which grew to be the largest of the base hospitals in Thailand, was very carefully controlled by the Japanese and it proved to be extremely difficult to establish links and to supply large sums of local currency. However, due to the efforts of Mrs Clark – after her release from internment – and the bravery of Kru Chalat Watanachau, a teacher in her mission, this was eventually achieved. Unfortunately, this required the co-operation of various POW 'racketeers' in the camp who had to be given a 10 per cent commission for bringing in the money. This payment was approved by Lieutenant-Colonel J. D. Sainter, the camp commandant, but others thought the amount excessive.

Another officer, Lieutenant-Colonel Parker, also attempted to raise money through other contacts, primarily for himself and his friends. These were largely unsuccessful but, nevertheless, it was he who was arrested by the *kempeitai* after two men were apprehended outside the camp. This then led to all outside transactions coming to an end and only 600 out of a planned 20,000 ticals delivery from the 'V' organization ever reached the hospital administration.[22]

The Heath and Hempson operation also relied very heavily upon large numbers of Thai citizens who were motivated either by a desire to help their former friends, who were now in trouble, or purely by their humanitarian instincts. One who acted from both of these reasons was Nai Boon Pong although he had little or no contact with any Europeans prior to the outbreak of war. This was not surprising for he was born in Kanchanaburi which, in 1906, was a quiet and isolated backwater. It was there that he was brought up and where he established himself in business as a general merchant. In the mid-1930s he attempted to set up a buying agency in Bangkok, but finding this unprofitable he returned to Kanchanaburi and devoted his time to placing his store and wholesale activities on a sound financial basis. The success of these ventures then enabled him to take a part in the local administration and he served as mayor for several years.

Boon Pong was, therefore, living and working in Kanchanaburi when he learned of the plan to build the railway. Then, when the construction of the camp at Chungkai was started, he became personally involved because the land on which it was proposed to site the cemetery was owned by his mother. The negotiations over this transfer brought him into contact with the Japanese and he was subsequently able to obtain their permission to supply the prisoners' canteens at a number of camps.

It was while on a visit to Chungkai that he recognized Corporal R. C. H. Johnson, an Anglo-Thai who was a former employee of the Anglo-Siam Corporation, whom he had known during his time in Bangkok. Johnson told him that many men were dying from diphtheria and asked him if he could secure any medicine. As a result Boon Pong approached a Chinese doctor in Bangkok and, after purchasing small quantities of the requisite drugs with his own money, was able to hand them over to Johnson on a later visit. Boon Pong was then asked if he could arrange to change cheques for the POWs; as he had insufficient funds he attempted to persuade other Thai and Chinese merchants in the capital to help with this work.

These efforts had two consequences. The first of these brought him into contact with Nai Olarn who, like Johnson, was a former employee of the Anglo-Siam Corporation. By this time Olarn was working for the Siamese government service but nevertheless, at great risk, he took it on himself to go to Kanchanaburi and check upon Johnson's story. When he became aware of the full extent of the problem he got in touch with R. D. Hempson, whom he knew well from when they were colleagues working for the same firm. The 'V' organization, then in its early days, was quickly convinced of the need to provide help and a viable system was rapidly evolved. Thus Heath and Hempson acquired the necessary cash and drugs and Olarn moved these items to Kanchanaburi. There they were received by Boon Pong who stored them until it was possible for him to make arrangements for their transfer to their final destinations in the camps.

Boon Pong's initiative in seeking support in Bangkok also had the result of putting him in touch with Mr Albert Tanner. This gentleman who, like Peter Heath, was employed by the Borneo Company, was of Swiss nationality so was never interned. He therefore enjoyed a freedom of action which was denied to many of his friends, and he made full use of his favoured position to alleviate their situation. His continuing links with his business associates made him aware of Boon Pong's difficulties so he sent a message and a meeting was quickly arranged. Until this took place Boon Pong had to resort to walking from company to company in an effort to exchange POW cheques for local currency. However, once Mr Tanner became involoved this dangerous practice was stopped. Instead, Mr Tanner accepted all of the cheques himself as well as any items of jewellery that prisoners wished to use to obtain credit. Boon Pong's task thus became simpler, though the process of carrying contraband in and out of a wide variety of camps remained an extremely risky business.

The extent of the assistance provided by Mr Tanner is not fully documented:

> The method of procedure for trading cheques was each cheque, accompanied by a covering letter, was taken by an agent to Bangkok where it was sold, chiefly by Mr A. Tanner of the Borneo Company. The ticals in the majority of cases duly arrived – approximate rate throughout 300 ticals for £25 sterling.[23]

Over £1129 was obtained in this way and used to promote the welfare of those in the camps. In addition, a substantial amount of money was secured by advances made on a private basis, but this cannot be properly quantified. Most of the official and private cheques were exchanged via the services provided by Boon Pong but it should not be thought that he was the sole channel for these transactions. Nai Lee Soon, who acted as a contractor to Chungkai camp, also provided a link with Mr Tanner and was responsible for cashing cheques and smuggling 'V' money on to that site.

The concern which Boon Pong felt for the prisoners was translated into action in a number of ways. His journeys to Bangkok to liaise with Mr Tanner and to arrange supplies with the 'V' organization formed only a small, though vital, part of his enterprise. His store in Kanchanaburi became a regular point of contact with the prisoners and was, in fact, the headquarters of all of his business and extraneous activities. This was in spite of his need to maintain friendly relationships with the Japanese, which meant that they frequently visited his premises whenever their duties brought them into the town. Most POWs became aware of his presence from his many appearances in their camps. These were ostensibly to supply the canteens or to trade food for cash and valuables but were, of course, to help cover his illicit traffice with the camp administration. Yet even the 'commercial' side of these ventures provided a real service to the prisoners, for Boon Pong was frequently the only real link which those in the up-country areas had with the outside world:

How, amid disease, slave labour and the perpetual monsoon rain, did we keep our sanity? God knows it was difficult, but we still could laugh and smile even if it wasn't normal laughter. In the first place Boon Pong, the Thai canteen contractor, who was one of the staunchest pro-British friends we ever had, used to bring supplies by barge and 'Pom-Pom' right up to our area [Dha Khanun, otherwise known as Takanum at the 218-km mark] and beyond. His prices were always the lowest, and his profit of the slightest. The voyage up from below was hazardous and long, but Pong brought us food, news, and sometimes even free drugs. As we got undernourished and desperate, so he advanced us generous sums against watches, rings and cigarette cases. If we valued them, he said, tell him so and he would keep them for us till we were free men. Friend of ours though he was, we could hardly credit that, but in August, 1945, he was as good as his word and he redeemed the precious personal belongings of all who came to claim them.[24]

Not all prisoners thought that Boon Pong's prices were quite as reasonable as has been suggested, but all were convinced of his bravery and of the value of his visits. These two characteristics were clearly demonstrated during an incident at Wampo:

135

One day I was called out unexpectedly and marched to the guardroom: the Japs appeared to be very worried about something. There, beautifully dressed and sitting at his ease in a chair, was Boon Pong: apparently he had arrived at the camp and asked for Captain Pavillard very casually, as if social calls were commonly paid on prisoners of war. The Japanese could not imagine how a well-dressed Siamese civilian knew my name or the fact that I was at Wampo; they seemed very angry and my explanations did not please them at all. But Boon Pong saved the situation by saying he had ten thousand duck eggs for sale; he gave each guard a dozen eggs and after that it was a very simple matter to arrange with the administration that he would sell the rest of them to us at five cents each.[25]

Although one source claimed that Boon Pong was a major in the Thai Army who had been seconded for this task, it is certain that he was just an extraordinary Thai citizen who acted from altruistic motives. It is pleasing to note, therefore, that after the war Boon Pong's efforts were marked by the award of the George Medal for Bravery and that he also received substantial, tangible recognition from the prisoners (see below, p. 208).

This brief account of the work of the 'V' organization would not be complete without recording its attempts to enlist the support of Herr Lenzinger, the Swiss consul. At an early stage he was asked if he would provide funds to help the POWs but he replied that he could not do so as it might jeopardize his neutral status. This would then weaken his position with the Japanese and would lessen the possibility of his being able to obtain permission to provide official aid at a later date. For the same reason he refused to guarantee any funds which might be raised locally, but he did let it be known that in his view the British government would recognize all such commitments after the war. He also made it clear that he would do his best to ensure that the British government was kept fully informed of the situation.

The tacit support of the Swiss consul was an important factor in helping money to be raised within the international community in Bangkok. By May 1943, Herr Lenzinger was prepared to take a more active role and with the encouragement of the British government he sanctioned a small amount of unofficial aid to the camp at Chungkai. He also approved a regular monthly payment to assist Thai and Chinese POWs, neither of whom were recognized by their respective governments and who were completely without funds. Later in the year the consul was given permission to send some official help to the camps, but the amount was inadequate and it proved to be difficult to ensure that these supplies arrived without interference from the Japanese. Although

136

great efforts were made to increase the flow of supplies, little progress was made and as late as November 1944 official help still only amounted to 80,000 ticals a month (approximately £4000) and was so inadequate that additional emergency funds had to be found.

In these circumstances the work of the 'V' scheme remained as vital as ever and was continued with only one short break until the Japanese surrender. The increasing difficulty of raising funds was partly offset by the willingness of the expatriate firms, particularly the Borneo Company, to underwrite the operation, although they themselves were in dire financial straits. However, the increasing inevitability of the Allied victory created an easier atmosphere in Bangkok and this enabled the organization to maintain its self-imposed tasks until they were no longer necessary. As the up-country camps were closed the need changed, but right until the end many prisoners continued to require the support which only the bravery of Messrs Heath, Hempson, Olarn, Pong and Tanner could supply. Toosey was convinced that without this external assistance the death rate in the camps would have at least been double and he spoke for many when he wrote to 'V' after he had heard that Tamarkan base hospital was to close:

Parcels T^I and T^{II} Received. Camp Dispersing. Money not required until further notice. Very many thanks. You have saved many lives.[26]

8

The final phase

The move from Tamarkan

Colonel Toosey was wrong in suggesting that Tamarkan was about to close. However, the completion of the railway in October 1943 was to mark the beginning of a series of changes which were completely to alter the personnel and character of the camp. The end of actual construction meant that the majority of prisoners were no longer required up-country. Consequently it was decided that they should be redeployed in other areas, either where they could make a further contribution to the Japanese war effort or, at least, where they could hinder it as little as possible. As a first step this policy resulted in a massive movement of troops down to southern Thailand where supplies were more plentiful and where it was easier to exercise control. A further aspect of this programme was to see many of these prisoners moved to work in Japan, although large numbers were inadvertently sunk *en route* by the activities of US submarines. These decisions were to lead to a fundamental change in the function of Tamarkan and then to the transfer of Toosey to a different venue.

In accordance with the overall Japanese plan, many men moved out of Tamarkan during October and November. Some of the 'fitter' troops were sent to the north to assist with repairs and maintenance, but most were transferred to nearby camps such as that at Chungkai. The steady reduction in numbers together with Japanese intentions for the future use of the site meant Toosey's presence was less important and it was made clear that he would soon be placed in charge of another establishment. Toosey fully expected that this would be at Nakhon Pathom where what was to become the largest of the base hospital camps was just beginning to be developed. However, this was not to be, for members of the Japanese administration at Nong Pladuk had worked with him on previous occasions and put in a request for his services.

Accordingly, after dividing the remaining 'V' funds on an equitable basis, Colonel Toosey and Captain Boyle were moved to Nong Pladuk on 10 December 1943.

The ending of Toosey's organization at Tamarkan and the subsequent transfer of most of its remaining prisoners then left the site free to accommodate other troops. In January 1944 it was occupied by men from a variety of Australian units who had been working under appalling conditions on the Burmese sector of the line. Amongst those who remained in the camp was the senior medical officer, Major Moon, who was thus able to continue his fine work – this time with his Australian compatriots. The better food and conditions at the bridge camp quickly reduced the death rate, so at the end of the month a section of the medical staff was moved to the new site at Nakhom Pathom. This group was headed by Lieutenant-Colonel Albert Coates, who was appointed SMO and who was later to be also appointed as camp commandant. Under his guidance the camp developed so that it could cope with 10,000 patients, and with the aid of many brilliant doctors – including the well-loved 'Weary' Dunlop – a tremendous amount of useful work was accomplished.

A year at Nong Pladuk

The camp at Nong Pladuk had been established in June 1942 (see above, p. 92), and had since been commanded by Major W. E. Gill of the 137th (A) Field Regiment RA. During this period he had stood up to the Japanese on many occasions and was widely regarded as a dedicated officer who always did his best for the men in his charge. Gill's efforts had taken their toll on his health and he was quite prepared to hand over his responsibility when Toosey arrived. He was subsequently to play a useful, though subordinate, part in the administration of the camp.

In December 1943 the camp accommodated about 4000 men, which included mainly British and Dutch troops as well as a few Australians and Americans. These were housed in a mixture of wooden and bamboo huts, covered with atap, which were generally in a satisfactory condition. The marshalling yards that, together with a series of engineering workshops, provided the basic reason for the camp's existence, lay within a few yards of the prisoners' living space and the whole was protected by a battery of Bofors guns manned by renegade Indians.

Toosey's assumption of authority at Nong Pladuk coincided with the appointment of Major Ebiko as the new commander of the Japanese group controlling all POWs in Thailand. Toosey quickly discovered that Ebiko was a sincere and tolerant man, and as he permitted personal interviews it became possible to reduce the friction which always existed

139

with local Japanese administrators. In fact relations with the camp staff were usually harmonious, and Lieutenants Osato and Katagiri (later replaced by Suzuki and Takasaki) and senior NCOs Saito and Watanabe seldom interfered with the prisoners' internal arrangements so long as their schedule of work was satisfactorily completed. By previous standards this was regarded as very moderate and mainly consisted of loading and unloading trains and maintaining the track in the nearby yards. A 9- or 10-hour day was quite common, but the pace was seldom excessive and a regular holiday was given each week.

Toosey's administration included Major Lees and Captain Boyle, who had worked with him on earlier occasions. They were joined by Major R. A. N. Davidson of the 4th Gurkha Rifles who became camp adjutant, Major R. S. Sykes of the RASC who became messing officer, Lieutenant J. Fullerton of the 137th (A) Field Artillery who took responsibility for the canteen, while Lieutenant H. L. Payne, also of the 137th, continued to take charge of the daily working parties to Hashimoto's yards. A. McTavish of the 2nd Argyll and Sutherland Highlanders completed this team, by acting as camp RSM. The backing of this strong group enabled Toosey to concentrate on what he regarded as the essentials of his task. Thus, apart from keeping a watchful eye on his 'executives' and undertaking a weekly inspection, most of his time was spent in negotiating with Japanese officials at both the local and group levels. The success of these tactics meant that the area of the camp was increased by about a third; sporting and cultural activities were extended; Japanese 'propaganda' newspapers were acquired on a regular basis; and the purchase of drugs and medicines was allowed through official sources in Bangkok.

Although the latter concession was on quite a small scale it helped to supplement the items secured when contact was re-established with the 'V' organization. The rations were also improved with the aid of funds received from this source, and with the additional benefit of tiny quantities of Red Cross supplies no one was ever seriously hungry. The canteen, of course, made a useful contribution in this area, and morale in the camp, which reached a peak of over 8000 men, was further aided by the provision of a small 'hospital' under the control of Major E. A. Smyth, FRCS, RAMC, and even more by the regular receipt of increasingly better news from the battle-fronts. The continued operation of illegal radios provided one, highly dangerous, source of information. Another was the Thai newspapers which were smuggled in and translated by a team led by Major R. C. Laming of the 3rd Indian Corps. Taken together these gave a fairly accurate picture of world events and reports of such items as the 'D'-Day landings in June 1944 gave all prisoners something real to give substance to their hopes of ultimate freedom.

140

From the foregoing it would appear that life at Nong Pladuk was quite tolerable, and by the standards of many of the jungle camps there was indeed much for which to be thankful. There was, however, another side to the picture which ensured that the true situation was much less sanguine than has been suggested. One, relatively minor, irritant concerned a series of swindles which resulted in a reduction of the prisoners' rations and the simultaneous enrichment of a number of Japanese and Korean NCOs. These had a long history stretching back to the beginning of the camp and included the issuing of stores which were much smaller than the official allowance: in one typical case margarine cans which were clearly marked as containing 13.2 kilos had to be accepted as if their contents weighed 19 kilos. Another racket involved the supply of vegetables. The Japanese authorities allowed a flat rate per head for the purchase of these items but did not specify the varieties to be bought. By providing a mixture with a predominance of the cheaper vegetables the ration sergeants and, sometimes, their supervisors could retain large sums for their own use.

A similar system also operated with firewood – the best quality was paid for and the cheapest variety supplied – while men passing through camps were always claimed for but not subsequently put on the ration strength. Rackets of this type abounded and in the working camps undoubtedly resulted in a significant reduction in the food available to feed the prisoners. At Nong Pladuk the more favourable situation meant that the effects were considerably less harmful but even there the loss of a 25 per cent vegetable peeling allowance must have had a serious impact on the welfare of the prisoners.

Of more immediate concern were a number of incidents between the POWs and their guards. Under Toosey's administration the number of minor disputes appears to have been kept at a fairly low level, but two serious confrontations did take place. In the first of these CSM Dooley. an Australian, was subjected to such a severe attack by Sergeant Ejima that his spinal column was nearly severed. Dooley then spent several months in hospital, but his ultimate fate has not been recorded. On the other hand the subsequent history of his assailant is quite clear, for Sergeant Ejima was hanged as a war criminal in March 1946.

The other serious incident involved Sergeant C. W. J. Pratt of the 80th Anti-Tank Regiment, RA:

In June 1944, while holding a concert for the men in one of the huts, I was stopped by a Japanese sentry who ordered me with two other men to report to the guardroom. There I was searched and then kicked in both legs and beaten round the face at least a dozen times by the Guard Commander, by name Takamini. The Interpreter was then

141

sent for and I was told to relate what the concert was about. The Guard Commander accused me of insulting a Japanese Sergeant during the Concert which, of course, was not true. Thereupon another Japanese soldier rushed out from the guardroom and immediately started kicking me in the privates, just above the bladder and all over the abdomen, and hitting me in the face. I fell to my knees and he still kept on kicking me. He kicked me all around the guardroom and then I told the Guard Commander that I would swear by anything he chose to produce what I had said was true. He then made me take the oath and left me alone. The Japanese soldier, who rushed from the guardroom and assaulted me, had no connection whatever with my alleged misdemeanour. He was one of the guards on duty at the time and, overhearing the allegation made against me by the Guard Commander, acted on his own initiative. Either Takamini had not the wish to restrain this man or he was too weak and irresponsible to do so.[1]

The injuries suffered by Sergeant Pratt proved to be both severe and long lasting, and when he made his statement 15 months later he was still not fully recovered.

The allied air attacks on Nong Pladuk

Regrettable though these incidents were, they paled into insignificance when compared with the horrific events of September and December 1944. These arose from the Japanese policy of siting POW camps next to targets of military importance. It was generally believed that the Japanese thought that this would deter Allied air attacks, but whether this was the official reason is not certain. What is without question is that at Nong Pladuk the prisoners were to pay a high price for the Japanese decision to place their living space in close proximity to a major strategic objective.

The obvious risk of this policy struck Toosey immediately on his appointment to Nong Pladuk, and he made repeated requests that the prisoners' accommodation be moved to a safe distance from the marshalling yards and workshops. The only replies he received were: 'The British have no aircraft left' and 'The Air Force know of the location of your camp'. Toosey remained unconvinced, and with the evidence supplied by increasing Allied air activity was able to obtain permission for slit trenches to be constructed. However, he was obliged to place these close to the base of the huts and once the rainy season began their presence threatened to undermine these structures. Thus the trenches had to be filled in and all men were instructed that in the event of an air raid they were to remain within their huts.

In spite of all protests this regulation was strictly enforced and was to be the principal cause of the heavy casualties which Nong Pladuk suffered when the inevitable attack eventually took place:

On the night of 6/7 September 1944, bombers passed over the Camp, turned and began a long attack on railway sidings concealed in trees about half a mile from the Camp. A petrol train and some ammunition were completely destroyed and most of the sidings completely and permanently wrecked. During the raid one bomber dropped two sticks across the Camp, possibly in error, possibly directed at the Anti-Aircraft position. One bomb wounded several officers, of whom one died and one lost a leg; two other bombs fell on the central hut of the Camp and immediately outside the Hospital, respectively. These two caused over 400 casualties, including over 90 killed and died of wounds. Many men had taken the meagre protection of shallow ground depressions and drains, but the vast majority were in huts in accordance with Japanese orders. Rescue and medical work was magnificently carried out by POWs One Japanese preferred human duty to self-protection – Sergeant Watanabe, I. J. A., administrative NCO of the camp, proceeded at once to the bombed area, himself carried to the Hospital one of the first casualties and assisted generally in directing POWs to drains while the raid proceeded.[2]

This bald account necessarily omits any reference to the indescribable confusion and chaos after the bombs were dropped. Great passions arose, which varied from the despair and frustration of the prisoners at being subject to such heavy punishment by their own side to the fear and hatred of many of the Japanese and, especially, Korean guards. In these circumstances a major confrontation could easily have developed, as can be seen by one incident in which Toosey

was with a party laying out the dead men in front of our little chapel, when a Korean soldier came along and told me to move them somewhere else. I looked him straight in the eye and told him to buzz off, which he did. He was drunk and very frightened.[3]

Fortunately the camp authorities quickly adopted a more conciliatory attitude and permission was given for slit trenches to be built and to be occupied by the prisoners when air raids were expected. However, the Japanese still refused to relocate the camp, although they took the precaution of moving their own accommodation to the furthest possible point away from the railway. A second attack, which caused little damage and no casualties, emphasized the dangers and after strong representations by Toosey the huts nearest to the track were evacuated and, in effect, the camp was moved back about 200 yards from the track. These measures, although beneficial, were not sufficient and additional casualties were caused during the third raid on 3 December 1944:

> One evening at 6 p.m., twelve four-engined bombers suddenly appeared making for us from the direction of Bangkok. We looked up and saw bombs coming out, and made for the trenches. It was a masterly bit of bombing: the railway sidings and workshops 10 yards from the Camp were completely demolished but, unfortunately, six bombs landed in the Camp, including one on the Hospital, one on the Cookhouse, and one in a slit trench. So died nine more, including [Major] Paddy Sykes, one of the finest characters in the Camp, and loved by all, officers and men alike. Out of cussedness, a direct hit on the Nip shelter, full of dwarfs, exploded on impact and killed no one.[4]

The net effect of these raids was the almost complete destruction of the marshalling yards and workshop facilities at Nong Pladuk. This was achieved at the cost of 104 prisoners killed and over 400 wounded. The Japanese reaction came in stages. First there was the small move away from the track. Then the numbers were reduced and No. 1 and No. 2 POW camps were united on a slightly less vulnerable site. Finally, when the Japanese realized that Nong Pladuk was too conspicuous a target to justify rebuilding, it was decided to disperse the troops to other camps in the area. As part of this process Toosey and his fellow officers were ordered to concentrate at a new establishment which was being set up at Kanchanaburi.

The progress of the war

The attacks on Nong Pladuk and the subsequent reduction in its scale of operations were only a small factor in the decision to move Colonel Toosey to another camp. The overriding consideration was the intro- duction of a new Japanese policy aimed at concentrating all commissioned ranks on one site. This was, in fact, an extension of an earlier instruction which, in July, 1942, had segregated all officers over the rank of lieutenant-colonel from their units. Japanese thinking at that time was that the removal of the senior men would prevent the prisoners from retaining any real cohesion. They quickly discovered their mistake, for the 'junior' officers filled the breach very adequately and the military efficiency of the troops was little impaired. By the time that this was fully appreciated the Japanese had learned the value of maintaining existing army structures and were quite content to work through the 'regular channels'. This practice continued without change until late in 1944

144

when the Japanese came to the conclusion that the excellent relationships which, in spite of all their efforts, continued to exist between officers and men must be ended. The solution which was then decided upon meant that all officers would be separated from their men, who were to be left under the control of their NCOs. The first part of this policy saw the development of an existing site at Kanchanaburi as an 'officers only' camp; the second part resulted in many groups of other ranks being moved to eastern Thailand, while some were returned to Singapore and a few went on to work in Japan.

The basic reason for the change in the Japanese attitude towards the prisoners lay, of course, in the declining fortunes of the Axis powers on virtually all of the world's war-fronts. The Italian government surrendered soon after the invasion of southern Italy in September 1943, and although Rome was not liberated until June the following year the American and British units were already beginning to pose a threat to the north of the country. In practice the drain on German resources imposed by the Italian campaign considerably reduced the size of the forces they could muster to oppose the 'D'-Day landings on 6 June 1944. This then proved to be an important factor in the liberation of France and by January 1945 the Germans had been pushed back to their own western frontier everywhere except in the Netherlands. By the same date the Russians had completed a year of almost continuous progress, so that East Prussia was largely in their hands and the Red Army had crossed the border into Germany proper at many points. The Third Reich also suffered severely throughout 1944 from the constant air attacks. British Bomber Command pounded it by night and the US Eighth Air Force by day. As a result the Ruhr was badly damaged and many cities like Hamburg almost totally destroyed.

The difficulties of the Axis powers in Europe were repeated in both the Pacific and Burma fighting zones during the year that Toosey spent at Nong Pladuk. The invasion of the Gilbert Islands in November 1943 was followed by the capture of the Marshall Islands only two months later. Then in June and July 1944 came the attack on the Marianas Islands of Saipan, Guam and Tinian. Once they were secure the American task force moved on to take Morotai and Peleliu and, on 20 October, landings began on the island of Leyte in the central Philippines. By the end of the year this was also in US hands and excellent bases were available for the imminent attack on Luzon and the great prize of Manila.

The rapid contraction of their defensive ring in the Pacific was made even worse by the enormous losses sustained by the Imperial Navy in attempts to regain their previous ascendancy at sea. The first of these occurred in mid-1944:

145

[Admiral] Nimitz employed no less than fourteen battleships, fourteen cruisers, twenty-six carriers and eighty-two destroyers in the Marianas campaign. Hirohito sent out from the Philippines, to seek a 'decisive battle', almost all the expendable remnants of the Japanese fleet: four battleships, nine carriers, seven cruisers and thirty-four destroyers. In the Battle of the Philippine Sea on June 19–20, three out of five of Japan's heavy carriers were sunk and almost 400 of her 473 carrier planes were shot down. Nimitz lost about 100 of his 956 airplanes and none of his ships.[5]

This disaster was to be compounded during October 1944, when in the Battle of Leyte Gulf the Japanese lost a further three battleships, one fleet carrier, four light carriers, six heavy cruisers, four light cruisers and seven destroyers. As only minor damage was inflicted upon the American fleet this marked the end of Japanese capacity to mount an effective challenge at sea. Instead future attempts to keep the invader away from the homeland were to be based almost entirely on air power. It was hoped to make full use of the 'unsinkable carriers' – the many islands that abounded in the seas around Japan. These plans included proposals to employ special attack units that would carry out crash dives on enemy ships. The adoption of these suicide tactics made it clear that the authorities in Tokyo fully realized that only such a *kamikaze* (divine wind) could now save the nation.

Earlier in 1944 it had appeared that one war-front did offer some hope for a counter-offensive that would help to restore Japan's fading morale. This was on the Burma–India border where substantial Japanese forces were available and where it was believed that the Allies were still relatively weak and not fully organized. Accordingly an army of 155,000 men was ordered forward to invade India. This involved the crossing of a wide band of mountainous countryside that was almost totally devoid of either tracks or inhabitants. As it was not possible to live off the land and as it was not practical to establish anything more than rudimentary supply routes, Japanese hopes rested on the capture of the British railheads and store depots at Imphal and Kohima.

The three Japanese divisions plus one recruited from Indian POWs that formed the attacking force successfully crossed the frontier, and by the end of March both Imphal and Kohima were cut off from their bases in Bengal. In accordance with the tactics devised by General Slim, the defenders in these areas did not attempt to withdraw but were supplied by air until reinforcements arrived. The Japanese units surrounding them received little in the way of either food or ammunition, and towards the end of April they began to falter. After a further period of heavy fighting some Japanese began to withdraw and by June the retreat had become a general one.

The repulse of the Japanese attack on India was to have far-reaching implications. Their enormous losses, subsequently confirmed at over 65,000 men, and the extent of the disorganization of those units that were able to return to their starting-lines meant that henceforth the Japanese were in a considerably weakened state. The Allied forces, in contrast, had received a great boost to their confidence and it was widely thought that this was the opportunity to begin the reconquest of Burma. The Allies now had the immense advantage of almost complete mastery in the air, so that by December 1944 the British 14th Army was everywhere approaching, or had reached, the banks of the Irrawaddy. Thus in Burma, as in all other theatres of war, the year which Toosey spent at Nong Pladuk ended with the Imperial forces in disarray and with little prospect of achieving anything more than delaying the defeat which seemed increasingly inevitable. However, while other fronts were crippled by a shortage of reinforcements and supplies the Japanese Army in Burma did have the advantage of a relatively secure supply line via the railway to Bangkok and Singapore, so was not so deeply affected by the continuing losses suffered by their mercantile marine. On the other hand the existence of the new line ensured that any attack from Burma into Thailand would be bound to follow this route. In these circumstances the Japanese authorities became increasingly nervous of the presence of large bodies of POWs in what were becoming potentially dangerous areas and decided that they must be relocated. It was as a part of this process that Toosey was ordered to move to the recently established 'officers only' camp at Kanchanaburi.

The officers' camp at Kanchanaburi

It is generally agreed that the camp in which Toosey found himself at the end of 1944 was one of the smallest and dirtiest of all the fixed camps in Thailand. It was away from the river and consisted of a bare, muddy, patch without any trees to provide shade. The total area amounted to only 325×150 yards and as a third of this was occupied by the Japanese the 3000 Australian, British and Dutch officers were a tight squeeze. Many found the site claustrophobic, for it was surrounded by a bamboo fence, with only a single gate, and had an average density of a mere 10 square feet per man. The accommodation was equally sparse and at first consisted of a single row of a dozen long huts, with one at each end adapted to form respectively a store and a hospital. Consequently the first few weeks proved to be rather difficult.

When Colonel Toosey first arrived at Kanchanaburi he played no part

147

in the organization of the camp. At that time the prisoners did not have a single commandant but were represented by a committee of seven officers – two Australian, two British, two Dutch and one American. This was a very cumbersome arrangement, as Toosey discovered when, at the suggestion of Lieutenant-Colonel Swinton (the senior British officer), he was made one of the British Army's representatives. The difficulties of control then persuaded the Japanese to re-form this archaic system and, on instruction from their area headquarters, Toosey was appointed as the sole liaison officer.

Before agreeing to accept this position Toosey was careful to consult the senior members of the four nations concerned and it was only with the support of the Australian Lieutenant-Colonel McEachern, the British Lieutenant-Colonel Swinton, the Dutch Lieutenant-Colonel Metzer and the American Lieutenant-Colonel Tharp that he agreed to undertake this onerous task. He was then given the assistance of British and Dutch adjutants – Majors Noble and Van Gulyk – who were both extremely able men. This was particularly fortunate, for, as Toosey later recorded, dealing with an awkward set of Japanese officials and attempting to reconcile conflicting interests within the camp was one of the most difficult experiences of his life.

The major problem was not, in fact, the physical conditions within the camp. Space always remained at a premium but after a 2-month building programme the standard of accommodation was felt to be relatively adequate. This work was completed entirely by the prisoners themselves but once it was finished their duties were comparatively light. A simple hospital was also constructed and sufficient drugs were obtained to provide a moderate service. Rations were supplied in reasonable quantities, and with the development of an excellent canteen the camp came to be regarded as one of the best-fed in the whole of Thailand. A limited amount of entertainment and sport was permitted and, although only very little in the way of cultural activities was allowed, life at Kanchanaburi should have been quite tolerable. That it was not was due entirely to the character and attitude of the Japanese camp staff.

The commander was Captain Noguchi, whom Toosey once described as 'an arrogant sadist of the worst type'.[6] His second-in-command was Lieutenant Takasaki, who had little authority and contented himself with agreeing with Noguchi on every occasion. Because of his habit of waddling around in field boots he was always known as 'The Frog'. The camp adjutant, Lieutenant Matsushita, was quite an agreeable man and did his best to help the prisoners, but he was frequently overruled by his superiors. The Japanese officers were assisted by a number of NCOs. These were also a mixed group – Warrant Officer Nomura and Sergeant Shimojo were extremely harsh, although the latter was felt to be a highly efficient soldier, while Sergeant Fujii was universally regarded as a decent and friendly person.

Noguchi lived in a wooden house within the camp and appears to have spent his time in devising ways to make the prisoners' lives as unpleasant as possible. Known as 'Nog', he insisted that he and all other Japanese officers and NCOs be saluted or bowed to at every meeting. These regulations might not seem to be too unreasonable, but Noguchi crept about the site dressed in a standard uniform without insignia or his sword clearly attempting to trap unwary or preoccupied POWs. In the early days he was frequently successful and then personally beat the offenders with a steel ruler, often causing serious injury. When these tactics lost their edge Noguchi introduced a series of rules which laid down severe penalties for petty misdemeanours such as smoking outside the huts, and in one incident all officers were confined within their living quarters for 14 days because a few cigarette ends were found on the floor of their accommodation.

Noguchi imposed so many rules that some were bound to be broken. As the penalties for even minor infractions were so heavy, the effort of attempting to keep within the law proved to be an immense burden and a feeling of tension developed and gradually poisoned the atmosphere. These circumstances led, inevitably, to a major clash, which was perhaps what had been intended. The dispute itself concerned the demand of a Japanese medical orderly for water from a number of British officers who were working the pump. As this was during the time allocated to the British for the drawing of water this was refused and the camp interpreter was asked to convey this message. Captain W. M. Drower duly translated and added: 'British Officers were not batmen to Nip privates.'[7]

When this incident was reported to Noguchi he ruminated over it for 2 days before deciding that he would make a serious issue of the matter. Drower was sent for and accused of insulting the whole Japanese nation. During this preliminary interrogation Drower was struck several times and he protested that the Japanese had no right to hit their captives. This then provoked a horrific scene in the camp office:

> Noguchi himself, aided by the Frog and the Japanese orderly
> sergeant, beat Reeves [a pseudonym for Drower] across the head and
> face with a dummy wooden rifle, and after a merciless thrashing
> which Reeves took standing rigidly to attention as best he could – they
> only wanted him to threaten back and they'd have shot him – they
> tripped him on the floor and the three of them jumped on top of him,
> hit and kicked him, and ended up by rolling on the floor with him in
> pure hysteria. All this before the British Camp Commander [Colonel

Toosey]. Reeves was then sent off to the 'No Good House', a dark cell at the back of the Nip guardroom, and there he was kept with no medical attention, a plate of rice and some water once a day, with no blankets, no mosquito net, and no facilities for washing or shaving.[8]

On the following day Noguchi apologized to Toosey for losing his temper and attacking Drower. However, this was only for the form of the punishment and Noguchi continued to maintain that Drower was guilty of a serious offence and nothing would persuade him to order his release. He then introduced even stricter regulations so that the lives of the prisoners were made even more miserable and for a 10-day period anyone not working was restricted to his hut and could leave only to obtain food or to use the latrines. Having failed to obtain the reversal of these orders, Toosey came to the conclusion that they were being provoked into mutiny so that the Japanese would have an excuse to shoot them all! He therefore counselled a cautious policy of compliance and the situation then gradually returned to its previous, less harsh, level of control. This slight relaxation did not extend to Captain Drower, who remained in close confinement.

As if these problems were not enough, the inmates of Kanchanaburi camp also lived under the constant threat of air attack and Allied planes were to be seen in increasing numbers on most days. These were usually on their way to targets further to the south, but the site provided a convenient grandstand for witnessing the regular raids on the bridges at Tamarkan 3 kilometres down the line. Regrettably, after a plane attempted to destroy a locomotive moving between the two camps, a number of bombs fell on the officers' quarters at Kanchanaburi and three of the Dutch prisoners were killed. In spite of all these difficulties, morale remained at a high level mainly because of the continuing flow of good news which reflected the further progress of the Allied forces. In these circumstances Toosey attached the greatest possible importance to the continued operation of the secret radio, and this was to bring him into conflict with some of his more senior colleagues in the camp hierarchy.

This situation arose because Toosey's position as the sole liaison officer did not give him unlimited authority over his fellow prisoners. His real responsibility was to act as a two-way channel of communication between the Japanese commander and the POWs' administration. This was controlled by the senior officers of the four nations confined within the camp, and Toosey was obliged to work in close association with its inner group. It should be appreciated that there were ninety-eight lieutenant-colonels within Kanchanaburi and that Toosey was one of the more junior of this number. Thus internal decisions were

150

sometimes made that Toosey did not support but that he would have found hard to resist. One such item concerned the radio receiver, which was operated by the Webber brothers – both of whom had served as captains in the Malay Regiment.

D. H. Webber and his brother, Max, were both captured at Singapore and after a stay at Changi were sent to work in Thailand. By February 1943 both were based at Chungkai and it was there that the two brothers – with the aid of an ex-BBC engineer named Tom Douglas – secured parts from which they were able to construct two small radios. The Webbers then used one of these sets to establish a news service, which was eventually to produce over 700 bulletins. The set was built into the bottom of a service water bottle, and as the top half could still carry liquid the finished product could only have been discovered by a particularly careful search. The torch batteries required to produce the necessary power were stored in a hollow length of bamboo which normally formed part of the structure of their hut, so was also unlikely to be detected. When orders came for the brothers to move from Chungkai to the officers' camp at Kanchanaburi, the bamboo was matched with another of similar size and used to form the sides of a stretcher on which they carried all their possessions.

Word had been received of the strictness of the regime at Kanchanaburi and officers were told to take nothing that might cause trouble. Captain D. H. Webber therefore approached Lieutenant-Colonel Owtram, who was in charge of his party. After Owtram had seen the arrangements for its concealment, he agreed that the radio should be taken to the new camp. Once safely installed, the Webber brothers resumed their previous activities and their flow of news, carefully released, provided the major source of external information during the early months of 1945. The increasing difficulties caused by Noguchi's intransigence then saw the development of a degree of nervousness amongst the senior officers and they decided that the 'canary' must be destroyed. This instruction was passed on to the Webbers by the Australian leader, Lieutenant-Colonel McEachern. They immediately protested that they had not been consulted and argued that as they were taking the greatest risk they should have the final say. This view was rejected and after further arguments they were threatened with court-martial if they refused to obey the order.

As a result of the subsequent uproar Colonel Toosey went along to see the Webber brothers and discussed the whole matter with them. After they had confirmed that they were determined to keep the radio at work irrespective of the risk, he explained that the real problem was that some of the senior officers were afraid that should the Webbers ever be caught with the 'canary' and be tortured then they might name one of

151

their seniors as being ultimately responsible for it. Toosey then asked them to promise that if they were caught and tortured and had to reveal the name of the senior officer responsible for them and the radio they would give his name and nobody else's. Toosey's acceptance of this grave responsibility filled the Webbers with respect and admiration.[9] All concerned appreciated that Noguchi would take a most severe view of these activities if they were discovered. They also knew that two officers had been killed for this very offence actually in Kanchanaburi when, during the previous year, it was being used as a working camp.[10]

As a result of Toosey's intervention the radio was kept in operation for several more months and was stopped only when its batteries became exhausted and new ones could not be procured. News from outside then became very difficult to obtain, although by then it was obvious to all but the most pessimistic that the war was drawing to an end. However, the lack of detail was extremely frustrating and it was not until much later that Germany's surrender on 8 May 1945 was finally confirmed. Even then the information was obtained quite by accident and via a most unlikely source. It came about when Toosey asked Noguchi, who was visiting Bangkok, to obtain some violin strings for the camp orchestra. This, at a price, he agreed to do, and on his return produced a neatly wrapped parcel (for which he charged the equivalent of £30 sterling). This proved to contain the required item, but of even greater significance was the inner wrapping, which was found to consist of a page from a local Thai newspaper. This not only provided solid information of the end of the war in Europe but also recorded the recapture of Rangoon.

External events were clearly moving to a climax and they now exerted a direct influence on the lives of the prisoners, for in June 1945 orders were received that all officers were to be moved to a new camp at Nakhon Nayok in eastern Thailand.

9

The last days of captivity

Japan's increasingly desperate position

During the early months of 1945 Japan's military situation was rapidly approaching its final crisis. In the Pacific the year opened with the invasion of Luzon and early in March Manila had been secured. Shortly afterwards all resistance on the island of Iwo Jima came to an end and this was followed by the invasion of Okinawa on 1 April. These developments meant that the ineffectual long-range raids on Japan by planes based in China could now be superseded by aircraft operating from much more convenient fields which were quickly established in the newly won territories. In Burma the Allied – mainly British – forces continued to make rapid progress and, on 2 May, Rangoon was recaptured. The speed of this advance left many Japanese units cut off on the wrong side of the Sittang River, so throughout June and July they made many attempts to cross it and withdraw to Thailand. These tactics led to further heavy casualties and those troops which did manage to reach the border were badly disorganized and in no condition to continue the fight. However, those formations which had escaped encirclement and been able to retire in good order had already been moved back into northern Thailand and were being re-formed as an effective fighting force. The chief factor making this possible was the existence of the Thai–Burma railway.

The achievement of the railway

Although the Japanese conquest of Burma in 1942 had been accomplished without the aid of proper communications, this was possible only because the British forces then available were too weak to make the campaign a long one (see above, pp. 84–85). Once Rangoon had been captured the Japanese found it easy to supply their troops by sea and it was the British who found it difficult to keep an army in the field. However, the growing intensity of Allied air attacks on Rangoon and the sea routes to Singapore and the heavy toll of shipping taken by American submarines gradually made this route more and more hazardous. Thus the Japanese were increasingly obliged to rely on their newly constructed rail link with Thailand for the bulk of their stores and ammunition. As the British were equally dependent upon the Indian rail network, the subsequent struggle for Burma was to be greatly influenced by the relative efficiency of the two competing supply routes.

The retreating British forces had been obliged to give up the whole of Burma and had established their new defensive line along the Indian border. The need to supply and reinforce these units provided a major logistical problem, for there was no through road and the only link with Calcutta – the nearest port – was via rail and river. All items destined for the war zone had to be first carried by broad-gauge railway for a distance of 235 miles and then transferred to a metre-gauge train which ran for a further 215 miles to Pandu. At that point the coaches and wagons had to be carried across the Brahmaputra River on barges and reassembled on the far side for the final 150-mile run to Dimapur, which acted as the main base for the central front. From there all supplies to Kohima and on to Imphal had to be transported by road.

This line had been constructed to cater for the Assam tea industry and in peacetime it had a daily capacity of about 600 tons. By 1943 this had been raised to approximately 2800 tons per day but as demand had also increased enormously this was still inadequate. The need to provide for the growing British and Indian forces from Dimapur and to cater for Chinese units from the terminus at Ledo was made even more onerous by the requirements of the American Air Force, both for its own use and for onward transmission to China. The challenge was eventually met by procuring 4700 fully trained railwaymen and a number of powerful locomotives from the United States.[1]

These additional resources enabled the daily throughput to be progressively improved so that by the end of hostilities this had reached 7300 tons per day. These impressive figures were further increased by improvements to river transport, while a programme of road building enabled the supplies to be taken forward from the base areas to the fighting zones. These facilities were never entirely adequate but the availability of a limited amount of air transport proved to be of inestimable value in overcoming the deficiencies which frequently arose.

When the Thai–Burma railway came into full service towards the end of 1943 it quickly became the principal channel through which the Japanese forces were to be supplied. Although originally planned to provide a throughput of 3000 tons a day, the target had already been reduced to 1000 tons by the time it was completed (see above, p. 98).

Mr Futamatsu thought that the actual performance was only 300 tons a day during 1944 and many prisoners have written about the wobbly track and the lack of power of the wood-burning engines and of the consequent need to push whole trains round bends and up hills.

When the prisoners themselves were obliged to ride on the track they had constructed, they did so with great apprehension:

> During our original march up-country we had experienced the fatigue and rigours of travelling over broken country, but the prospect of a return trip on the crazy railroad we had helped to build was more terrifying than the dense jungle paths and the mountain ledges, gorges and swollen rivers. We had no faith in the track and knew only too well where the many dangers lurked.[2]

From many such anecdotal accounts it might be thought that the line built at such high cost in human misery was a failure or, at least, completely ineffective. This judgement is very far from the truth, as the records of the 9th Railway Regiment clearly indicate. These show that in the period from December 1943 to August 1945 a total of 299,550 tons of military supplies were delivered to Burma. A further 5260 tons of commodities including various mineral ores, oil pipes and refining machinery were also taken into the country. This suggests a daily average of about 370 tons a day, but as little was carried in this direction after April 1945 the true figure is close to the claim of staff officers of the Burma Army that about 400 tons per day were received. These conclusions are further supported by the number of trains which actually completed their journeys into Burma. The statistics state that between 2.43 and 2.725 trains ran each day. As each train was made up of 20 wagons, and each wagon carried 10 tons, the average load amounted to 200 tons. This would suggest that daily tonnages of approximately 468–545 could have been delivered. The reason that they were not was, of course, that the railway was also transporting large numbers of troops.

During the first half of 1944 all troop movements were into Burma and the railway is reported to have carried seven or eight complete divisions as well as many corps and army personnel. However, details have survived only in respect of the Retsu Butai of the 31st Division, of the Okami Butai and 168th Infantry Regiment of the 49th Division and of the entire 53rd (Yasu) Division. The only men returned to Thailand in this period were those who had been wounded, and in the course of the whole campaign 10,000 casualties were evacuated by this route. Then, after the disastrous attack on India, most of the defeated units used the railway to escape into Thailand. These began their retreat in

February 1945, when the Isamu (2nd) Division was carried back and this was followed by the Taka (5th) Air Division, Hayashi HQ (15th Army), Matsuri (15th) Division, the Aoba and Chu Brigades, the railway specialists themselves and the naval troops who formed the rearguard from May to August.

From the foregoing it will be seen that the 'prisoners' railway did, indeed, play a significant role in the Burma campaign. Without it the Japanese would have found it virtually impossible to reinforce and supply their forces and would certainly not have been able to consider an attack on Imphal and Kohima. Then, when it became necessary to bring their troops back from Burma, the railway not only had sufficient capacity to meet all demands but did so in a way that enabled these units to retire in good order. Thus the Japanese were quickly able to reorganize what might otherwise have been a demoralized rabble and within a very short time possessed an army that would have been very difficult to move from its new defensive positions. These, as might have been expected, were along the line of the railway. A system of fortifications was constructed at the Three Pagodas Pass, and a series of anti-tank ditches and obstacles were set up on lengthy stretches of the track. In addition Nong Pladuk and Kanchanaburi were re-formed to provide protected camps, although these were primarily to deter the possibility of an airborne assault.

If the British had attacked, either via Three Pagodas or by invading western Malaya, they would have faced a formidable task. Allied HQ were, of course, well aware of these developments and used every ounce of their air power to frustrate Japanese intentions. The result may fairly be described as a draw. The damage inflicted by air attacks certainly prevented the railway from achieving its full potential but could not, apparently, stop it from functioning as Japan's major artery of communication with Burma. In its own way, the Thai–Burma rail link made just as great a contribution to the Japanese effort as the Indian network made to the British.

Air attacks on Japanese communications

The Eastern Air Command (EAC) had been organized in December 1943 to control and co-ordinate the US Tenth Air Force and the RAF's Bengal Command. This was to remain in being until Rangoon was captured in May 1945, and during this period it was responsible for all operations within its area. Allied strength rose dramatically in 1944 so that in the wider theatre of China, Burma and India the number of American aircraft increased from approximately 1500 to over 4000. This growing power was reflected in Burma where the EAC's joint units could call on only 900 planes in September but more than 1500 by the end of the year. By then its superiority over the Japanese was complete, for the enemy could muster only 160 planes in October and, in spite of every effort, a bare 300 in December.

A series of concerted attacks on Japanese airfields in Burma made then untenable and by the beginning of 1945 virtually all of their remaining aircraft had been withdrawn to Thailand. Allied planes then took advantage of this situation to provide close support for the advancing ground forces, innumerable missions being flown to act as aerial 'artillery' against defensive positions and troop concentrations. Of equal importance was the work of the Combat Cargo Task Force, which in the months from October 1944 to May 1945 carried nearly 380,000 tons of supplies and 339,000 men to the forward areas and successfully evacuated 94,000 casualties. The troop and cargo planes of the Tenth Air Force, with many fewer aircraft, moved 211,000 tons and 225,000 personnel in the period July 1944 to April 1945. In addition, the US and British air forces made a sustained effort to disrupt Japanese communications at both the local and distant levels.

The EAC's operational directive No. 16, issued on 18 October 1944, stressed the importance of destroying enemy ports and shipping and the railway routes which brought supplies and troops into Burma. The docks and workshops at Bangkok and Rangoon were made the object of heavy raids and smaller raids were undertaken against the waterfronts at Mergui and Victoria Point. However, the ever-growing weakness of the Japanese mercantile marine gradually led to a greater emphasis on the railways, particularly the bridges which ultimately provided the only real links between Burma and the outside world.

Part of this task was completed by the B-29 'super-fortresses' of the 20th Bomber Command which, though based in India and China, were not part of the EAC structure. While these long-range planes dealt with such targets as Kuala Lumpur and Singapore, the B-24 Liberators of the EAC's Strategic Air Force concentrated on middle-distance objectives, including the marshalling yards at Bangkok. These squadrons also attacked and eventually brought down the Ban Dara bridge on the Chiengmai line. This railway had acted as the main artery for the Japanese invasion of Burma in 1942 (see above, p. 84) and, although its effectiveness had been limited by the failure to construct a proper road across the mountains to Kawkareik, it still offered a minor escape route via northern Thailand. Having to a large extent closed this loophole in early November, the allies then concentrated all efforts on those lines still controlled by the Japanese in Burma and on their link through the Three Pagodas Pass to Nong Pladuk.

The Allied air offensive against enemy communications then swiftly accelerated. Technical devices to make the bombs more effective against railway tracks were also introduced. The 688 bridges on the Thai–Burma line were naturally a prime target and those to the north of Three Pagodas were especially vulnerable – some had to be rebuilt no fewer than ten times. This bombing campaign reached its peak on 24 April 1945, when a force of forty planes smashed thirty and damaged a further seventeen bridges on the line between Thanbyuzayat and Kanchanaburi.

A major reason for the increasing success in attacking bridges and other key points on the railway was the development of a 'dive- or glide-bombing' technique in which all pilots of the 7th Bomb Group were trained by Colonel Alness during April 1945. The personal experience of one of the Liberator pilots involved confirms the value of these new tactics:

> Back at our home base a practice bridge was built. The abutments were made of 50-gallon oil drums. A single-bomb release button was put on the pilot's control wheel. Bombardiers were not carried on the B-24s for these practice missions. Each pilot was given 12 sand-filled bombs to practice his technique on the bridge. Because the nose of the plane obstructed the view on a low-level flight, we were forced to use a diving approach to the target. We flew in a circle at an altitude of 500–1,000 feet and then dived the plane at a speed of about 300 mph toward the bridge. The pilot pulled out of his gradual dive at 50–100 feet above the bridge and pressed the special bomb release button on the control column. It was all guesswork, for there was no bombsight; the pilot dropped the bomb where he thought it might be effective. I noticed a row of rivets in front of my seat extending out across the nose of the plane. This was my bombsight. As that row of rivets seemed to scoop over the bridge abutment, I released the bomb. In 12 runs I got 11 bombs right on the target, winning for my flight engineer a case of beer from the ground crew. Other pilots had similar success. With delayed-action 500-pound bombs and the diving attack with the B24, the railroad bridges of Burma fell with astounding success.[3]

As these raids were made with increasing frequency they had a serious impact on the throughput of the system. Bridges that needed to be rebuilt and breaks in the track and embankments all took time to be restored to working order. Repairs to damaged locomotives and rolling stock could also be a lengthy process and many were so badly affected that they had to be abandoned. On the Burma side of the frontier approximately 30 engines and 150 wagons were completely destroyed, and while no details have survived for the Thailand sector it is certain that its statistics would have been very similar. The effects of bombing were supplemented by numerous strafing attacks. In about half of these cases the train would stop and the crew would take cover. Thus, apart from the physical damage, the disruption to schedules was enormous and the process of rearranging services made incredibly difficult.

In spite of these enormous problems the Japanese engineers, with the aid of largely POW labour, did manage to keep the route open and it was never out of commission for very long. In the absence of air cover and a paucity of effective anti-aircraft guns, policies of concealment and rapid renovation appeared to offer the best hope of limiting the damage, and these did eventually enable the railway to function sufficiently well to perform its essential tasks. Thus when raids were particularly heavy, damage to the trains was kept to a minimum by limiting their movement to the hours of darkness. Camouflaged spur lines were then constructed to shelter locomotives and wagons during the daytime and these proved to be an effective method of protecting the rolling stock. Little, however, could be done to disguise the track and bridges; the only solution was to accept that they were likely to be attacked and to be prepared to repair them as quickly as possible.

This tactic was helped by the abundance of labour and by the stockpiling of the necessary materials, including large quantities of pre-cut timber. Thus breaks in the track seldom took more than one or two days to put right and even major attacks on railway yards and junctions could usually be dealt with inside a week. As 680 of the 688 bridges on the line were constructed of timber this also caused few difficulties for locally produced softwoods could always be readily obtained. Bridges of up to 25 feet were normally re-erected in four days and even those of 40 feet were renovated within a week. In some circumstances it was more convenient to build a new bypass: pressure of work usually ensured that this was never as solid as the original construction but it still performed the same task.

The evidence of a Japanese labour officer of No. 4 Special Railway Unit confirms these points from his own experience:

In 1944 I was in charge of maintenance of the section of the line between Neekey [Nikhe] and Plankashi [Purankasi], a distance of about 100 kilometres. Labourers were dispersed in about sixty camps in this section, about ten thousand in all. The chief task was the repairing and rebuilding of timber bridges of which we had more than 200 to look after.

Rebuilding of a bombed bridge started without delay and continued night and day until the job was completed. The average moderate-sized bridge took about a week to rebuild. While the construction was in process, a gang of coolies was employed in unloading trains on the one side of the gap and reloading trains on the other. Generally it took about four hours to unload one train.

The Neekey bridge was destroyed three times. It was the longest in length. By working three shifts daily with about 500 men in each shift we were able to rebuild the bridge in about two weeks. We have had as many as twenty bridges hit in one day.[4]

The few bridges built of steel and concrete posed more awkward questions, for the re-erection of fallen sections required specialised skills and equipment, while the replacements themselves were hard to find or fabricate. The 'permanent bridge' over the Kwae Yai at Tamarkan proved to be the principal example of a structure of this type with all its advantages and disadvantages. Its strength of construction made it more resistant to air attack but once it was seriously damaged it was extremely difficult to put it back into operation.

The route chosen for the railway required a major crossing over the Kwae Yai. The erection of this 'permanent' bridge had been preceded by the completion of a wooden structure but once the main bridge was fully operational it coped very easily with the demands made by the railway so the wooden structure was allowed to fall into disrepair. Then, as the prospect of Allied air attacks became a real possibility, this period of neglect came to an end, for the wooden bridge clearly offered a useful option which could be pressed into service in an emergency.

The first reconnaisance flight over Tamarkan took place on 19 January 1943, before the 'permanent' bridge had been completed, and attacks on the line began only two months later. However, these tended to be on the Burma sector of the railway, where there was an abundance of more convenient targets. In addition, the need to provide the maximum amount of aid to the Chinese during the earlier part of 1944 meant that many American planes had to be diverted to that war zone. In these circumstances the Japanese authorities were led to believe that the bridge at Tamarkan would not be attacked on any scale so, although an anti-aircraft battery was installed, it was thought that it would only have to deal with single planes operating at extreme range – if at all!

The deterioration of Japan's military position was not obvious either in Thailand or on the Burma front at the beginning of 1944 but nevertheless some preparations were put in hand during the spring. The value of this policy became apparent when the US Air Force resumed its air offensive at the end of September 1944, for it quickly became apparent that the Kwae bridges were regarded as prime targets.

When Colonel Toosey had been obliged to help in the construction of the bridges at Tamarkan he always had one thought to console him. He was quite convinced that if the Allies ever gained sufficient strength to

160

win the war then the demolition of these prominent structures would be well within their capabilities. The first major raid after the return to full strength was the unfortunate attack on Nong Pladuk on 6/7 September where, although the target was badly damaged, over ninety prisoners were killed and a large number injured (see above, p. 143). Then, on 29 November, Liberators of the 493rd and 9th Squadrons of the 7th Bomb Group, USAAF, made a determined effort to bring Toosey's forecast to fruition. The planes dropped their bombs in a tight pattern from about 8500 feet but, in spite of at least one direct hit and many near misses, the spans of the steel bridge remained intact.

The failure of this attempt led to a follow up raid on 13 December 1944:

> The 436th and 492nd Squadrons were to attack the ack-ack sites of the steel bridge while the 9th was to attack from high level. Two other Liberators were then to low-level the bridge from 200 feet. The attack was carried out as planned, but the steel bridge withstood all the explosions.[5]

Another raid was arranged for 23 January 1945, when the 9th and 436th Squadrons set out to bomb the bridges. Bad weather and malfunctions of various types meant that only one plane reached the site and the bridges again remained intact. Enormous problems were encountered in the attempt to maintain these air attacks over very long distances. The fact that they were continued owes much to the determination and calibre of the pilots and their crews.

One such officer was Captain Carl H. Fritsche of the 492nd Squadron, which at the end of 1944 was based at Madhaiganj near Asansol about 100 miles to the north of Calcutta. He relates that with the addition of two bomb-bay tanks his Liberator had a range of about 3000 miles at its cruising speed of 225 m.p.h. This was sufficient to reach most targets in southern Thailand, including the Bangkok dock area, and also brought the Kwae bridges into range. These missions, however, involved flights of up to 18 hours and as most of this time was spent crossing the Bay of Bengal and the Andaman Sea at a height of only 50 feet in order to stay under any possible radar screen they imposed very heavy strains on both men and machines. Although the B-24 could fly on three engines, the hazards of mechanical failure were always present on trips of such magnitude. These risks were increased by the frequent spells of bad weather and by the dangers posed by enemy guns. Fortunately, by the time that the bombing campaign was reaching its climax few Japanese fighters remained in the area, so there was little to fear from that quarter.

In spite of all these actual and potential problems, all four squadrons of the 7th Bomb Group were involved in a further raid on Tamarkan on 5 February. Considerable damage was caused to the protecting gun positions, and the embankment and track leading to the bridges was badly knocked about. Once again, however, the structures themselves remained in being. This failure prompted a swift response to what was now becoming a personal challenge to many of the air crews involved and a raid was organized to take place only 4 days later. This was undertaken by eight planes of 9th Squadron and this time two sections of the wooden bridge were destroyed. However, the steel bridge was still in full working order, so yet another attack was ordered by the now completely frustrated Colonel Harvey T. Alness.

This raid took place on 13 February 1945, and the first strike was made by four Liberators of the 493rd Squadron all armed with four 1000-pound bombs. They approached the target in single file at a height of 300 feet. As the leading plane reached the site it released its cargo of high explosives and then veered sharply to the left and closer to the ground in an attempt to avoid the enemy's gunfire. In that instant the tail gunner saw that one of the concrete piers was crumbling and that two of the spans were falling into the river. As this Liberator then climbed away it was seen that the centre of the steel bridge had been demolished and that, in addition, the second B-24 had scored a number of direct hits on the already damaged wooden bridge. These successes were also witnessed by the third and fourth aircraft in the group and they turned away without bombing, but a following flight of six more Liberators of the 9th Squadron, including one commanded by Colonel Alness, pressed home their attack and further hits were reported on both of the bridges.

At the time it was thought that the bombs of the 9th Squadron had brought down a third section of the steel bridge and this claim was repeated in Carl Fritsche's authoritative account of the raid. Further research has revealed that although the 9th Squadron did cause severe additional damage it did not bring down another span. However, the net effect of the attack was the same, for both bridges were now breached and the throughput of the railway was considerably reduced. The Japanese reacted by arranging for barges to ferry loads across the Kwae Yai, but as this was a cumbersome and time-wasting process they simultaneously began a crash programme of repairs.

Within six weeks photo reconnaissance showed that the wooden bridge had already been mended and was back in service. Some reports have suggested that POWs assisted in this work, but Mr W. L. Davis, who was employed on the maintenance of the bridges, has stated that after the successful raid of 13 February the prisoners were kept away and all repairs were undertaken by Japanese personnel. In any event, the link across the Kwae Yai had now been partially restored. The weakness

162

of the damaged structure meant that it was not strong enough to bear the weight of steam locomotives, but diesel cars were permitted to cross and loaded wagons could be pushed over, one at a time, by hand.

As soon as it was appreciated that the wooden bridge was back in operation, arrangements were made for a further attack. This took place on 3 April when six Liberators of the 436th Squadron were instructed to undertake this mission while other aircraft from the 492nd Squadron were ordered to 'divert' the ack-ack gunners. The leading B-24 scored a direct hit on the eastern side of the bridge and as the following planes inflicted even more damage a large gap quickly appeared as a whole section was destroyed. Once again the crossing of the river could only be made by barge and once again the Japanese engineers were faced with the thankless task of patching up their now considerably battered charges.

According to Mr Davis, the wooden bridge was not repaired after the raid on 3 April. If this were true it would be very surprising, for the restoration of this structure was purely a question of time and effort. Other reports indicate, however, that the wooden bridge was put back into some form of working order. Perhaps the truth is that, when this attack took place, work on restoring the 'permanent' bridge was at such an advanced stage that it was decided that it should be completed before the task of rebuilding the wooden bridge was attempted? The work on the steel frame presented special problems, for no metal spans were obtainable. These were eventually solved by the use of timber sections, which once again enabled light traffic to cross the Kwae Yai. It seems likely that once the steel bridge was back in service further effort would then be directed to the reconstruction of the wooden edifice and both were reported to be in operation by the middle of June.

The capture of Rangoon and the reduced requirement for aircraft in Burma enabled the US Tenth Air Force to transfer many of its units to China. As a result only the 493rd Squadron remained to continue the strategic bombing campaign on Japanese communications. Thus the task of making what proved to be the last raid on the site at Tamarkan was entrusted to the RAF. British air strength had been gradually built up and six squadrons, equipped with Liberators, had been operating alongside the four American squadrons since 1944. Two of these, the 159th and the 356th, were now selected to attack the two bridges across the Kwae Yai. The raid took place on 24 June and when the planes finally left the scene three spans of the steel bridge had been broken and the wooden bridge had been breached in two places. The official records indicate that the bridges had been intact prior to the attack and this view is supported by photographs taken before and during the raid.

The RAF raid marked the finish of the wartime careers of the bridges over the Kwae Yai. As the withdrawal from Burma was virtually complete by this time there was less pressure on the railway, and with many smaller bridges down along the length of the remaining line to the Three Pagodas Pass it is thought that barges were sufficient to deal with the reduced level of traffic. Thus if efforts were made to rebuild at least the wooden bridge, these were not pursued with any great vigour and little progress had been made when the war came to an end.

The disruption to Japanese communications of which the bridges formed an important part was not achieved without the payment of a heavy price. During the period from January 1944 to April 1945 the Strategic Air Force lost a total of sixty-three bombers in this work – thirty–four British and twenty-nine American. However, the damage inflicted on the enemy was enormous and proved a significant factor in the victory of the land forces. General Slim was certainly most grateful for the overall contribution of the Allied air forces, and stated:

> Never, I believe, was air co-operation closer, quicker or more effective; never was it more gratefully appreciated than by the Fourteenth Army and its commander.[6]

The Camp at Nakhon Nayok

When, in June 1945, Colonel Toosey was informed that Kanchanaburi was to be closed it was stated that this was because the officers were to be moved to a more roomy and comfortable site. The real reason was, of course, very different. So long as this and other camps were located along the route of the railway they were in the direct path of the invading forces whose arrival could not be long delayed. Thus large bodies of prisoners posed a threat to the Japanese rear which, it was thought, might have been exploited by the dropping of arms or even the arrival of airborne troops. Some weight might also have been given to two additional factors. If existing camps were dispersed and their organizations disrupted, the concealment of war crimes would obviously be made easier, and if the prisoners were placed in areas well away from the fighting zone, they might have a value as potential hostages.

The Japanese plan was that the officers would move to their new site in parties of 400, and they suggested that Toosey should lead the vanguard. He could have protested and argued that he would be better employed at Kanchanaburi but after discussing the matter with his senior colleagues it seemed sensible that he should leave with the first group. Many of the prisoners in the officers' camp were elderly or infirm and Toosey's tactics were aimed at reducing the burden on them as much as possible. At the age of 40 he still regarded himself as a comparatively young and healthy man and thought that by arriving at an early stage he would be able to influence the design and layout of the new establishment. Accordingly he arranged for his position as liaison officer to be taken over by Lieutenant-Colonel Swinton and then selected 400 of the fittest men to accompany him. He trusted that with their co-operation it would be possible to provide at least some facilities for the less fit and well who were to follow at regular intervals.

Toosey and his party left Kanchanaburi on a wet evening on 28 June 1945. His account of the subsequent journey is typical of the muddle and delay which prisoners always seemed to experience during wartime trips organised by the Japanese:

We left Kanburi [Kanchanaburi] at 2200 hours arriving at Nong Pladuk-40 kilometres away at 0300 hours the next morning, travelling 30 to an open luggage truck. At Nong Pladuk we were allowed off the train to sleep and eat our haversack rations. It was pouring with rain: we had no cover. At 1100 hours we entrained again, this time in enclosed luggage trucks, and arrived at 1300 at a blown-up bridge across a river East of Nakhon Pathom where we had to unload our baggage, carry it across a very dangerous foot-bridge some 2'6 wide, over the river, and camp down for the night in the open alongside the blown-up bridge. Fortunately it did not rain although the tide came up and flooded a large part of the Camp.

At 1100 hours next morning we entrained again for Bangkok arriving at 1800 hours. We sat alongside the Station, which had been heavily bombed, until 0100 hours the following morning when we were put on to 5 barges, packed like sardines in a tin. We were towed down the river to some go-downs [warehouses] about 10 kilometres from Bangkok where we unloaded the barges and attempted to get some sleep lying on the concrete floor. Some of the buildings were partially open to the weather from bomb damage. Here we were well fed from the Cookhouse of an O.R.'s Camp which was situated in a neighbouring go-down. We made contact with them and found them to be in good order although nervous since they were forced to remain in the go-down during air raids. We attempted to put this matter right but without success. We stayed there one further night and after our short rest were put on a train at 1100 hours in the morning to be slowly moved to Bangkok. There we were shunted about for several hours arriving at our final destination at 0100 hours on the following morning. Feeding arrangements on the train were haversack rations: on this occasion we were permitted to purchase fruit from the Thais.

On arrival at the final station we unloaded the trucks, heavy baggage was put on 2 lorries and at 0200 hours we started on our 41 kilometre march. Since we were all fit men this march was not difficult except for the first 4 hours when we marched in a typical monsoon deluge. Feeding arrangements, for the Japanese, were good, food being sent from an O.R.'s camp twice during the day, but the march arrangements were most inefficient and stupid. We arrived at the O.R.'s camp at 2000 hours where we were given a meal and spent the night. We had some 25 blister-casualties: most officers had not marched far for some considerable time, but generally speaking the party was quite fit.[7]

On his arrival at what was referred to as Nakhon Nayok (it was actually 41 kilometres from the station of that name) Toosey found himself in an area of virgin jungle at the base of a long line of hills. The site was 17 kilometres from the nearest village and the only approach was along a 3-kilometre track that was only wide enough for a single person. In these unpromising circumstances Toosey was instructed to prepare to receive the balance of the officers from Kanchanaburi. Knowing the Japanese practice of moving men at short notice, Toosey asked the advance party for a special effort and began by dividing them into two groups of equal size. One section cleared the site of lalang grass while the other made a series of journeys along the track to bring in luggage and tents from the road. By the end of a very long day these ancient Indian-pattern tents had been erected. They were not waterproof but fortunately a period of dry weather made this of less significance than would otherwise have been the case.

Having established a temporary base, the next task was to construct a road to the camp. This involved an enormous amount of hard labour, but 4 weeks after their arrival the track had been transformed so that it was fit for motor vehicles. During this period all daylight hours were spent at work, and with the return of the rain the entire party became permanently soaked. The tents provided little protection but the building of huts could not be undertaken until the road had been constructed. These were then erected at a rapid rate out of local materials, but as a stream of fresh parties were arriving it was difficult to supply proper accommodation for all and it was not possible to construct sleeping platforms. Nevertheless all incoming officers were met and assisted on the last stage of their journey and then found a place out of the incessant downpour. Many of the older officers were in an exhausted state and had been roughly treated by their Korean guards, so this reception made a great deal of difference to their welfare.

As the construction of the camp proceeded, an administrative structure

166

gradually developed. At first the Japanese camp staff consisted only of Lieutenant Takasaki and Sergeant Ido, although these had the assistance of a number of Korean guards. Colonel Toosey built up his organization to include Captains Boyle and Wood, while Captain Alting von Geusau represented the Dutch personnel. These two groups worked reasonably well together. The major difficulty was the shortage of rations. Only small quantities of stew and rice were provided and this was insufficient for men performing hard physical labour. As only rice was available locally and everything else had to be brought from Bangkok, food remained a problem throughout the existence of this camp. However, Toosey's pressure resulted in the establishment of a canteen and the eggs and fruit which this spasmodically provided at least partially filled the gap.

A further difficulty which could not be resolved was the site of the camp itself. It was quickly discovered that it had been placed right in the middle of a Japanese defensive position and that over 30,000 fighting troops were actively preparing to resist the Allied attack when it reached this area. It was widely thought that the Japanese Army intended to make its final 'decisive stand' in the hills to the north of Nakhon Nayok. The fate of the prisoners in such an event was ever-present in the minds of Toosey and his colleagues. However, such considerations were soon forced into the background for, early in August, Captain Noguchi arrived from Kanchanaburi. Up to that point there had been few incidents, for the effort required to construct the road and build the camp had fully occupied both the prisoners and their captors.

Noguchi's presence immediately produced a charged atmosphere and this was given real substance after two officers were caught receiving messages from a Thai while *en route* to Nakhon Nayok. Although both were severely beaten by the *kempeitai* before being delivered to the camp, Noguchi took it upon himself to continue the punishment and they were ordered to stand in front of the guardhouse. They had been standing there for 3 days (together with three other ranks who were being punished for unrelated offences) without being given either food or water and were in a state of near collapse when news arrived that Japan had capitulated and that the war was over.

10

Freedom at last

The coming of peace

By the summer of 1945 Japan was in desperate and terminal difficulty on all fronts. The last of the Imperial Navy, including the remaining super-battleship *Yamoto*, had been sacrificed in a futile and suicidal gesture off Okinawa during April and the remaining troops on Okinawa were being urged to fight to the death. This instruction was followed so literally that resistance on the island was prolonged until 2 July. Although 12,000 Americans were killed during this campaign, the defenders lost 110,000 men while a further 75,000 civilians also paid the ultimate price for their emperor.

Large numbers of Japanese troops remained in various parts of the Pacific theatre, but the lack of communications meant that they could play no effective role in future events. This was also the case with the Southern Army, which was ordered to hold its ground in Malaya, Thailand, Indo-China and the Dutch East Indies with whatever it could command locally. The situation on the Chinese mainland had remained fairly static since the Japanese advance to the south of Hankow in June 1944. Although the Imperial Army in China had subsequently been weakened by the transfer of many units to Formosa and the Ryukyu Islands, it still remained a formidable force that was quite capable of dealing with any attack which might be delivered by its divided opposition.

However, this relatively sanguine position began to change when, on 5 April 1945, the Soviet Union announced that it did not propose to renew its neutrality pact with Japan. The conclusion of hostilities in Europe then increased the fear that Russia might join in the war by attacking Manchuria. It was accepted that this was a risk which had to be run since Japan's sole priority at this stage was to organize her remaining strength so as to provide the maximum resistance to what was regarded

168

as the inevitable invasion by American forces. By midsummer the country was in a state of siege and under constant attack from the air. This process had been gaining momentum since 12 October 1944, when the first of the new B-29s arrived on Saipan in the Marianas. Only 5 weeks later, over 100 of these super-fortresses attacked Tokyo and, although little was achieved, the stage was then set for the development of a massive programme of raids which was to devastate most of the enemy's towns and cities.

The rapid build-up of numbers and the establishment of closer and more convenient facilities enabled an increasingly large series of attacks to be undertaken. These attempted to cripple Japanese production by the dropping of high explosives on specific industrial targets. Some disappointment was felt in respect of the results that were achieved by these tactics and so a new policy was adopted. This was entirely on the initiative of General Le May, the commander of the B-29 Groups in the Marianas, and came into effect on 9 March 1945. On that night the bombers were loaded exclusively with incendiaries and these were directed towards the poorer residential districts in the south-eastern sections of Tokyo. The consequences of this fire-raid were horrific, for there were thousands of wooden buildings, all in close proximity to one another, and no fire lanes had been cut through this densely packed area. It took 4 days before the last of the flames could be extinguished and by then 16 square miles of Tokyo had been gutted, nearly 80,000 people had been killed and more than 1 million had been left homeless.

The fire attacks on Japan's capital were followed by similar raids on Nagoya, Osaka and Kobe. Significant damage was caused to industrial capacity but this was achieved only at the expense of thousands of civilians who died in what remained of their homes. These attacks by heavy bombers were gradually supplemented by those from shorter-range aircraft and, after the capture of Okinawa was assured, by the full weight of the US 3rd Fleet. This was organized into three battle groups and when the British Pacific Fleet arrived in mid-July this was formed into a fourth task force. Thereafter the Japanese mainland was subjected to constant raids by carrier-borne aircraft and, in addition, many coastal sites were bombarded by the Allied battleships and cruisers. Little resistance was encountered – the Japanese were keeping any last reserves for use against the invasion forces – and both planes and ships enjoyed complete freedom to select and destroy their targets.

These blows to the Japanese military and economic systems were exacerbated by the simultaneous reduction in the capacity of the Japanese mercantile marine, which meant that during the last months of hostilities Japan was effectively cut off from her overseas possessions and armies. American submarines had already taken a substantial toll of

Japanese shipping on external routes and after May 1945 they also operated within the Sea of Japan. This was a logical move for by then the only remaining links between the home islands and the outside world were to Korea and northern China via the Shimonoseki and Tsushima Straits. A series of mine-laying raids on the ports which could contribute to this trade and the effects of the losses caused by submarine meant that by July even this route was at a near standstill.

Japan's isolation from her overseas supplies of food, fuel and raw materials led to desperate shortages of all items that were essential to the prosecution of the war. In spite of these manifest problems, there was little thought of surrender. Instead, efforts were made to convert acorns into food to offset the effects of the smallest rice harvest since 1905, and attempts to combat the lack of oil were concentrated on the production of aviation spirit from the roots of pine trees. Every possibility was investigated to ensure that any invading force would pay a high price for any success it might achieve. However, the collapse of production and internal communications, together with the incessant air attacks, led inevitably to the disintegration of the social structure and to the near breakdown of the central administration. This dire combination of circumstances and forecasts then encouraged the first, hesitating, steps towards what was hoped to be a negotiated settlement with the Allied powers, but at the same time the final plans for the defence of the homeland were being organized under the code name of 'Operation Decision' (*Ketsu-Go*).

It is doubtful if even at this late stage in the war the Japanese authorities appreciated the magnitude of the forces to be brought against them. The Allied navies were already dominating the seas round the home islands and their aircraft had gained almost total superiority over huge areas. These carrier planes were being supported by fighters based on Iwo Jima and by heavy bombers using the many airfields developed in the Marianas. A further sixty air groups, comprising 240 squadrons, were in process of being established at new facilities being constructed on Okinawa and its neighbouring island of Ie-shima and these were scheduled to be fully operational by the date of the invasion.

These vast naval and air forces were thus well placed to cover the landings of the fourteen divisions of the US 6th Army to which was allocated the task of seizing the southern part of Kyushu, planned for 1 November. These were almost all battle-hardened troops, lavishly supplied with the latest weapons and equipment. Had resistance been stronger than expected, a further three divisions per month could have been delivered to the area from the massive armies being built up for the coming invasion of Honshu. It is difficult to see how the Japanese could have provided effective opposition for very long for, although Japan had mobilized an army of over 2.5 million, of which two-thirds were to be used in Kyushu, their quality was uncertain and many units were poorly equipped. A civilian militia of 28 million had also been authorized and was in the process of being organized. However, this was being supplied with only the most primitive of arms, including spears and bows and arrows, and it cannot now be determined if this would have proved an effective guerrilla force or merely a disjointed rabble. In addition, by the beginning of August approximately 800 fighters and bombers had been put in a state of readiness and were dispersed on concealed airfields in many different parts of the country. It was realized that this number could do little to influence the course of events, but great hopes were placed on the special *kamikaze* units which by then had been provided with an estimated 3000 planes. With the benefit of hindsight, the weight of evidence indicates that the American invasion would have succeeded. The only real question was, at what cost?

As early as July 1944, Japan's declining fortunes had led to the resignation of General Tojo as prime minister. His successor, General Koiso, was regarded as a moderate but, as all of his activities were constrained by the need to retain the approval of the armed forces, there was little scope for those who favoured an end to hostilities. Nevertheless he did establish a Supreme Council for the Direction of the War and attempts to begin negotiations were made via contacts in Russia, Sweden and China. When these failed during April 1945 Koiso felt obliged to resign.

Koiso's replacement was Admiral Suzuki. As he had not been involved in the decision to enter the war, he was thought to be a man on whom the Allies might look with some favour. The position of the 'Peace Party' within the Supreme Council was therefore improved and its freedom of action was further strengthened by a reorganization of its secretariat, which ensured that policies could be resolved without undue outside pressure. These changes enabled new contacts to be made through unofficial channels in Sweden and Switzerland; when these came to nothing another approach was made to Russia. When this, in turn, was rebuffed, a drastic reappraisal of policy and resources became necessary. This was presented to the Supreme Council on 6 June, and it became evident, even to the 'War Party', that the war was lost. However, a majority thought that it was still worth while struggling on in order to obtain better terms from the Allies.

When it became clear that the battle for Okinawa was lost, another meeting of the Supreme Council was held. This agreed that further attempts to persuade Russia to negotiate should be made and this course of action was approved by the emperor on 22 June. The Soviet ambassador in Tokyo was immediately approached but no reply was received until 18 July and even then for only called further clarification. This finally convinced the Supreme Council that the Russians were being deliberately obstructive and that no help could be expected from that source. Indeed, it quickly became obvious that a Russian attack on Manchuria was now only a question of time.

Japan's disappointment at these developments was compounded by news from the Potsdam Conference that at the conclusion of their meeting the Allies had issued a proclamation which threatened the complete destruction of Japan if she did not accept 'unconditional surrender'. In fact the terms were less harsh than had been anticipated and appeared to give some hope that the emperor's position might be respected and that Japan would eventually be allowed to seek her own destiny. The Supreme Council met on 27 July to consider its implications but although a majority thought it could form the basis for discussions the service chiefs demanded its rejection. The result was an inconclusive statement to the press which implied that the government intended to ignore the Allied initiative; the United States therefore took the view that the terms had been rejected, so pressed on with plans to drop the newly available atomic bomb.

It was at the Potsdam Conference that Stalin informed the Western Allies that Japan had been making overtures for a settlement and that as he regarded them as a device to secure Russian collaboration he had merely kept them going without any commitment. These messages were being monitored by the Americans, so this information came as no surprise. Stalin had realized that Japan's position was becoming so difficult that she might choose to accept the terms being offered and that in this event he would have little say in the subsequent negotiations. He therefore ensured that the Japanese were kept waiting for a final reply to their requests until 8 August. This was the date, which had been carefully brought forward, on which the Soviet Union was ready to begin hostilities.

While the Russians were making their final preparations to enter the war, the Americans dropped the first atomic bomb on Hiroshima. Early reports, received in Tokyo on the afternoon of 6 August, suggested that it had done enormous damage but that it was no worse than many of the fire raids which had already been endured. It was not until the 8th that it was confirmed that it was an atomic device, and there was still no real understanding of the problem of radiation which was to follow. In many respects the event was overshadowed by the announcement that Russia had declared war and that Manchuria and southern Sakhalin, the furthest north of the Japanese home islands, were already being invaded.

The need for peace was now obvious to all members of the Supreme

Council, but disagreement about the exact terms that would be acceptable and doubts as to how extreme elements would react prevented a
firm decision being taken. Details of the second atomic bomb, which
devastated Nagasaki, then added to the urgency but the council could
still not make a unanimous recommendation. In the event it was the
emperor who, on 10 August, made the final decision. After this had
been formally accepted by the cabinet, a statement was sent to all Allied
governments by radio. This stated that Japan was prepared to accept the
terms laid down at Potsdam providing the position of the Imperial
House was not jeopardized. After rapid consultation amongst the Allies
this condition was agreed to and the stage was set for the termination of
the Second World War.

Before steps to implement this decision could be taken, internal
difficulties inside Japan had to be overcome. As anticipated, a number of
the younger officers of Imperial General Headquarters and the War
Office attempted to disrupt the moves towards peace and it seemed
likely that a *coup d'état* could be expected. It was against this background
that Emperor Hirohito took the unprecedented step of broadcasting to
the nation. To most Japanese he was a mystical figure, greatly revered,
whom the vast majority had never seen, and the effect of hearing his
voice and learning his views was enormous. The population at large
then accepted the need to surrender – many with intense relief –
and opposition to the policy quickly petered out. However, it was
necessary to convince the field commanders that this was the Imperial
wish, for, away from the devastation of the Japanese cities, there were
still many who thought that the war could be won or that all should
perish in the attempt. To meet this difficulty the Emperor sent three
Imperial princes by air to the principal overseas command centres.
When one of these arrived at the HQ of the Southern Army in Saigon
and confirmed the official edict, the POWs in Thailand were once again
free men.

The ending of captivity

The prisoners in Thailand knew little of these events in Tokyo but were
well aware that the end of the war could not be long delayed. The
evidence provided by the daily presence of Allied aircraft was there for
all to see, and for those still based on or close to the railway the
damage caused by these raids was very apparent. For those officers
who still remained at the camp at Kanchanaburi the successful attacks
on the Kwae bridges were a particularly strong indication of the
increasing power of the Allies. Those, like Toosey, who had already
made the journey to Nakhon Nayok had seen the extensive damage

caused in Bangkok and many POWs have commented on the systematic destruction of the bridges they had to cross to reach their destination.

By early August rumours of impending peace were rife but life still went on as what passed for normal in the POW camps. Noguchi's departure had left Lieutenant Matsushita at Kanchanaburi, so it was he who had the task of organising the remaining officers into parties and sending them in a pre-determined sequence on to Nakhon Nayok. He was quickly prevailed upon to improve Captain Drower's diet but all attempts to persuade him to release this now desperately ill prisoner were unsuccessful. The POWs were now without a link to the outside world, for no further batteries could be secured for their radio. However, in the hope that fresh ones might be obtained in Bangkok the set was sent on to the new site at Nakhon Nayok. As usual it was concealed in an officer's water bottle and on this occasion travelled as part of Noguchi's personal effects.

The ending of radio reception did not mean a complete break with all news, for pamphlets dropped by Allied aircraft and contacts with local civilians enabled the prisoners to keep track of major events. The Korean guards were an increasingly useful source of information and it was through them that the first real intimation of the Japanese surrender was heard at Kanchanaburi. This report was received on 14 August but on the following morning the 6th Party, which was due to move to Nakhon Nayok, was still ordered to move its gear and equipment to the railway line. While this was being completed numerous Thais walked past. All were extremely excited and many gave the 'V' sign and others spoke of the war being over. The news was greeted with considerable scepticism but when Nai Boon Pong cycled past and whispered the same message it seemed it might be true. There was no official confirmation of the event by the time that the train was due to leave. Some prisoners thought they should delay their departure until the situation was clarified, but with the Japanese still very much in control it was finally decided that it could only be to their advantage if they went as far as Bangkok.

A further long and anxious night was passed by those still at Kanchanaburi. Then, as nothing was mentioned by the Japanese on the following morning, the whole of 16 August passed very slowly in an atmosphere of mounting anticlimax. It was not until early in the evening that all hut commanders were called to a meeting with the camp administrators. When this was over each returned to his own accommodation and made his individual announcement that the war was over. A deep silence then fell over the whole area but when a single voice began the singing of the national anthem this was quickly taken up by the entire camp. Many of the officers then moved to the parade ground where they sat in the moonlight and sang all their old favourites. This spontaneous action was followed by a drift back to the huts where the news of the day could be more quietly digested.

When Lieutenant Matsushita had informed the prisoners' leaders of Japan's surrender he had pointed out to them that he did not know if the fighting units in the area had received specific orders and urged that all personnel should remain in the camp for the time being. This was agreed to on the condition that a delegation be allowed out to negotiate for food with the Thai authorities and that the prisoners should forthwith be responsible for their own internal discipline. One further matter was dealt with as soon as this handover was accomplished: Captain Drower was released from his 'cage' and, to everyone's satisfaction, housed in Noguchi's personal quarters. At this stage he was extremely weak and apart from suffering from blackwater fever was thought to be on the point of madness. After an immediate blood transfusion and a night's sleep he was found to have begun a remarkable transformation. This progress was subsequently maintained and in spite of his 77 days in appalling conditions he eventually made a full recovery. The following day, the 17th, saw the first fruits of freedom. Those prisoners who were scheduled to move to Nakhon Nayok refused to go and the Japanese did not attempt to insist. Boon Pong produced a constant flow of food, which immediately transformed the diet and eating habits of all in the camp. Arrangements were also made for specially detailed officers to listen to the BBC news in the governor of Kanchanaburi's house, so all aspects of world events quickly became known. However, these concessions could not disguise the prisoners' real wish to move out of the camp. The presence of many armed Japanese and Thais made this potentially dangerous and Lieutenant-Colonel Swinton attempted to keep everyone inside. This policy would soon have resulted in confrontation with the mass of officers but as Swinton received permission to transfer to Bangkok within 24 hours of the surrender the situation did not arise. Instead his successor, Commander Alexander of the Royal Navy, took a different view and arranged a pass system so that all could visit the local town in a controlled manner. It was soon discovered that British military personnel had been training 'Free Thais' close to Kanchanaburi and when these were contacted the ex-POWs knew that their captivity was definitely at an end.

At Nakhon Nayok the lack of a working radio and the absence of a neighbouring town meant that news about the progress of the war was difficult to obtain. The only real source of information was that brought by new parties when they arrived from Kanchanaburi. Their accounts of continued Allied bombing and of the damage they had witnessed *en route* added to the general belief that the fighting had entered its final phase, but they could contribute little in the way of solid facts. This lack of definite evidence plus the heavy workload restricted serious discussion but the majority of the prisoners remained extremely sceptical of the various rumours which regularly swept the camp. Toosey also adopted a 'wait and see' policy, for his naturally optimistic nature had been severely tested by a major attack of pneumonia which almost cost him his life. This was his only serious illness while he was in captivity and he had begun to think that he was immune from tropical complaints and malnutrition. He now realized his mistake and intensified the tactics which had brought him so far – each day was to be lived for itself and he tried to devote little thought to either the past or the future.

Toosey's sickness only kept him out of action for about a fortnight and he then made a rapid recovery. However, the attack left its mark and it was partly for this reason that he took less notice of the increasingly persistent reports that the war was about to end. Then towards the middle of August a party arrived led by a lieutenant-colonel in whom Toosey had great faith. This officer was quite convinced that events had already come to a head, for he had seen many Thais openly defying the Japanese in a way which would have been unthinkable on earlier occasions. Information from this source had to be taken seriously and in spite of his reservations Toosey found his expectations being raised. Nothing further occurred for several days and in his isolation he attempted to put the matter out of his mind and concentrated on the business of building and running the camp. Then on 15 August he was summoned to meet Lieutenant Takasaki, the second-in-command, in his office.

At this stage Toosey had no reason to think that this was anything but a routine meeting and this belief was apparently confirmed when he saw that two officers and three other ranks were still being punished by being obliged to stand to attention outside the guardroom. However, once he entered the building he could see that circumstances had changed, for a new mat was produced for him to sit on and he was offered fresh Chinese tea to drink. Takasaki then told him that Japan had been forced to surrender because of the use of a weapon of terrible magnitude. He went on to say: 'Now we are friends, we can shake hands.' Toosey replied:

> Before I do that I want to know what happened to those officers who escaped from Tamarkan camp.[1] Did you shoot them and cut their heads off on your own initiative or had you orders from above?[2]

Takasaki stated that he had issued these orders on his own authority. Toosey did not believe him, but nevertheless refused to take tea with him. Instead he proposed that he should now take over the camp. Once Takasaki had agreed, Toosey moved outside and, finding that all the Japanese seemed to have disappeared, he instructed the prisoners still standing by the guardroom to dismiss. After a brief word with his 'command group' Toosey then called for a general parade. Twelve hundred excited officers immediately rushed forward, for the absence of guards and the early return of many of the working parties had already led to considerable expectations.

Colonel Toosey then made a brief announcement that the war was over. No one was concerned that he was unable to supply any further details. All were just content to savour the moment and then join in the singing of 'Land of Hope and Glory', 'God Save the King' and 'Jerusalem'. Little else could be achieved that night but by the following morning when a second parade was held Toosey had already made a number of arrangements. A detachment of guards, armed with sticks, were already manning the gate and keeping a watchful eye on the commandant, Captain Noguchi, who had now reappeared. Another group were engaged in examining the camp stores to see what food and clothing were available and a Japanese truck had been sent to the nearest village with British personnel to buy as much food as the funds formerly held by Noguchi could buy.

By the time that Toosey addressed the second parade he had decided the way in which he thought it would be wise to proceed. He therefore informed the officers of the steps he had taken and told them that for a start there would be no outside work and rations would be greatly improved. He went on to say:

I propose to keep the discipline exactly the same as I have done throughout three-and-a-half years and I am in charge and you will, I'm sorry to say, still have to do as you are told: I warn you against two things, that is indiscriminately going out of camp to get food for yourselves or getting mixed up with women, because the last thing I want is to get a lot of you full of venereal disease before we go home and before I'm going to allow you to make contact with women I'm going to make arrangements to have an air-drop and get some proper supplies so that if you wish sexual intercourse you can do it in safety.[3]

As the vast majority of the now ex-prisoners were in a deplorable physical shape these restrictions caused only small resentment. The lack of any nearby centres of population and the presence of large numbers of still armed Japanese fighting troops made ventures outside the camp unattractive (although a few celebrated their freedom by making brief excursions). Accordingly the efforts to improve conditions inside the site were given the highest possible priority and supplies of additional rice and vegetables, together with cattle 'on the hoof', were quickly acquired. In many other camps huge quantities of Red Cross parcels were quickly discovered and distributed, but at Nakhon Nayok none was in store. This meant that clothing was in particularly short supply and everyone, including Toosey, possessed only a ragged pair of shorts and a pair of wooden 'clompers'. A few still retained shirts and hats of various descriptions but in that climate it had been found that these were not absolutely necessary.

Of greater importance was the need to satisfy the prisoners' desire for news. At many camps large backlogs of mail, some letters dating back to 1942, could be quickly released. This was not the case at Nakhon Nayok and it was to be some time before mail could be sent on from other areas or fresh personal contacts established with home. In these circumstances the renewal of radio reception assumed major significance and the set sent by the Webber brothers from Kanchanaburi was quickly assembled and prepared for service. Captain Boyle then visited Noguchi and demanded a battery. The Japanese commandant was very reluctant to believe that a wireless existed and was astounded to be informed that it had been brought in as part of his own kit. However, he duly produced a suitable battery and the camp was quickly brought up to date with world affairs. Unfortunately, although news could now be freely received, there was no way of contacting the authorities outside Nakhon Nayok and for a few days no official link could be established.

The aftermath of captivity

The ending of the war came so suddenly that this was a time of great confusion in Thailand and the other remnants of the Japanese empire. Thus it was some days before all of the camps could be located and contacted by Allied personnel. This came about in a variety of ways. At Kanchanaburi the 'underground' forces were already in position but in most places Allied officers had to travel long, dangerous distances by road to give their instructions to the Japanese and to discover the needs of the ex-POWs. Nakhon Nayok was a particularly difficult journey from Bangkok and in the centre of Japanese defensive positions. Consequently, while a single American paratrooper who had lost his way must be regarded as the first 'outside' visitor, real contact was achieved only after a light plane landed close to the camp. Toosey then provided a list of requirements and these were dropped by a transport aircraft the following day.

Some groups of prisoners were not located so quickly. As late as 23 August the administration at Kanchanaburi was notified to expect up to 1500 POWs who had been working on the Thai-Burma border. Until a few days earlier these had been digging tank-traps and building artillery embankments at breakneck speed in an effort to strengthen Japan's defensive positions near the Three Pagodas Pass. They worked from dawn to dusk and the combination of a tiny diet, minimal accommodation and the constant attacks of flies and insects made their life a living hell. All this was during the height of the monsoon and even after the surrender the only concession was to push everyone onto the trains as they became available. The journey south proved to be the last straw for some and of the 700 who arrived in the first party only the fittest could walk. The remainder had to be carried the few yards into the camp where they were immediately given the best of food and attention. A second party followed soon afterwards. This included a few stronger individuals but all were in a filthy state, dressed in rags and suffering in varying degrees from fever and malnutrition. The availability of food and medicine rapidly began the process of restoring these men to some kind of health. This was greatly helped by their knowledge that the war was over; unfortunately it had come too late for a number of their comrades.

The possibility of incidents such as this and the uncertainty felt amongst the general disorder gave Toosey much food for thought. He then decided that it would be wise to return to their units those officers who had been in charge of camps, so that they would be in a position to protect their own men. With the presence of many responsible and capable administrators at Nakhon Nayok Toosey felt able to include himself in this category, and as soon as contact was made with the outside world he handed over his command and commandeered a Japanese truck to take him and a number of other officers to Bangkok.

On arrival at the Thai capital Toosey found everything in a great state of confusion. It proved to be extremely difficult to obtain information as to the whereabouts of his regiment and while enquiries were under way he was 'billeted' in a go-down, or warehouse, in the dock area. It was there, after several unsuccessful days, that Toosey heard his name being called by a tall, lanky figure. This proved to be Peter Heath of the Borneo Company, who introduced himself by saying, 'I am "V" of the "V" organization.' A party was quickly arranged and that night Toosey and Heath collected Boon Pong and went out for what turned out to be a tremendous celebration:

> I have to admit I'd had very little alcohol, if any, for three-and-a-half years and I got completely tight – I was driven home in the pouring rain in a rickshaw still singing to myself.[4]

With the aid of Peter Heath, Toosey found that his former unit had been moved to a site at Ubon, close to what was then the border between

Thailand and French Indo-China. It would have been extremely difficult for Toosey and his party to travel to this camp by road and it was not certain how long they would have to wait for an aircraft to become available. Fortunately Mr Heath was able to use his influence to obtain the use of a locomotive from Thai Railways and Toosey, with his fellow officers and batman, made the 300-mile journey in a train which consisted of just one carriage. A message had been sent on ahead so that when the group arrived at Ubon station they were met by a smart-looking soldier – it was not until later that it was learned this man's kit had been borrowed from a large number of other individuals. Toosey was then driven the short distance to the camp in a jeep. It was the first time he had been in a vehicle of this type.

> On arrival at the camp I received the most wonderful reception you could believe possible. It took me quite some time to get through the large cheering crowd to the Japanese office to find out what had been going on and there I met a very dejected Japanese officer. I asked the Regimental Sergeant-Major who had been in charge of the camp what had happened. He said, 'Well, Sir, the Australians have already written two of them off and the Dutch (who, incidentally, had not been the bravest of prisoners), wished to write the whole lot off' and I said:
>
> 'What about our men?' 'Oh,' he said, 'their attitude is quite simple – they say let the silly little devils go, we [just] want to get home'.[5]

Toosey was accompanied by twenty-nine other officers who were all quickly reunited with their particular units. However, Toosey found that the existing organization and discipline were extremely good, and it was only necessary for him to take formal charge. This was largely due to the sound work of RSM A. McTavish of the Argyll and Sutherland Highlanders and of Warrant Officer S. J. Slotboom of the Dutch Army. These two men had been running the camp very successfully and in Toosey's view they had coped very well. Their only major disappointment was when a Dutch prisoner and an Australian prisoner were caught attempting to escape and in spite of all efforts were subsequently executed.

Although Toosey did not reach the camp until 28 August he was still surprised to find that Allied personnel were already in touch with the POWs at Ubon. He later learned that Force 136 had been dropped into the area 6 months prior to the end of the war and had been secretly based in the barracks of local units of the Thai Army. During this period it had been gathering intelligence and relaying this back to India by radio. The unit had also kept a discreet watch on the prisoners and once the Japanese surrender was officially announced immediate contact was made. This enabled small quantities of food and drugs to be brought on to the site and news of the outside world was quickly made available to an eager audience. Toosey's arrival had been notified to Force 136 – he was transported from the station to the camp in their jeep – and a meeting was soon arranged. Toosey was then introduced to Lieutenant-Colonel Smiley of the 'Blues' and to Major Griswold of the US Air Force. A young officer named Lockett was another member of the group and he provided an unexpected link with home as he was a distant relative of Toosey's wife.

Colonel Toosey and his fellow officers were well received by the men from whom they had been separated in December 1944, and it was decided to mark the occasion by a grand parade of all ranks. This was organized by RSM McTavish in an atmosphere of immense good humour, which was further heightened when Toosey informed the assembled men that an air-drop would take place on the following day. Colonel Smiley was then invited to inspect the parade and this he did with great ceremony. However, the sight of so many ragged 'scarecrows' who in spite of their many ailments and malnutrition were standing to attention with enormous precision and pride is said to have affected him so deeply that he found it difficult to conceal his tears.

Supplies from India, arranged through Colonel Smiley's radio, were accurately parachuted into the camp and shortages of food and clothing quickly became a thing of the past. Toosey records that the 'drop' was a wonderful sight, only marred by the injury to a Dutchman who dashed out to seize one of the first packets and was hit by a later one and received a broken jaw. As at Nakhon Nayok, Toosey was particularly anxious to prevent an outbreak of venereal disease:

> I knew the neighbourhood was rife with it, as were most places where the Japanese had been, and I therefore said to David Smiley: 'We must make some arrangements' and he said, 'Well, we'll have a go.' So we sent a signal to Delhi – 'Please send 10,000 French letters at once.' They arrived the next day. I believe that the message was received by a girl wireless operator in the Royal Air Force. She must have been astonished at our virility after so many years in captivity![6]

The increasingly favourable conditions in Ubon were at first threatened by the presence of large numbers of fully equipped Japanese troops. A decision was then taken in Bangkok that these should be disarmed and Colonel Smiley was instructed to make the necessary arrangements in respect of the division based in his area. At his request Toosey accompanied him to the Japanese HQ where a very tough-looking general was still in command. A brief show of aggression persuaded this officer to co-operate and after a fairly tense few minutes he produced a bottle of excellent Scotch whisky and everything was settled in an amicable manner. As a result his troops gave up their weapons and, by agreeing to remain in their barracks, effectively became prisoners themselves.

With this potentially dangerous situation defused Toosey was able to concentrate on his prime task. The good offices of Force 136 ensured that he was soon on friendly terms with the Thai governor, the officer in charge of the local Thai Army units and the Chief of Police. With their aid, the flow of food and other supplies into the camp was steadily increased and all ranks were invited to a series of entertainments. Toosey found the Thai population to be especially helpful and the Thai Army went out of its way to provide many scarce items, which were invariably supplied free of charge. However, this relatively comfortable life did not alter Toosey's belief that he should press for the earliest possible date for his unit's repatriation. Radio communications gave him the impression that if he did not make a fuss then the authorities would be quite content to leave them where they were for the present. He therefore persuaded Colonel Smiley to fly him to Bangkok in the small plane he had at his disposal and while there managed to press the claims of his men with both General Evans and Colonel Clague, the officer in charge of RAPWI.[7]

The point Toosey wished to impress on those responsible for the evacuation of the former prisoners was that his group should not be discriminated against because they were well behaved and causing no problems. This argument must have carried much weight, for soon after his return the long-awaited order to move to Bangkok was received. On their arrival at the capital, motor trucks took the men directly from the station to the airport. The delight felt by this progress was little reduced by the absence of covered accommodation at the new site, for the weather was warm and all knew that the next stage in their homeward travels could not be long delayed. In fact most of the men were to spend only two or three days in the open before being ferried, twenty at a time, by Dakota aircraft to Rangoon. It was during this period that Colonel Toosey was to spend many hours finalizing his reports on 'Malay and Thailand POW Camps' and on 'Ex POW Finance' as well as making his recommendations in respect of those Japanese whom he wished either to indite or to exonerate as war criminals.

The return home

On arrival at Rangoon Colonel Toosey, like all of his men, was given his first real check-up in hospital. Only a few of the more serious cases were detained, since it was thought that what was most required was a period of peace and quiet and an improved diet. These conditions were easily met in the transit camp where the men were sent to await further instructions. This was a reasonably pleasant place but all were impatient to be off and it was not made clear how long they would have to wait for a ship to take them home. Toosey's enquiries could discover no great sense of urgency and it also transpired that the provisional plan provided for units to be broken up into small parties and then moved as vessels became available. It was in these circumstances that Toosey heard that (Sir) John Nicholson, an old friend from the Ocean Steam Ship Company in Liverpool, was currently head of the Ministry of War Transport in India. He promptly sent a cable asking if it would be possible for his men to be kept together, pointing out that as they were used to his control they would undoubtedly behave much better if this could be arranged.

It cannot now be determined if this message affected the issue or expedited matters, but in the event it was not long before the Pacific Steam Navigation Company's SS *Orbita* arrived in Rangoon and Toosey and his entire party were ordered to embark. By chance this was the very vessel on which Toosey had travelled back from South America in 1929 (see above, p. 15) and to his surprise he found that both the bar-room steward and his bedroom steward were still serving on board. By another strange coincidence the ship's commandant was a man named Ratcliffe from whom Toosey had purchased his house in Hooton in 1936 (see above, p. 17). It was from this officer that he learned of the death of his brother, Arthur, who had been killed in France soon after 'D'-Day.[8] By then he had already received a number of letters from his wife but she had decided not to include this piece of bad news for fear that it would upset him.

The voyage home in *Orbita* proved to be a smooth one and Toosey noted with pleasure the way in which the good food, fresh air and rest gradually improved the health of all on board. There were a few incidents in which men who had been subjected to the harsh discipline of the Japanese slowly began to reassert their personalities. In one early case the captain's cabin had been rifled and the presents he had bought for his wife had been removed. This could have led to strong repressive measures, which would have spoiled the atmosphere for the remainder of the journey, so Toosey decided to intervene. He knew immediately who was responsible, so said to Ratcliffe:

'Look, I can put this right for you provided I am allowed to be the commandant of the ship from now until we get home.'

To this he agreed so I got on the blower and I said this:

'I am going to empty the alleyways for half an hour. If the Argylls do

183

not return the silk stockings and other things they have taken from the
Captain's cabin in that time, they will get no more beer for the rest of
the voyage. You know who is speaking to you and you know that I
mean what I say.'[9]

This appeal, and threat, produced the right response and the booty
was returned. Under Toosey's guidance the troops then settled down
for what turned out to be an enjoyable 8-week trip. Calls at Colombo
and Suez were followed by a leisurely, almost idyllic, cruise along the
length of the Mediterranean. Then, after a brief stop at Gibraltar came
the turn to the north and a run along the coast of Portugal to the Bay of
Biscay. As the weather grew colder the excitement of the returning
prisoners gradually rose and this was to reach a peak as *Orbita*
approached British waters. Unfortunately this pleasurable anticipation
was to be marred in many cases by news of domestic tragedies at home:

Men received cables or letters from their wives saying they had left
them for other men or some had died and so on and so forth and it
was really very sad. I remember clearly one Scottish soldier, a Gordon
Highlander – a great big man – coming to see me and showing me a
cable from his wife which read:
'It is no good you coming back to me. I have married an American
soldier.' He was obviously very upset so I did my best to console him.
I did however say to him, 'How long ago did you see your wife, Jock?'
and he said, 'Seven years, Sir.' You see he was a regular soldier and
had been stationed in India without his wife and then the war broke
out and they had been separated for this great length of time.
I said to him, 'You know, one can hardly blame her, after all you
have left her for a very long time.'
I then said: 'Stop worrying about it. You will find there are just as
good fish in the sea as those that have come out!' At which he smiled
and recovered his equanimity.[10]

As SS *Orbita* picked up her pilot at Port Lynas off the Isle of Anglesey
these private sadnesses were submerged in the general feeling of relief
and joy. The vessel then came directly up the River Mersey and tied up
at Liverpool's landing-stage. Within a very short time relatives were
allowed on board and Philip and 'Alex' Toosey were together after a
separation of over four years. These final arrangements had been made
for Mrs Toosey by Alan Tod, with whom Philip had worked for so long
before the war (see above, p. 15). He, however, refused to join them and
instead waited for a long time at the bottom of the gangway to say: 'It's
wonderful to see you again. We are all so proud of you.'[11]
Colonel Toosey, like all ex-POWs, was immediately given a physical

check-up. He was taken to a medical centre at Huyton on the outskirts of Liverpool. Preliminary examinations showed no particular problems in his general health and after 24 hours it was agreed that he should leave on the following morning. His satisfaction at this decision was somewhat modified by the feeling that little attention had been paid to the possibility of tropical disease and he feared that many of his men might have complaints that would be overlooked. Nevertheless he allowed himself to be reassured by the medical staff and then telephoned his wife to come and collect him.

That night a splendid meal at the Adelphi Hotel marked the end of his full-time Army service and next morning Alex drove him to 'Heathcote'. The first sight of his home was not too pleasing, for a large bonfire was burning where he had remembered a beautiful tennis court. He quickly learned that this had been dug up to produce potatoes and other vegetables. He then noticed a great 'Welcome Home' banner strung across his front doorway. It seemed that all of Hooton Village was there to greet him, but it was to his three children that he first turned. Only Patrick, the eldest, could recognize him but as he hugged Gillian and Nicholas this was the moment when he really felt that the war was over.

11

The post-war era

Resumption of Toosey's career

Toosey's readjustment was more difficult than his family's. Although reasonably fit and rapidly returning to his pre-war 12 stone – he weighed only 7.5 stone when he was liberated – he found it hard to settle. Thus, in spite of Baring Brothers' offer of 6 months' paid leave, he found that 3 weeks of holiday were quite enough and he then decided that it was time to go back to work.

The war period had seen a considerable contraction of Barings' activities in Liverpool and no preparations had yet been made for the resumption of the branch's peacetime business. It was on this task that Toosey set his sights. As a first step he secured premises at 68–70, the Cotton Exchange Building, so as to provide a more convenient base. He then assisted Sir Alan Tod to recruit a number of new staff, including Tod's own nephew, Ian Tod, and a major effort was then made to re-establish contact with the firm's previous customers.

This was to be an extremely tortuous process, for many companies were still at an early stage in reorganizing their affairs and most were not sure of their future plans. In addition the announcement of government measures to retain the wartime controls on cotton imports meant that much of Barings' potential business would be permanently lost. The prospect of losing what had accounted for 90 per cent of the branch's income meant that a fresh niche would have to be found within the city's financial structure. Considerable efforts by Tod and Toosey, working together, gradually solved this problem and an entirely new business was eventually evolved. These fresh initiatives included the provision of financial and investment advice to both companies and individuals, the acceptance of short money deposits, a small commodity-financing business, some dealings in foreign exchange and the management of the Albany Investment Trust.

186

The success of these developments owed much to the hard work put in by Tod and Toosey, but their task was greatly eased by the availability of the resources and expertise of the entire Baring Brothers organization. This was, of course, a two-way process and in 1947 Toosey undertook an extensive tour of South America which was to benefit both the Liverpool and London offices of the firm.

In the course of time Toosey took more and more responsibility for the running of the branch and in 1962, on the retirement of Sir Alan Tod, succeeded him as Liverpool agent. There can be no doubt that Toosey's energy and drive did much to ensure that the firm's post-war operations became and then remained highly profitable. During the same period his personal career also went from strength to strength for as he became better known to the business community he was offered and accepted a whole range of directorships and other appointments. All of these required the approval of his employers, but as it was appreciated that they would usually help to generate additional business this was invariably given. It might be thought that this situation could, on occasions, create a conflict of interest, but Toosey's innate common sense, his judgement of what was fair and his rapport with his superiors in London as well as with members of the Baring family ensured that this did not occur. Indeed he was always proud of the excellent relationship he enjoyed with everyone in the company and, in turn, found that the firm was ever ready to consider requests for aid when Toosey found worthy causes that needed support. This was, in fact, a frequent occurrence, for in spite of his active business career Toosey was also extremely busy in a number of other areas. Shooting appears to have been Toosey's sole sporting and social interest, for his private life was completely dominated by three very demanding pursuits – the reorganization of the Territorial Army, the well-being of those who had been prisoners of the Japanese and, bound up with this, the encouragement of the Liverpool School of Tropical Medicine.

Toosey's post-war association with the TA began when he was telephoned by Sir Douglas Crawford and informed that the government had decided to re-establish a number of the old regiments. Crawford had been asked to command the local medium artillery group and immediately offered Toosey the task of re-creating the 368th Regiment. Toosey was happy to accept this new challenge and quickly demonstrated that his former enthusiasm remained undiminished. He was to remain with this unit from 1947 to 1950 before being transferred to take over the 287th Regiment on a temporary basis. Then, with the retirement of Douglas Crawford, Toosey was promoted to brigadier and placed in charge of the 87th Army Group Royal Artillery.

In 1954 Toosey decided that it was time for him to stand down. This was the end of his active service with the Territorial Army, although he was to remain as an honorary colonel of the 368th Regiment until 1970. He was awarded a CBE in 1955 to mark his outstanding and long-lasting contribution to this voluntary organization.

Foundation of the FEPOW Federation

Toosey's other major concern, which was to remain with him for the rest of his life, was for the welfare of those who had served and suffered with him in the Far East. His return home had been marked by a flood of letters, which included many from those who had shared his captivity. At first these were primarily designed to maintain links with someone they respected and trusted, but as time went on they increasingly requested advice and guidance.

In those early days the only specific organization dealing with this kind of problem was the ex-British Prisoner of War Association. This catered for all POWs, irrespective of the theatre in which they had been captured, but there was a general feeling that the particular needs of those who had been the 'guests' of the Japanese were not fully understood. Toosey's appreciation of this situation convinced him that a separate body should be set up and from the start he insisted that General Percival was the only man who should act as its leader. Percival was very reluctant to accept this position and did so only after Toosey had pointed out that if he did not it might fall into the 'wrong hands'. (By this Toosey was implying that the new association could be used for political purposes – something both men were strongly opposed to.) Percival eventually agreed to become the first president of what was then known as the Far East Prisoners of War Federation (FEPOW) (later changed to the National Federation of Far Eastern Prisoners of War Clubs and Associations of Great Britain and Northern Ireland).

The new organization came into being in 1947, with Toosey being elected to serve as Percival's deputy. Thereafter both men worked extremely hard to see that local associations took firm root and their encouragement did a great deal to help FEPOW develop into what was to become probably the most vigorous and effective of the ex-servicemen's associations. The federation's leaders rapidly became the spokesmen for the prisoners on all national issues. Thus within a very short period it was necessary to set up a subcommittee to express the former prisoners' demand for compensation for their wartime sufferings. This then organized what was to prove a long campaign before Parliament agreed to accept the principle that the Japanese must be obliged to make some degree of reparation for their misdeeds. This approval was gained in 1951, so was just in time to be made a part of the peace treaty which was completed with Japan during the following year. The effect of this was that enemy assets which had been frozen in Britain could now be seized and distributed. In addition, ex-prisoners and civilian internees were to receive a share from those Japanese assets which had been frozen in other Allied and neutral countries. It took some time for these items to be liquidated and the amount per person was not large, but it was widely felt that a small measure of justice had at long last been secured.[1] The decision to divide the compensation received from the sale of Japanese assets on a per capita basis to all living FEPOWs did much to foster the spirit of comradeship which has since characterized the federation.

Work of the Liverpool School of Tropical Medicine

The establishment of the FEPOW organization also helped to reduce Toosey's worries in respect of the welfare of 'his men' but it did little at first to solve another of his problems. Toosey had always been critical of what he regarded as the superficial nature of the medical inspection of the returning troops. However, it was only when he noticed that a former prisoner appeared to be going into a decline that he felt compelled to take some action. Suspecting that the disease had been picked up in the Far East, Toosey called at the Liverpool School of Tropical Medicine and was able to arrange for the man to be examined. It quickly transpired that he was suffering from amoebic dysentery and although it was possible to treat this successfully it was clear that it would have been far better if his illness had been diagnosed at an earlier date.

This incident led to the development of an 'unofficial' system under which at least 600 FEPOWs were examined and, where necessary, treated. It was then decided that the scale of this operation was such that it ought to be organized in a formal manner, and this was greatly facilitated by the friendship which Toosey had struck up with Professor Brian Maegraith, who was the dean of the school. Under this arrangement all FEPOWs could have regular examinations and the school was notified if any were ever admitted to a Liverpool hospital. In return the school always informed the federation's welfare officer of any difficulties so close contact could be maintained with each individual member and his family. This system proved to be so helpful that it was subsequently extended to other parts of the country, with other centres being set up at Roehampton Hospital and in Edinburgh. The resulting tests showed that a large proportion of the ex-POWs were still affected by serious diseases which they had acquired during their captivity. This led to such an immense increase in the number of claims for disability pensions that the Ministry of Health and Social Security established a special unit to deal with the rush of applications.[2] When Toosey himself thought he

189

would set an example he received the usual thorough examination. He was subsequently given both good and bad news: on the one hand it was discovered that his health had been badly undermined by his wartime experiences; on the other this meant that he qualified for a 100 per cent pension, which he was then to draw with considerable satisfaction for the remainder of his life.

Colonel Toosey's association with the Liverpool School of Tropical Medicine and his increasing eminence in the business community then led to an invitation to join the Appeal Committee which Sir John Nicholson ran for the school in 1964. Toosey's commercial connections proved to be very valuable and with the aid of Baring Brothers he was able to solicit a large number of substantial donations. The skill and enthusiasm which he demonstrated in this matter greatly impressed those concerned with the running of the school. Consequently, when Sir Geoffrey Bates decided to retire in 1965, Toosey was elected president in his place.

In the same year Toosey was appointed to act as High Sheriff of Lancashire. This was a major honour and a clear indication of the regard in which he was held by the community. It also meant a considerable amount of extra work, but he took this in his customary stride and it was not allowed to detract from what he regarded as his prime obligations to the FEPOW Federation. These were becoming even more important because of the failing health of General Percival, and when he died in January 1966 Toosey was elected president.

Toosey's life at this time was particularly rewarding but also highly stressful. His business career demanded constant attention but he still managed to contribute a considerable amount of his time and energy to FEPOW affairs and to the Liverpool School of Tropical Medicine. In addition he continued to play an important role as a Justice of the Peace and also assisted in the management of many voluntary bodies, including the Personal Service Association and the Disablement Advisory Committee. Although approaching his mid-sixties Toosey still felt reasonably fit and believed that a busy life was a happy one. The only difficulty he ever experienced was an occasional spell of breathlessness after heavy exertion. In the spring of 1969 these minor attacks became rather more frequent and long-lasting, but they gave no real indication of the event that was soon to end his active participation in virtually all of his areas of interest.

Toosey's heart operation

In spite of his experiences in captivity and of his disability pension Colonel Toosey remained comparatively healthy throughout the post-war period. The exception to this run of good fortune came in the late

1950s when it was discovered that he was suffering from tuberculosis. This gave him no particular trouble and the treatment consisted of little more than rest. On medical advice Toosey subsequently arranged to have an annual check at University College Hospital so as to guard against a recurrence of this disease and it was during one of these examinations that his heart complaint was diagnosed. He was quickly admitted to the Heart Unit at Sefton General Hospital and after exhaustive tests he was told that something was wrong with one of the valves of his heart. Toosey was still feeling reasonably comfortable at this stage and after a week's rest he was discharged. Unfortunately he was soon obliged to return and then spent 4 months in bed. There was no specific treatment and as the days dragged by Toosey felt increasingly weaker and depressed. Then, after a heated altercation between 'Mrs T.' and the medical staff, Toosey was visited by a new consultant surgeon, David Hamilton, who explained that the only hope was for a plastic valve to be fitted, but that this operation had never previously been performed on anyone over the age of 60. As Toosey had by then turned 65 it was not thought that he would survive the ordeal. When Toosey said that if there was any chance, that would be preferable to the alternative of a lingering death, Dr Hamilton agreed to make further tests. When these were completed he informed Colonel and Mrs Toosey that he was prepared to go ahead but that the odds were three to one against a successful outcome. Toosey then turned to his wife and said:

'Well that's a fair bet rather than just dying slowly, isn't it?' and she said: 'I've always been prepared to take a gamble. Let's have a go at it!'[3]

The operation was performed at Broadgreen Hospital in Liverpool on 2 February 1970, and proved to be even more gruelling than the surgeon had anticipated. Toosey later learned that his heart had stopped three times during the fitting of the replacement valve and that on the third occasion he had been saved only by such heavy pounding that two of his ribs had been cracked. Nevertheless the surgery was successful and although it took 6 weeks for Toosey to recover he was then allowed to return home to his beloved 'Heathcote'. Even then he was confined to bed for most of the day and it was some time before he felt able to attempt any activities outside his home. Thus although his life had been spared it was clear that he would never be able to resume his former way of life and that he would have to settle for a much quieter existence.

Borrowed time

Colonel Toosey's gradual return to health was regarded as something of a miracle by his doctors and after the operation he always considered that he was living on 'borrowed time'. Although he was determined to make the most of this second chance, he quickly realized that he would have to come to terms with his changed circumstances. This view was further strengthened after a sudden, frightening relapse which fortunately responded to a period of enforced rest and, thereafter, he tried to restrict his activities to bare essentials. Needless to say he was extremely grateful to the Heart Unit and once he felt well enough he attempted to repay his debt by raising funds to provide an additional intensive care unit, to become known as the 'Gunner Ward' at Broadgreen Hospital.

As his recovery continued Toosey found that his remaining activities were well within even his reduced capabilities. Thus these involved no particular strain, but the proposed visit of Emperor Hirohito to be made a Knight of the Garter was another matter. The news of this event aroused great passions within FEPOW and there was a considerable danger that some members of the federation might use the occasion to remind the public of their treatment during the Second World War. The view of the executive, strongly backed by Toosey, was that this was the Queen's private business and, even if it were thought that she had been badly advised, any demonstrations would cause great embarrassment and, in any event, be counterproductive.

It was against this background that Toosey attended the federation's 19th annual conference in May 1971. Although still far from well he made an impassioned speech against any protests and the executive was subsequently backed by a large majority of the delegates. This effort took a tremendous amount out of him but he reaped his reward when the Emperor's stay in London passed off without any incident provoked by members of FEPOW. Toosey later received a letter from Lord Mountbatten in which he mentioned that he had informed the Queen

of your remarkable success in discouraging any demonstrations. I thoroughly understand how frightfully bitter most of the FEPOWs must still be feeling. At all events I feel I must write a line to express my deep appreciation to you and all FEPOWs for their statesmanlike attitude.[4]

Colonel Toosey's illness meant that it would have been extremely difficult, if not impossible, for him to have undertaken all the duties expected from a president of FEPOW. As the federation was anxious for him to continue both for his sake and their own purposes, Toosey was elected patron and in the mean time Harold Payne (with whom he had worked so successfully at Nong Pladuk) took over as president.

The conference left Toosey very weak and he found it necessary to spend many weeks almost entirely in bed before he could recover a semblance of his former strength. Thereafter he was obliged to husband his remaining power very carefully and, although he would not always admit it, from this point onwards he became increasingly frail. As if to compensate for his diminishing input, the last few years of his life saw Toosey add considerably to his previous honours.[5] Thus in 1972 he received the Mary Kingsley Medal from the Liverpool School of Tropical Medicine and this was followed, in 1974, by the award of an Honorary LL D by the University of Liverpool. In the same year he also obtained his greatest tribute when he was made a knight and became Sir Philip Toosey.

A time for reflection

I was eventually to complete no fewer than forty-six taped interviews with Philip Toosey. In the process I got to know the man, as well as his life's work, extremely well and I am convinced that in addition to providing an essential record they also had a valuable therapeutic value for the colonel himself. In retrospect it can be seen that the period after his operation provided Toosey with much time for contemplation and that the interviews brought many incidents into sharper focus.

Colonel Toosey was not especially critical of the military authorities who were responsible for the defence of Singapore and Malaya. He regretted, but could understand, the policies which had led to Britain's weakness in the 1930s and appreciated that in the difficult days after the fall of France little could be spared for the Far East. The German attack on Russia which led to the massive diversion of aircraft and tanks that it had been intended to send to Malaya was particularly unfortunate – it meant that the British forces possessed ample facilities and manpower but lacked the essential weapons which would have made them into effective fighting units. However, Toosey was sure that the decision to try to keep the Soviet Union in the war was the right one, especially as it was made at a time when the US Pacific fleet appeared to guarantee immunity from any potential attack. Given the British strength actually available when the Japanese chose to begin their operations, it was Toosey's view that the invasion was almost bound to succeed. But he continued to feel that with better intelligence much more could have been done to exact a higher price. In particular he thought that a more logically organized command structure and a closer co-operation between the fighting services and the civil administration would have been enormously beneficial. If these changes had been allied to the establishment of clearer, realistic objectives, then many fundamental mistakes could have been avoided. Toosey none the less remained convinced that the best that might have been achieved would have been to delay the Japanese programme. This would have gained vital time elsewhere, so should not be dismissed as unimportant, but, in view of Japanese naval and air superiority and the disparity in the numbers of trained and experienced troops, Malaya, and then Singapore, would still have fallen.

Colonel Toosey's interest in the campaign and the general strategic situation was much less than in what followed the surrender. His major concern was for the many thousands of POWs who died, quite unnecessarily, while in Japanese hands. He appreciated that some deaths were inevitable, but was anxious to learn why only 4 per cent of American and British troops failed to survive in German camps while nearly 29 per cent of the American, Australian, British, Canadian and New Zealand captives did not return from their confinement in the east.[6] These bare statistics would seem to indicate that Nazi Germany had a more caring attitude than Imperial Japan but this is too simplistic a view. While the Third Reich certainly appears to have looked after its Anglo-Saxon prisoners moderately well, its treatment of Poles, Russians and, of course, Jews was a different matter. On the other hand, Japanese treatment of their captives during the Russo-Japanese War of 1904 was marked by great chivalry and this continued after the Japanese seizure of Tsing-Tau from the Germans during the First World War. However, the treatment of their opponents in the 'China Incident' was quite the reverse and culminated in the appalling massacres at Nanking in 1937. Thus while it seems obvious that national attitudes, influenced by their respective cultures, may play a role in determining the treatment of captured troops, it appears that it is government policy which is the significant factor in many particular cases.

Toosey never believed the allegations that the Japanese High Command found the large numbers of prisoners taken at Singapore such an embarrassment that it decided upon a policy that would gradually eliminate them. The directives of the Prisoner of War Bureau and of the POW Management Section issued in Tokyo can be interpreted in this way, but a more reasonable conclusion is that the Japanese had decided to make their captives work and if this had the effect of increasing the death rate that was just unfortunate. There were, of course, many incidents of deliberate brutality by both individual Japanese and Korean guards, but for every prisoner killed or injured in this way many hundreds died from malnutrition and tropical disease largely resulting from neglect and indifference.

Toosey was well aware that the Japanese had a different view from that in the west on the value of human life and he had witnessed the savage discipline which they imposed on their own troops. He also knew of the way in which local labour, especially the Tamils but including some Chinese and Malays, had been recruited to work on the railway and had subsequently died in their tens of thousands. Consequently he was prepared to accept that the Japanese intention was to make use of those captured at Singapore in any way that would be beneficial to their war effort. The possibility of heavy casualties would not be a consideration, for men who had surrendered in battle were of little consequence and could, therefore, be regarded as expendable. Nevertheless this was a long way from a policy of annihilation and when rations were cut from already low levels Toosey was usually prepared to believe that this was due to logistical difficulties, or graft, rather to deliberate intent.

Toosey's understanding of this situation was based on the common observation and widely held opinion that the individual's chance of survival declined in proportion to his distance from Singapore. Thus according to this theory those prisoners who were to spend all their captivity in the Changi area were likely to suffer least and those, like Toosey, who were to remain in the relatively cultivated zone of lower Thailand would not be too badly off. It was to be those units which were sent into the tropical forests and mountain regions of upper Thailand and Burma that were to be the worst affected and of these it was those men furthest away from the two base camps who were to endure the most.

As the statistics which are available do not give the place of death they cannot offer positive proof. However, as they are arranged on a monthly basis and as the highest figures are to be found in the period August–October 1943, when the construction was about to join up at the 262-kilometre point, the theory is given considerable support.[7] The overall figures show that, of the 61,806 Allied prisoners employed in building the railway, a total of 12,399, or just over 20 per cent, died while engaged in this task. However, separate details of 'F' and 'H' Forces, which worked on a particularly inaccessible stretch of track to the north of Nikhe, show that they had lost 4789 out of a total of 10,628 men. Even this death rate of over 45 per cent was exceeded at Sonkrai camp where a part of 'F' Force suffered 1175 fatalities from an original strength of 1602 – the equivalent of 73 per cent.[8] While it may be argued that the heavy casualties experienced by these two forces were worsened by the fact that they came directly from Changi so were totally unprepared for jungle conditions, the statistics do, again, suggest that those prisoners obliged to work at the greatest distance from civilization were indeed those at the greatest risk.

Toosey's belief that difficulties of supply played an important role in raising the death rate in the more remote areas did not, in any way, provide an excuse for Japanese mismanagement. As the military authorities were primarily responsible for the sending of both POWs and local labour to these regions it was their undoubted duty to ensure that adequate supplies of food, medicine, clothing and housing were available.

The fact that desperate shortages of these items were the norm shows a degree of bureaucratic inefficiency that is quite uncharacteristic or can be explained only by a total indifference to human suffering and to the higher priority frequently given to materials necessary for the actual construction. It was also very obviously counterproductive, as can be seen from the official statistics for locally recruited labour. Those relating to workers from Malaya, Java, Thailand and French Indo-China indicate that 91,112 were induced to join and that 32,996, or 36 per cent, died during their period of service.[9] Details for civilian labour secured in Burma are not so precise. The target of 177,300 was never reached and it appears that only 91,836 actually arrived at the base camp at Thanbyuzayat. The overall death rate for these personnel is not known, but the records of the Japanese 9th Railway Regiment suggest that the figure for the 45,000 who were employed on the Thai side of the border was only 7 per cent. However, this figure relates to only an unspecified 1-year period and may have been selected so as to provide the most favourable possible impression. The same table shows death rates of 26 per cent for other labourers, 17 per cent for POWs and only 4 per cent for members of the Japanese Army.

From the foregoing it is clear that, while all reports state that medical provision for Japanese army and civilian personnel was very limited, it was better than the non-existent facilities provided for everyone else. In addition, the Japanese received the best of whatever food was available and were usually much fitter than other workers when they were posted to the railway and began their tour of duty. The token aid given to POWs and to the labour recruited in South-East Asia meant that there was a lack of the barest necessities for these groups and this inevitably resulted in heavy fatalities. Thus the tremendous efforts made by the Japanese to obtain labour to supplement the exertions of the Allied prisoners was largely unproductive, for the majority quickly became ill and disillusioned and those who survived were in no condition to make a real contribution to the work of construction. It might be argued that a smaller number of fitter men who could have been more easily supplied might have completed the task more quickly. However the Japanese on the spot were not consulted and were only required to follow the instructions of the *Daihon'ei* in Tokyo. The High Command was, of course, very anxious to see the railway in operation and its only solution to potential delay was to order the transfer of more prisoners and the recruitment of additional local labour.

The fact that Imperial HQ took a strong and continuing interest in the project made it difficult for a pragmatic and flexible approach to be adopted. Had Japanese managerial genius been allowed to flourish unhindered at the regional and local levels, at least one authority is convinced that many lives could have been saved and the railway built more quickly, cheaply and strongly than was actually the case. The lack of effective control and direction within Thailand and Burma was compounded by the directives from the centre, which assumed a total disregard for all previously accepted international legal obligations. This was apparent not just in the early, victorious, stages of the war, when no one expected to be called to account, but as late as midsummer 1945, when the defence works at Three Pagodas and the escape road being constructed at Mergui[10] were both the scene of excessive brutality and impossible working conditions.

Colonel Toosey was not aware of these structural difficulties in command but he was very concerned with their consequences, for his position brought him into contact with many different groups of Japanese all of whom were attempting to fulfill their respective tasks to the best of their ability. His early links with 'fighting troops' caused no particular problems, but his subsequent relationships with Japanese and Korean guards were to lead to many serious incidents. He quickly learned that this was mainly due to the differences between the eastern and western cultures and to the lack of effective communication. Having appreciated these points, he attempted to understand the thinking behind many apparently stupid decisions and also encouraged his interpreters, especially Captain Boyle, to be as precise as possible. This did not end the difficulty but it minimized the risk of misunderstandings and in some cases, as with Sergeant-Major Saito, a kind of rapport was gradually evolved.

In retrospect Colonel Toosey felt that he had been reasonably adept at coming to terms with his captors and thought that the tactics he had followed had been of some help in keeping down the level of fatalities. He had always attached great importance to the maintenance of strict discipline, for he believed that military routine gave the men something to hold on to. He subsequently felt that this view had been fully justified when he learned of the chaos and very high death rates in many of the camps occupied by Asian labourers. Toosey also considered that the dedication and ingenuity of the medical staffs played a vital role in keeping casualties to a minimum and thought that the achievements of doctors such as Albert Coates, 'Weary' Dunlop, Arthur Moon and Stanley Pavillard had never been sufficiently recognized.

With hindsight he could see how the work of these devoted men had been significantly aided by the 'V' Scheme, for it was the drugs and food which this brought into the camps which enabled medical treatment to be successful. Consequently he felt an immense debt of gratitude to those civilians like Peter Heath, Boon Pong, Lee Soon and Albert Tanner who had been prepared to risk their lives in order to preserve the health of others. Lastly, Toosey genuinely thought that the self-esteem and general good nature and common sense of the troops was a major ingredient in maintaining their will to live. The self-help epitomized by the development of gardens where all kinds of exotic and basic foods could be produced – usually with the advice of Dutch colonials – is a good example. Many prisoners knew that the possibility of enjoying the fruits of their labour was remote because they would almost certainly be moved on before the crops would be ready, but this did not prevent much work being undertaken. Evidence of this kind of spirit was some small reward for Toosey's own endeavours in those camps where he was responsible for the welfare of the occupants.

Toosey and the atomic bomb

In the post-war era Toosey gave a great deal of thought to Britain's need for an independent nuclear deterrent and to the advisability of utilizing atomic energy to produce electricity for the national grid. He was quite prepared to accept that there were many sincerely held views on these matters and he had no quarrel with those whose opinions differed from his own. However, he regarded these topics as quite distinct from the decision to drop the two atomic bombs in Japan in 1945 and strongly objected to this being included in the same debate. In his mind there was never any doubt that it was only the intervention of the bombs which saved his life and in this matter it seems certain that he was reflecting the belief of the vast majority of men who were held prisoner in all parts of the Japanese Empire. This was a subject which he was to consider very thoroughly during his period of 'borrowed time' and, having examined all available sources of information, he came to the conclusion that his original feelings had been completely justified.

The Japanese had ordered the digging of an enormous trench at the officers' camp at Kanchanaburi, as Toosey was aware, and in the absence of any other logical explanation he, and the occupants, had been convinced that in the event of an Allied attack it was to be used as a mass grave. 'Think we'll be in the ditch tonight?' was a common query. This question presupposed that at the appropriate moment the Japanese would liquidate their prisoners by lining them up at the edge of the trench and machine-gunning them from their already prepared positions. The situation of Toosey's final camp at Nakhon Nayok in the middle of a defensive stronghold also seemed to imply that few POWs would survive if the area were ever to be invaded. Although this circumstantial evidence may have seemed overwhelming at the time, no documentary proof has ever been discovered to confirm that it was the Japanese intention to dispose of their captives in Thailand in this way. However, the belief was universal and widespread and covered all regions where troops were held captive. Writing about his imprisonment in Java, Laurens van der Post confirms that this view was universally held. Indeed, he states that secret orders from Field-Marshal Terauchi were quite explicit in laying down that all POWs were to be killed in their camps as soon as the Allies began their final assault.[11] The plans indicated in this document called for all captives to be concentrated in a few convenient locations where it would be easy to follow the instructions at the appropriate time. In his case Laurens van der Post found himself pushed, together with 7000 others, into a reformatory and prison which had been constructed to hold only 120 boys. This confirmation of Japanese intention then led to the formation of a desperate plan that would be used in the event of a general massacre. This involved the organization of a number of the fitter men and the acquisition of many stones which would have to serve in the absence of other weapons. It was not thought that this would provide an effective defence, but it was hoped that it would enable a few of the inmates to survive.

The evidence for the island of Formosa (now renamed Taiwan) is more specific because a document has survived for this area.[12] This lays out quite clearly the methods that were to be employed in the killing of the prisoners when the time and circumstances were deemed to be appropriate. The way in which this document came to be discovered is well described by Jack Edwards in his recent book on his life as a POW and its aftermath. The former RSM was a prisoner of the Japanese at Kinkaseki in Formosa for several terrible years. In February 1946 a series of fortunate circumstances enabled him to return to the mine where he had worked under such extreme conditions. To his great surprise he found that the camp records had not been properly destroyed and amongst them was a written order dated 1 August 1944 which instructed that all POWs were to be killed if Allied forces approached the area.[13]

Although quite precise and not capable of any different interpretation, these orders, like those quoted by Laurens van der Post, may not be regarded by everyone as conclusive evidence. The prisoners, however, remain convinced that they show quite clearly the real intentions of their captors and point out that the order quite specifically calls for no traces to be left. The implications of this suggest that no further debate is possible on this topic. (Copies of the document found at Kinkaseki may be examined at the Imperial War Museum, London, and at the Nissan Institute, Oxford; a translation appears in Mr Edwards's work, *Banzai You Bastards*, pp. 260–1.)

POWs' apprehensions about their ultimate fate would have been further increased had they been aware of the events in February 1945, when approximately 5000 western internees and captured troops were liberated in Manila. Captured papers suggested that they were to be killed but this was in fact prevented by the unexpectedly rapid advance of the American forces. From this time onward many incidents are on record from places as far apart as Borneo and the Philippines of prisoners being disposed of by their guards. Whether this was as a result of a secret telegram sent by the War Ministry from Tokyo cannot now be confirmed, although the text would suggest that this was the case. For Toosey, the truth or otherwise of these shreds of evidence of official involvement was unimportant. All that concerned him was that many POWs were killed during the last few months of the war and there was every reason to expect that this would continue and intensify in the event of heavy fighting near their camps.

Toosey's opinion that the dropping of the atomic bombs was completely justified on this account was further strengthened when he learned of the events which then followed. It appeared that even after this traumatic shock it was difficult to convince many regional commanders that they must surrender. Accordingly it was necessary for members of the Royal Family to visit all important HQs to ensure that the Emperor's wishes were fully understood. In the case of South-East Asia the man in charge was Field Marshal Terauchi and it was only after Prince Chichibu, the Emperor's brother, had seen him in Saigon that he agreed to order his forces to surrender and only then, according to records found at his HQ, that orders to kill all prisoners were finally rescinded. Thus Toosey's basic conviction received added confirmation that without the Bomb the problem of enforcing a cessation of hostilities would have been even greater and that the prisoners would have been the principal losers in the general confusion.

Having satisfied himself that the use of atomic weapons had been clearly beneficial for all those held captive by the Japanese, Toosey was then faced with the moral dilemma of balancing the potential loss of their lives against the actual losses at Hiroshima and Nagasaki. This simple argument, although sometimes put to him, was not really a logical one, for it implies that these were the only gainers and losers. This was obviously not the case and many other aspects would need to be included before a true balance could be reached. The most significant of these would be the additional casualties which non-nuclear air raids and the ongoing blockade would have cost the Allies and the Japanese. Then, if the conflict had still not been resolved, there would be the need to apportion the immense casualties which both sides (including the civilian population) would have suffered from the invasion of Japan scheduled for 1 November 1945.

When Colonel Toosey considered these two alternatives he quickly discovered that either would have cost both sides far more casualties than those actually caused by the employment of the atomic bomb. The easier option, that of continuing the existing programme of bombing and blockade so that Japan was effectively isolated from the outside world, would have resulted in the deaths of many Allied servicemen. *Kamikaze* attacks had already led to the loss of 34 American ships while a further 285 had been damaged. It was known that the Japanese were assembling large numbers of these planes for the final defence of their homeland and it is certain that they would have exacted a heavy price if the fighting had not come to such an abrupt end. However, even if it were to be considered that this was a cost which had to be endured, it seems extremely unlikely that this policy would have caused Japan to surrender. The universally held view is that, without the use of atomic weapons or a physical occupation, the war would have dragged on for a considerable time. It is widely believed that the fanatical element amongst the Japanese forces was still so strong that it would have been impossible for the emperor to have acted in isolation. And it seems quite probable that any sustained attempt to gather influential counsellors of like mind would have resulted in his, and their, assassination.

From the foregoing it is clear that the only real non-nuclear alternative would have been a full-scale invasion of Japan. Although the overwhelming power of the Allied forces would certainly have led to an ultimate victory, the campaign would have been long and difficult. Estimates of likely casualties vary between the 0.5 million anticipated by the American President[14] and the 1 million expected by his Secretary of State for War.[15] These figures can be regarded as only very general guidelines in an unpredictable and volatile situation, but there can be no doubt that Allied losses would have been extremely heavy. These potential casualties, plus the saving of the lives of Japan's many prisoners, may be thought to be of sufficient weight to convince the unbiased reader that, on balance, the dropping of the atomic bomb was justified. However, the most telling argument has still to be included:

the people who would have suffered most ... were the Japanese. One American incendiary air raid on the Tokyo area in March 1945 did more damage and killed and injured more Japanese than the bomb on Hiroshima. Even greater groups of American bombing planes would have hovered over Japan, consuming the land, its people and its food, with blast and fire, leaving them no place to hide, no chance to rest, no hope of reprieve. A glance at the chart kept in the Headquarters of the U.S. Strategic Air Force at Guam, with its steeply ascending record of bombing flights during the summer of 1945 and scheduled for the next month or two, leaves visions of horror of which Hiroshima is only a local illustration. Observations of the plight of the country and its people made soon after the war ended left me appalled at what those would have had to endure had the war gone on.[16]

In retrospect it is quite clear that the gradual loss of Japan's earlier conquests, the defeat of her armies overseas, the destruction of her air force and navy and even the obliteration of all her chief cities by July 1945, were still not sufficient to persuade enough men of influence that the war must be ended. Arguments that the offering of softer terms than 'unconditional surrender' or that the imminent Russian invasion of Manchuria would have materially changed this situation seem unrealistic in the circumstances. It is now certain that it was only the psychological shock of the atomic bombs that enabled the Emperor and the 'Peace Party' to act, and without this dramatic event it is difficult to see how the opposition of the military leaders could ever have been overcome until a successful invasion had been completed.

Toosey's welcome for the use of the atomic option during August 1945 was therefore based on the knowledge that it had played a vital part in preventing the almost certain massacre of himself and his fellow prisoners. This view was subsequently strengthened when he learned that its employment had saved far more lives than it had taken. Thus, to his mind, it was an act that was clearly beneficial to all except the unfortunate inhabitants of Hiroshima and Nagasaki. Their horrific experience could, however, be regarded as the price which had to be paid in order to resolve the constitutional impasse and power struggle round the throne which were preventing the widespread desire to end the war from being realized.

The involuntary sacrifice of these citizens also had another, long-term aspect which was to have an important bearing on the future of their country. Had the war continued for any appreciable length of time, Japan would have been completely devastated and a legacy of bitterness might well have been created that could have retarded her recovery for many years. At worst this might have resulted in the establishment of a Communist regime and even at best it would seem improbable that Japan's economic and social development could possibly have been so rapid and fundamental as has actually been the case. For all of these reasons the dropping of the bombs received Toosey's unanimous approval when he was released from captivity, and continued to do so for the remainder of his life.

In the autumn of 1975, at the age of 71, Philip Toosey's health began to fail. Consequently when it became necessary for his wife to go into

Sefton General for a small operation it was decided that he should enter the same Liverpool hospital where it was hoped that he could build up his strength. However, after a sudden deterioration, he died in his sleep on 22 December.

After a private family funeral service Sir Philip was cremated and his ashes were buried at Landican on the outskirts of Birkenhead. As he would have wished, his grave was an unpretentious one that was virtually indistinguishable from many others in this very extensive cemetery. In contrast, the memorial service held at Liverpool Parish Church in January 1976 was a very large and public affair at which over 700 of his friends and former comrades gathered to pay their respects to this outstanding man. These included Sir Douglas Crawford (Lord Lieutenant of Merseyside), Councillor Owen Doyle (Lord Mayor of Liverpool), Mr Selwyn Lloyd (Speaker of the House of Commons) and Lord and Lady Pilkington. An address was given by Mr John Bromfield, one of Toosey's oldest friends, during which he quoted a testimony from Sir John Smyth:

> Toosey was with his men all the time, fought for them, worked for them, suffered for them, starved with them, was beaten up with them and for their own good bullied and tore strips off them – with the result that their morale remained high and their spirit was never broken.[17]

This assessment of Toosey's wartime activities followed the pattern of many similar tributes to him both in his lifetime and after his death. These came from a wide spectrum of society, and ranged from a speech made by the Duke of Edinburgh in which he referred to 'Brigadier Toosey's fine example and remarkable achievements'[18] to a letter received by the author from Private Hislop who wrote: 'He was a great man who always did his best for us.' David Boyle, who worked so closely with Toosey as his interpreter, saw him as a man 'determined to make the best possible answer to this life', while another fellow captive considered that he was a man of 'courage, simplicity and wisdom', and that 'he was invaluable'.[19]

On his return to civilian life Toosey was to make an equally strong impression. Sir John Nicholson thought he was a good judge of what was practical, had great independence of mind and always brought out the best in people. Toosey's attributes as a businessman were further reinforced, in Nicholson's opinion, by his strength of character and by his personal charm, and after his death he wrote:

> One could never recapture the magic of his company or describe the unique blend of sympathy and enthusiasm which instantly warmed everyone who met him. Like innumerable others, I count his friendship amongst the highest and happiest privileges of my life.[20]

203

Of course it was during his period as a prisoner of the Japanese that Toosey's character and strength of purpose received their most severe test. This was most carefully analysed by Ian Watt when, in an attempt to distinguish between the fiction of Pierre Boulle's novel and reality, he investigated the 'Myths of the Kwai'. Both Toosey and the imaginary Colonel Nicholson began with the resolve that the men under their command would survive with honour, but it was only Toosey who

> had the imagination to understand all the sides of the problem confronting him ... the engineering side, the labour-supply side, and above all the complex morale side as it affected the prisoners and their captors.

> Toosey knew that in a showdown the Japanese would always win, because they had the power, and no scruples whatever about how to use it. So, though a very brave man, he never forced the issue so as to make his captors lose face; instead he first awed them with an impressive display of military swagger, and then proceeded to charm them with his ingratiating assumption that no serious difficulty could arise between honourable soldiers whose only thought was to do the right thing.[21]

The bridge camp and other sites commanded by Toosey were large, permanent structures located in the more civilized part of southern Thailand. This meant that Toosey's technique for bridging the gap between himself and his captors could be given a fair opportunity to work. Thus at Tamarkan his relationship with Sergeant-Major Saito began rather coldly but the consequence of many hours of discussion in respect of working arrangements was that a genuine rapport developed on both sides. Toosey quickly realized that Saito's only desire was to complete the task he had been given with as little friction as possible and that he would respond favourably to any suggestion that helped him to achieve this object. Consequently it was relatively easy to persuade him to allow the British administration to have a bigger share in the organization of the work. This had the effect of transforming the prisoners' lives, for many of the previous misunderstandings and difficulties could largely be eliminated under this system. It did mean that collaboration with the Japanese became greater and that productivity rose a little, but no one regarded Toosey as 'Jap-happy' on this account. Everyone on the spot had by then realized

> that the real issue was not building the bridge but merely how many prisoners would die, be beaten up, or break down, in the process.[22]

The relationship between Toosey and Saito was crucial to these developments and, while they never became friends, their continued association led to a strictly formal but real understanding of each other's point of view. This process was also helped by discussions which were gradually extended to cover a wide range of topics and which, in Toosey's opinion, further reduced the risk of any serious misunderstandings. As Toosey would not have been prepared to compromise his principles it is fortunate that he found Saito to be a reasonable man who was only trying to do his duty. Proof of this can be seen by the events after the surrender when Saito, like all other personnel who had been associated with the camps, was screened to see if he had been guilty of any war crimes. No allegations had been made against him and no doubt he would have been cleared in the normal way, but Toosey's testimony helped to accelerate this process. David Boyle supported Toosey in this matter, later giving his opinion that:

> Saitō was hard but he was fair and could be trusted – and you could not say that about many of them. I remember Colonel Toosey once called a strike by the prisoners because a guard beat me up. Saitō got hold of the guard and beat the daylights out of him.[23]

After the hearing Toosey met Saito for the last time and discussed the reasons for the deaths of so many prisoners. Before leaving, Toosey remarked: 'God would decide who was in the right.' This was a phrase which Saito, who knew a little English, could still remember forty years later.[24] Clearly, even at this time, when Toosey could have been forgiven for adopting a vindictive attitude, he could still see the dilemma under which Saito had been obliged to work. His recognition of the conflict between duty and compassion was yet another example of his own generosity of spirit and of his understanding of the insoluble difficulties caused by the clash of eastern and western cultures.

Another impact of Ian Watt's article in the *Observer* was to make it clear that it was Toosey who had been portrayed by Alec Guinness in *The Bridge over the River Kwai*. This prompted Earl Mountbatten to write in the following vein:

> I realise that the film ... was wildly inaccurate, but I also heard that it was based on a legendary British hero. The film was so interesting that I had it down here at Broadlands to show the Queen, who was thrilled.
>
> I must confess that it was not until I had read this article that I realised that the true hero was yourself, and in a way that made much more sense than Alec Guinness's hero.
>
> I feel, as the Supreme Commander of those days, I really ought to write and thank you on behalf of the Command for all you did to keep morale going, and to save so many prisoners. What a wonderful story. Please accept my sincere congratulations.[25]

205

Apart from the film, the building of the Thai–Burma railway had surprisingly few long-lasting consequences:

At the end of the war the British army dismantled 3.95 km. of the railway at the Burmese/Thai border and eventually 300 km. was handed over to Thailand in 1945. After due consideration of the economic and political situation, the Thailand State Railway dismantled the remainder of the line from the [Burmese] border to Namtok [Tha Soe] station. The decision was then made to upgrade the remainder of the line to operational permanent way standard. The section from Nong Pladuk to Kanchanaburi was opened to traffic on June 24, 1949: that between Kanchanaburi and Wang Pho [Wampo] on April 1, 1952; and the last section between Wang Pho [Wampo] and Namtok [Tha Soe], on July 1, 1957.[26]

Part of this programme necessitated rebuilding the bridges at Tamarkan. This was undertaken by a Japanese firm as part of the reparations agreed by Japan after war:

However, as the 22 metre spans had proved an obstacle to the huge timber rafts plying the river, the two damaged piers were removed and replaced by a single support carrying two box-girder bridge sections. This enabled the navigable gap to be increased to 33 metres. The wooden bridge, being an even worse barrier to river traffic, was completely dismantled.[27]

The reopening of the railway as far as Namtok (formerly known as Tha Soe) means that the track is now operational for a distance of 130 kilometres from Nong Pladuk. As there are still few all-weather roads in this part of Thailand, the line performs a useful purpose in transporting children to school at Namtok, which also serves as a market centre for local products. In addition, the railway caters for a small but constant number of tourists who are anxious to ride on this historic route.

Thus it is clear that while the building of the railway did result in some long-term advantages to the local community these were very minor in character. Of course from the Japanese point of view the construction had been completely justified when, in the spring of 1945, the remains of its defeated army had been safely evacuated from Burma. Against these 'benefits' must be placed the enormous cost in human lives of both the Allied POWs and the Asian labourers. The workforce naturally had an entirely different opinion of the merits of establishing the rail link with Burma and this was compounded by the knowledge that the existence of the line which had cost the lives of so many of their friends was now making their own survival even less likely. This was because the Japanese troops that had been brought back to Thailand had been quickly re-formed into a strong fighting force and, but for the dropping of the atomic bombs, they would undoubtedly have given a good account of themselves had the proposed invasion of Malaya taken place on 9 September. In this event the prisoners would certainly have suffered further heavy casualties.

It will be appreciated that in these circumstances few FEPOWs could be expected to applaud the enormous technical feat which the completion of the railway represented. Their feelings on this subject were further strengthened by the legacy of ill-health and disease which they had brought back from their captivity, for these have proved to be extremely long-lasting. A number of ongoing investigations have shown that even 45 years after their release the former prisoners have above-average levels of psychiatric illness and significantly higher than normal rates of admission to hospital, and continue to suffer from a whole range of diseases which had their origins in the tropics.[28] And it is widely felt that, even amongst the body of men who exhibit no clinical symptoms, their quality of life and indeed their longevity have been drastically reduced by their wartime experiences. A major achievement of the FEPOW Federation under both Percival and Toosey, and subsequently under Payne, was the assistance which it could provide to alleviate these ongoing consequences of the Second World War.

Colonel Toosey saw the preservation of the lives of the men under his command as his first priority and with the aid of his colleagues he was remarkably successful in keeping casualties to the lowest possible level. However, much of the credit for enabling his policies to succeed must go to those civilians who at great personal risk operated the 'V' scheme and supplied essential quantities of drugs, food and cash. The bravery of Messrs Clark, Gairdner, Heath, Hempson, Hong, Millet, Soon and Tanner has already been recorded and it is pleasant to note that all survived the war without serious incident. Boon Pong, whose role was particularly important and dangerous, also escaped detection by the Japanese, although one account suggests that he was fortunate to survive after a post-war revenge shooting which left him for dead. All those prisoners who knew of the danger he had accepted on their behalf were saddened to learn that his neglected business had subsequently collapsed and it was decided to make a financial appeal on his behalf. This was organized by Colonels Lilley and Knights and resulted in the raising of a sum which is believed to have approached £40,000.[29] Boon Pong used this to establish his own small bus company in Bangkok and this then operated very successfully for many years.[30]

The welfare of his men was, as we have seen, always Toosey's prime consideration and a principle that appears to have guided all of his actions both during and after the war. This is made abundantly clear in a tribute by Selwyn Lloyd, who had himself enjoyed a distinguished career in the army before entering Parliament. His assessment also stressed his old friend's innate modesty and qualities of leadership and, in view of the aptness of his comments, Lloyd's opinion should be allowed to stand as Philip Toosey's final epitaph:

> Philip was a leader of men: he had the dynamic quality which made him a commander in the full sense of the word.
>
> Physically courageous, shrewd, cunning (for example, about the black market supplies which meant so much to the prisoners), psychologically a match for the Japanese in authority, he preserved not only many lives, but also high morale, dignity and discipline among men in dire adversity.
>
> After the war he has proved himself a wise and prudent leader of the Far Eastern Prisoners of War, never forgetting the sufferings of individuals but always remembering the wider national purposes.
>
> This is indeed a man, the like of whom this generation will not see again. Those of us who are his friends and many, many others regard him with respect and admiration, and when we think of what he suffered and achieved, we salute him with affectionate wonder.
>
> Yet for all the pleasure that they gave him, tributes like this and the sustained adulation of his fellow prisoners had no effect on his selfless modesty. Nor was his life distorted by memories of his extraordinary past. And we who were privileged to work with him remember that despite his habit of unchallenged command even his strongest convictions were cheerfully subordinated to the attainment of our common good.[31]

Capital Shure — p 91/93 — Guy Valery. "It knows?
Papers — p. 14 — reference p 139

Appendix

Letter to *The Times* of Friday 10 October from H. E. I. Phillips
of the 18th Infantry Division on the misuse of the 18th Division in
the battle for Singapore

See page 60.

Letters to the Editor

FALL OF SINGAPORE

FATE OF 18TH INFANTRY DIVISION

Sir,—Copies of *The Times* take some weeks to reach me, and for this reason I have only just read the letters by your various contributors on the fall of Singapore. I hasten to add my own comments. I was a member of the 18th Infantry Division. Originally destined for the Near East, it was diverted to India from South Africa in December, 1941. One brigade was immediately detached and proceeded direct to Singapore, arriving in mid-January; the remainder, having spent three weeks in India, arrived there at the end of the same month. The fortress fell a fortnight later, and the division, the first to leave England on the new establishment of 1941, had been prodigally thrown to the winds.

The division had been trained for mobile warfare against Germans and Italians. It knew nothing about the jungle or about the Japanese. In the short time after the change of destination it was not possible to obtain any authentic information about the Malayan terrain; nor were there any pamphlets available to show how a Japanese soldier was dressed, armed, and equipped, or to tell how he was accustomed to fight. Notwithstanding this all units of the division were committed to action immediately upon arrival, which in the circumstances was only to be expected.

But even then the division was not permitted to fight as a division. Already one brigade had been detached, and this was followed by the arbitrary creation of artificial "forces" constituted of units and sub-units drawn from its other formations. Thus battalions were divorced from brigades, and companies from battalions. Unnecessary difficulties of administration were created and the chain of command disrupted.

It is, of course, easy for those who have to do the fighting to criticize those who do the planning; but there seems in these circumstances to be some justification. We of the 18th Division wanted to know then, and still want to know now, who gave the order, and why, that a division untrained for Far Eastern warfare be sent to retrieve a situation which by the time of its arrival and, indeed, for some time before, could only be deemed irretrievable in view of the overwhelming superiority of the Japanese on land, and especially in the air. We wished also to know what justification there was for the ruthless tearing apart of units and sub-units. These seemed to us matters of strategy, perhaps even of politics. We knew our own tactical faults, and they seemed light in comparison. Not even General Percival's long-awaited dispatch can really give us the answer, although it should make interesting reading if only in view of the remarkable delay between its preparation and publication. Mistakes have to be made in war, and it cannot detract from the glory of our war leaders if these mistakes have to be divulged. It seems that the misapplication of the 18th Division was one such mistake, and it was a tragic mistake resulting in the subsequent death in captivity of more than one-third of the division's strength. If there was an error of judgment it should be publicly acknowledged; so much at least is due to the memory of those who died, and particularly of our gallant commander, General Beckwith-Smith.

There was no way of white-washing the fall of Singapore because there was no subsequent evacuation to glorify the military defeat, as there had been at Dunkirk. It was an unredeemed disaster. But this was no fault of the individual Imperial soldier, who fought as heroically and as dutifully there as in any other theatre of war. I speak only for the 18th Division, which was flung in when all was lost. There are others, no doubt, representing those who fought a running fight the whole way down the Malay peninsula, who may be tempted to add their voices to mine, and agree that some public statement should be made, perhaps a Commission of Inquiry appointed, to throw more light on the current of events contingent upon so important and so tragic an event in our military history.

I am, &c.,

H. E. I. PHILLIPS.

References

NOTE   In the references that follow, Colonel Toosey's initials, PJDT, identify manuscript material and transcripts of interviews bearing on his life and the experiences of POWs in Japanese camps during the Second World War. These files and tapes are all in the possession of the author.

Prologue

Sources

The principal items utilized for this section are to be found in the transcript of the author's taped interviews with Colonel Toosey (PJDT. 0) and in Toosey's 'Report on Malay and Thailand POW Camps' (PJDT. 3) (cited as 'Report').

Notes

1   Toosey interview, tape 20, p. 199.
2   Louis Allen, *Singapore 1941–1942*, (Davis Poynter, London, 1977), p. 270.
3   Toosey Report, p. 4.
4   See Map 3 on p. 88.

Chapter 1

Sources:

The main works used in this chapter are Colonel Toosey's unpublished 'Autobiography', in the possession of the author (PJDT. 1) and the following:
J. Gathorne-Hardy, *The Public School Phenomenon* (Hodder & Stoughton, London, 1977), p. 320.
History of the 359 (4th West Lancs) Medium Regiment, R. A. (T.A.) 1859–1959 (Tinling, Liverpool, 1959).
Rev. C. L. S. Linnell and A. B. Douglas, *Gresham's School: History and Register, 1555–1954* (Cowell, Ipswich, 1955).

Notes

1 Toosey, 'Autobiography', p. 9.
2 *History of the 359 (4th West Lancs) Medium Regiment.*
3 ibid., p. 58.
4 Toosey, 'Autobiography', p. 11.

Chapter 2

Sources

The principal works utilized in the writing of this chapter were the author's interviews with Colonel Toosey (PJDT.0), Toosey's unpublished 'Autobiography' (PJDT.1) and the *History of the 359 (4th West Lancs) Medium Regiment*. Specialist studies consulted included:

L. Allen, op. cit., Chapter 4, 'The Role of Thailand'
G. Bennett, *The Loss of the Prince of Wales and Repulse* (Ian Allen, London, 1973)
A. Bryant, *The Turn of the Tide, 1939–43* (Collins, London, 1957)
S. W. Kirby, *The Chain of Disaster* (Cassell, London, 1971)
Captain S. W. Roskill, *The War at Sea* (HMSO, London, 1954), Vol. I. *The Defensive.*

Notes

1 Toosey, 'Autobiography', p. 17.
2 *History of the 359 (4th West Lancs) Medium Regiment*, p. 83.
3 John Tilney, a great personal friend of Toosey, later became the MP for the Wavertree constituency in Liverpool.
4 Toosey, 'Autobiography', p. 24.
5 ibid., p. 26.
6 ibid., p. 27.
7 ibid., p. 29.

Chapter 3

Sources

In addition to the author's interviews with Colonel Toosey and Toosey's 'Autobiography' a large number of sources that deal with particular topics have been utilized in the production of this chapter. These have included:

L. Allen, op. cit.
S. Arneil, *One Man's War* (Alternative Publishing Cooperative, Sydney, 1980)
K. Attiwell, *The Singapore Story*, (Muller, London, 1959)
David Bergamini, *Japan's Imperial Conspiracy*, (Heinemann, London, 1971)
Russell Braddon, *The Naked Island* (Werner Laurie, London, 1952)
A. Bryant, op. cit.
Kate Caffry, *Out in the Midday Sun: Singapore, 1941–45*, (Deutsch, London, 1974)
W. S. Churchill, *The Second World War* (Cassell, London, 1948–54), Vol. IV, *The Hinge of Fate* (1951)
B. Collier, *The War in the East* (Heinemann, London, 1969)
R. Grenfell, *Main Fleet to Singapore* (Faber & Faber, London, 1951)
The Grim Glory of the 2/19 Battalion, A. I. F. (published in Sydney for the Regimental Association, 1975)

Jizo Hashimoto mss. These papers of a former major of the Independent Engineer Regiment of the Japanese 5th division include the diary of its late Commanding Officer, Colonel Tamura. A translation of this and of a series of questions put to Hashimoto has been kindly made available to me by Mr G. P. Adams of Poole, Dorset (PJDT.33).

Précis of lectures given by Lieutenant-General Heath of Changi on the Malaya Campaign (see PJDT.42).

S. W. Kirby, op. cit.

London Gazette, Second Supplement, 26 February 1948 (dispatch by Lieutenant-General A. E. Percival)

W. M. Naylor, 'The Fall of Singapore and After', unpublished mss by a young signaller in the 135th Regiment (see PJDT.16).

Official Diary of 135 (N. Herts Yeomanry) Field Regiment, R.A. (T.A.)

Frank Owen, *The Fall of Singapore* (Michael Joseph, London, 1960)

Lord Russell, *Knights of Bushido* (Cassell, London, 1958)

Sir William Slim, *Defeat into Victory* (Cassell, London, 1956)

Sir John Smyth, *Percival and the Tragedy of Singapore* (Macdonald, London, 1971)

A. Swinson, *Defeat in Malaya* (Macdonald, London, 1970)

Masanobu Tsuji, *Singapore: The Japanese Version* (Constable, London, 1962)

Notes

1 Toosey, 'Autobiography', p. 31.
2 ibid., p. 32.
3 ibid., p. 37.
4 After the war he became Canon Duckworth of Churchill College: in pre-war days he had coxed the Cambridge crew in the Boat Race.
5 K. Caffrey, p. 62.
6 Toosey, 'Autobiography', p. 43.
7 Records of the 11th Indian Division compiled by their CSO1, Colonel Harrison.
8 *The Grim Glory ...*, p. 300.
9 Toosey, 'Autobiography', p. 46.
10 ibid., p. 48.
11 D. Bergamini, pp. 3–48 and Lord Russell, pp. 39–52.
12 A. Swinson, p. 140.
13 Statement made by Major C. H. D. Wild and held as part of the Percival Mss. at the Imperial War Museum, London.
14 T. Ishimaru, *Japan Must Fight Britain*, (trans. G. V. Rayment) Paternoster Library, London, 1936.
15 Under the agreement with the Kremlin in the autumn of 1941, Britain was to supply, by June 1942, 2250 tanks, 1800 aeroplanes and 1800 bren-gun carriers – see A. Bryant, p. 324.
16 S. W. Kirby, p. 251.
17 M. Tsuji, p. 181.
18 ibid., pp. 128–9.
19 R. Braddon, p. 56.
20 S. W. Kirby, p. 253
21 The case against the civilian authorities made by Brigadier I. Simson, Chief Engineer of Malaya Command, is reproduced in L. Allen, op. cit., pp. 202–12.
22 S. Arneil, p. 18.

213

23 W. S. Churchill, p. 48. (This statement was modified in a footnote on the same page)
24 J. M. A. Gwyer and J. R. M. Butler, *Grand Strategy*, (HMSO, London, 1964) Vol. III of *History of the Second World War*, p. 283. (Quoted in S. W. Kirby, op. cit., p. 390)
25 John Masters, *The Road Past Mandalay* (Companion Book Club, London: original edition Michael Joseph, London, 1961), pp. 157–8.

Chapter 4

Sources

The author's interviews with Colonel Toosey, his 'Autobiography' and 'Report on Malay and Thailand POW Camps' form the basis of this chapter but this information has been supplemented by material from a wide range of other sources including:

G. P. Adams, *No Time for Geishas* (Leo Cooper, London, 1973)
A. Allbury, *Bamboo and Bushido* (Robert Hale, London, 1955)
L. Allen, op. cit.
S. Arneil, op. cit.
K. Attiwell, op. cit.
A. J. Barker, *Behind Barbed Wire*, (B. T. Batsford, London, 1974)
R. Braddon, op. cit.
J. Bradley, *Towards the Setting Sun* (Phillmore, London, 1982)
J. Coast, *Railroad of Death* (Commodore Press, London, 1946)
J. H. H. Coombes, *Banpong Express* (Wm Dressor, Darlington, 1948)
R. Hastain, *White Coolie* (Hodder & Stoughton, London, 1947)
W. M. Naylor, op. cit.
Official Diary of 135 (N. Herts Yeomanry) Field Regiment, R.A. (T.A.)
Author's interviews with Harold Payne.
Lord Russell, op. cit.
D. Russell-Roberts, *Spotlight on Singapore* (Times Press, Douglas, IOM, 1965)
Sir J. Smyth, op. cit.

Notes

1 A. J. Barker, p. 43.
2 Toosey, 'Autobiography', p. 49.
3 J. Coast, p. 11.
4 D. Russell-Roberts, pp. 149–50. It should be noted that many officers with regimental affiliations marched with their own units.
5 ibid., p. 150.
6 W. M. Naylor, p. 7.
7 A. G. Allbury, pp. 21–2.
8 J. H. H. Coombes, p. 62.
9 R. Braddon, pp. 153–4.
10 ibid., p. 158.
11 Toosey, 'Report', p. 1.
12 W. M. Naylor, p. 8.
13 ibid., p. 9.
14 R. Hastain, p. 99.

Chapter 5

Sources

Heavy reliance has been placed on information obtained from Yoshihiko Futamatsu, *Recollections of the Thai-Burma Railway* (translated by C. E. Escritt) and his *Materials about the Thai-Burma Railway*. These, together with the transcripts of the author's interviews with Mr Futamatsu and ex-Major R. Sugano in Tokyo in 1979, 1984 and 1986, are held in PJDT.36. Copies of Futamatsu's correspondence with C. E. Escritt provide further illumination of many aspects of the construction. Mr. Escritt's unpublished ms, 'A Japanese Engineer's Trace of the Thailand-Burma Rail Link in the Imperial War Museum', is held in PJDT.35 and has also proved to be extremely valuable.

The major sources from the British side are:

Lieutenant C. C. Brett, *The Burma-Siam Railway* (SEATIC Bulletin No. 246, October 1946)

S. W. Kirby, *The War Against Japan* (London, 1969), Vol. V of *History of the Second World War* (UK military series, 1957–69)

Other useful works for this chapter include:

J. Alford (ed.), *Sea Power and Influence* (Gower & Allanheld, Osmun, 1980)

D. Bergamini, op. cit.

K. Caffrey, op. cit.

B. Collier, op. cit.

C. A. Fisher, 'The Thailand-Burma Railway', *Economic Geography*, vol. 23, no. 2, April 1947, pp. 85–97.

L. Hall, *The Blue Haze: Incorporating a History of 'A' Force, Groups 3–5* (National Library of Australia, 1985)

C. Kinvig, *Death Railway* (Pan/Ballantine, London, 1973)

S. M. Morison, *History of the United States Naval Operations in World War II* (Oxford University Press, London, 1962), Vol. XV

S. S. Pavillard, *Bamboo Doctor* (Pan Books, London, 1970 edition)

R. D. Rivett, *Behind Bamboo* (Angus & Robertson, London, 1946)

Sir William Slim, op. cit.

J. Toland, *The Rising Sun: The Decline and Fall of the Japanese Empire* (Bantam Books, London, 1971)

Brigadier P. Young (ed.), *The Battle of Midway: World War II* (Orbis, London, 1983)

Notes

1   W. Slim, p. 14.
2   S. W. Kirby, *The War Against Japan*, p. 397.
3   C. E. Escritt, 'A Japanese Engineer's Trace', pp. 6–7.
4   *Barbed Wire and Bamboo* (official organ of the ex-POW Association of Australia), vol. 27, no. 4, August 1977, p. 7.
5   S. S. Pavillard, pp. 68–9, provides an account of his march towards Tardan in October, 1942, when the proposed road was still only a track.
6   C. C. Brett, p. 11.
7   ibid., p. 9.

Chapter 6

Sources

While interviews with Colonel Toosey, his 'Autobiography' and his 'Report' outline the essential framework, the works of C. C. Brett, C. E. Escritt and Y. Futamatsu (previously cited) provide much additional and useful material. Interviews with David Boyle (PJDT.18), Robert Hislop (PJDT.83) and Teruo Saito (PJDT.36) supply first-hand accounts of many incidents while a number of published studies also make helpful contributions to this chapter:
G. P. Adams, op. cit., is particularly valuable on life and work at Tamarkan.
J. Bradley, op. cit.
W. M. Naylor, op. cit.
Lord Russell, op. cit.

Notes

1   Toosey, 'Report'.
2   Toosey interview, tape 21, p. 208.
3   W. M. Naylor, pp. 11–12.
4   A plan of the steel bridge is held in PJDT. 36.
5   R. Hislop, letter dated 3 October 1979.
6   ibid.
7   W. M. Naylor, p. 11.
8   Toosey, 'Autobiography', p. 62.
9   ibid.
10 Interview with David Boyle, p. 13.
11 ibid.
12 Toosey, 'Autobiography', p. 63.
13 ibid., p. 57.
14 For details of one of the more promising attempts to escape see J. Bradley, op. cit.

Chapter 7

Sources

The major basis for this chapter is provided in the 'Report on Ex POW Finance' produced by Colonel Toosey in October 1945 (PJDT.4) (cited as 'Ex POW Finance'). A copy of this work is held in the Imperial War Museum, London. The author's interviews with Toosey, David Boyle (PJDT.18), E. P. Heath (PJDT.22), D. G. Horner (PJDT.24), W. E. Kirley, a former private in 3/20 Battalion of the AIF (PJDT.26), W. M. Naylor (PJDT.16), Boon Pong (PJDT.32), Colonel Sanderson, former captain in the 9th Battalion, Royal Northumberland Fusiliers (PJDT.27) and Lee Soon (PJDT.31) have supplied much useful information. This has been supplemented by a number of published and unpublished accounts, many not previously identified:
L. L. Baynes, *Kept – the Other Side of Tenko* (Book Guild, Lewes, 1984)
C. F. Blackater, *Gods without Reason* (Eyre & Spottiswoode, London, 1948)
C. E. Escritt, 'Note on the 'V' Organisation' (PJDT.35).
A. Gilchrist, 'Diplomacy and Disaster: Thailand and the British Empire in 1941', *Asian Affairs*, vol. XIII, 3 October 1982.
R. Grant, 'A War Hero named Boon Pong' (PJDT.32).

J. C. Hamel, *Soldatendominee* (N. V. Uitgeveri, W. van Hoeve, The Hague, 1948)
R. D. Rivett, op. cit.

Notes

1   J. Coast, op. cit., p. 96.
2   C. Kinvig, op. cit., p. 90.
3   The two scales are quoted in Toosey's 'Report', pp. 5 and 8.
4   ibid., p. 8.
5   Letter from Dr A. A. Moon to Sir John Smyth, 28 July 1972 (PJDT.2).
6   ibid.
7   L. L. Baynes, pp. 122–3.
8   ibid. p. 118.
9   R. Burton, *The Road to Three Pagodas* (MacDonald, London, 1963), pp. 121–2.
10 C. F. Blackater, pp. 117–8.
11 Letter from G. E. Downes to Sir John Smyth (PJDT.2).
12 Author's interview with Mr D. G. Horner (PJDT.24).
13 W. E. Kirley, transcript p. 4.
14 Author's interview with W. M. Naylor, (PJDT.16).
15 Letter from Dr A. A. Moon, op. cit.
16 Toosey, 'Ex POW Finance', letter to British Embassy, Chungking, 26 July 1943.
17 Letter from Dr A. A. Moon, op. cit.
18 C. F. Blackater, p. 120.
19 Letter from A. E. Knights to Toosey (PJDT.70).
20 Toosey, 'Ex POW Finance', ref. 31.
21 A. Coates and N. Rosenthal, *The Albert Coates Story* (published privately, Melbourne, 1980), pp. 131–2 and p. 145 give details of Mr and Mrs Clark's arrest and subsequent release.
22 Toosey, 'Ex POW Finance', incident re Colonel Parker at Nakhon Pathom.
23 ibid., Final Report.
24 J. Coast, op, cit., p. 123.
25 S. S. Pavillard, op. cit., p. 87.
26 Toosey, 'Ex POW Finance', ref. 33.

Chapter 8

Sources

This chapter utilizes much information from Toosey's 'Report on Malay and Thailand POW Camps' and his 'Report on Ex POW Finance'. This has been amplified by the author's interviews with: G. P. Adams (PJDT.33), C. E. Escritt, (PJDT.38), Sir Edward Dunlop (PJDT.20), T. Saito (PJDT.36) and D. H. Webber (PJDT.25).

The principal printed works consulted included:

J. and C. Blair, Jr, *Return from the River Kwai* (Simon & Schuster, New York, 1979)
G. K. Donaldson, *177 Wing: A Short History of the Work of 32, 62, 117 and 194 Squadrons* (published privately – a copy is in the author's possession).
John North, *North-West Europe, 1944–5* (HMSO, London, 1977)
J. Toland, *The Last 100 Days* (Arthur Barker, London, 1965)
G. Webster and N. Frankland, *The Strategic Air Offensive Against Germany*, (HMSO, London, 1961), Vol. III.

In addition studies previously cited by D. Bergamini, J. Coast, A. Coates and N. Rosenthal, B. Collier, J. H. H. Coombes and Sir John Smyth have proved very useful.

Notes

1 Toosey, 'Report', p. 11.
2 ibid., p. 13 (notes provided by Captain C. E. Escritt).
3 Toosey, 'Autobiography', pp. 66–7.
4 J. H. H. Coombes, pp. 141–2.
5 D. Bergamini, p. 1008.
6 Toosey, 'Report', p. 17.
7 ibid., p. 18.
8 J. Coast, pp. 222–3.
9 Author's correspondence with D. H. Webber (PJDT.25).
10 J. H. H. Coombes, p. 117.

Chapter 9

Sources

While the Toosey mss have been used as a framework for this chapter the material for the air attacks on the bridge has been based on the specialist works cited below. The SEATIC *Bulletin* produced by C. C. Brett (op. cit.) and interviews with W. L. Davis, Carl H. Fritsche and Douglas Williams have been essential for this section, while the details of the move to Nakhon Nayok owe much to the accounts written by C. E. Escritt, E. Gordon and C. Hugh. See in particular:

W. A. Craven and J. L. Cate (eds), *The Army Air Forces in World War II* (University of Chicago Press, 1953), Vol. 5
W. L. Davis, 'The Bridges on the River Kwai', *Aerospace Historian*, vol. 20, no. 1, March 1973
C. E. Escritt, letter to the author dated 14 March 1986 (PJDT.35)
Carl H. Fritsche, 'B.24 Liberator', in R. Highan and C. Williams (eds), *Flying Combat Aircraft on the USAAF & USAF* (Iowa State University Press, Ames, 1978), Vol. II
Carl H. Fritsche, 'Liberators on the Kwae', *Aerospace Historian*, vol. 30, no. 2, June 1983
E. Gordon, *The Miracle on the River Kwae* (Collins, London, 1963)
Charles Hugh, 'The Last Journey', *Blackwood's Magazine*, vol. 259, No. 1566, April 1946.
S. W. Kirby, *The War Against Japan*, Vols. II and V.
W. G. Ramsey (ed.) 'The Death Railway', *After the Battle*, no. 26, 1979 (this provides a first-hand account of a raid on the bridge by Lieutenant William Henderson).

Notes

1 Sir William Slim, op. cit., p. 170.
2 R. Hastain, op. cit., p. 177.
3 Carl H. Fritsche, 'B.24', p. 55.
4 C. C. Brett, op. cit., p. 14.
5 Carl H. Fritsche, 'Liberators on the Kwai', p. 87.
6 Sir William Slim, op. cit., p. 411.
7 Toosey, 'Report', p. 20.

Chapter 10

Sources

The author's interviews with Colonel Toosey, his 'Autobiography' and 'Report on Malay and Thailand POW Camps' (especially Appendix 'H') provide the background to this chapter. Additional material has been obtained from a number of works previously cited, by D. Bergamini, C. F. Blackater, J. Coast, B. Collier, J. H. H. Coombes, E. Gordon, S. W. Kirby, S.S. Pavillard, R. D. Rivett and the *History of the 359 (4th West Lancs) Medium Regiment*. A specialist work on the naval war in the east also supplied much helpful information:
S. E. Morison, *History of the United States Naval Operations in World War II* (Little Brown, Boston, Mass., 1960), Vol. XIV, *Victory in the Pacific*.

Notes

1   This is a reference to the execution of Captain Pomeroy and Lieutenant Howard. (See above, p. 112.)
2   Toosey, 'Autobiography', p. 74.
3   Author's interview with Colonel Toosey, tape 28, p. 277.
4   ibid., tape 27, p. 276.
5   Toosey, 'Autobiography', p. 76.
6   ibid., pp. 77–8.
7   Sir Douglas Clague's work in Bangkok has been the subject of research by Mr R. Hutchinson (PJDT.91).
8   Major A. D. Toosey, DC of 235 Battery of the 59th Medium Regiment RA (Philip's old unit) was killed on 15 July 1944.
9   Toosey, 'Autobiography', p. 81.
10 ibid., pp. 81–2.
11 Author's interview with Colonel Toosey, tape 29, p. 295.

Chapter 11

Sources

Material supplied by the Toosey archives has been supplemented by the author's interviews with David Boyle, 'Weary' Dunlop, Jack Edwards, Robert Hislop, Stanley Pavillard and Harold Payne. A wide range of general and specialized works have also been consulted including:
Count C. Beckendorf, *Half a Life: Reminiscences of a Russian Gentleman* (Richards Press, London, 1955)
D. Bergamini, op. cit.
D. C. Bowie, 'Captive Surgeon in Hong Kong', journal of the Hong Kong Branch, Royal Asiatic Society, vol. 15, 1975.
C. C. Brett, op. cit.
A. Coates and N. Rosenthal, op. cit.
E. E. Dunlop, 'Medical Experiences in Japanese Captivity', *British Medical Journal*, vol. II, 5 October 1946.
S. J. H. Durnford, *Branch Line to Burma* (Macdonald, London, 1958)
S. W. Kirby, *The War Against Japan*, Vol. V, op. cit.
S. Pavillard, op. cit.

J. Smyth, op. cit.
The Times, *History of the War* (London, 1955)

Notes

1 As part of this campaign General Percival, Colonel Toosey and Sergeant-Major Hastain had an interview with Mr Yoshida,the prime minister of Japan, when he visited London in October 1954 (PJDT.111).

2 D. L. Patrick and P. J. D. Heaf, *Long-Term Effects of War-Related Deprivation on Health* (British Members of World Veterans Federation, Haverhill, Suffolk, 1981)

3 Toosey interview, tape 45, p. 453.

4 Toosey scrapbook, leter dated 13 October 1971.

5 Colonel Toosey had been awarded the Territorial (Officers) Decoration in 1944 and the Distinguished Service Order in 1945. He was made an Officer of the British Empire in 1946 and a Commander of the same Order in 1955.

6 D. Bergamini, p. 960.

7 C. C. Brett, table 7, p. 24.

8 P. U. Coates and P. Neild, 'Up Country with 'F' Force'. Unpublished mss held by the author (PJDT.13).

9 C. C. Brett, p. 25.

10 Memoirs of J. M. Fram-Taylor, former CQMS in 9 Battalion Royal Northumberland Fusiliers (PJDT.96).

11 Laurens van der Post, *The Night of the New Moon* (Hogarth Press, London, 1970), p. 59.

12 I.M.T.F.E. International Prosecution Section, B. & C. Offences, British Division, document no. 2701 (certified as exhibit 'O' in document no. 2687) dated 1 August 1944. Copies of this document may be examined at the Imperial War Museum, London, and at the Nissan Institute, Oxford.

13 Jack Edwards, *Banzai You Bastards* (Corporate Communications, Hong Kong, 1986), pp. 260–1.

14 Harry S. Truman, *Memoirs*, Vol. I, *Year of Decisions* (Doubleday, New York, 1955), p. 417.

15 Henry L. Simpson, 'The Decision to Use the Atomic Bomb', *Harper's Magazine*, February 1947.

16 Herbert Feis, *The Atomic Bomb and the End of World War II* (Princeton University Press, Princeton, NJ, 1966), p. 192.

17 *Liverpool Daily Post*, 2 February 1976.

18 Address given by HRH the Duke of Edinburgh to the National Reunion of FEPOWs held on 4 May 1974.

19 Dr P. E. F. Routley, former major with the RAMC (PJDT.21).

20 Sir John Nicholson mss (PJDT.79).

21 Ian Watt, 'The Myth of the Bridge on the River Kwai', *Observer* Magazine, 1 September 1968, p. 7 (see also PJDT.7).

22 ibid., p. 8.

23 *Glasgow Herald*, 15 March 1974.

24 Author's interview with T. Saito (PJDT.36).

25 Letter from Lord Mountbatten of Burma to Toosey dated 6 September 1968.

26 Paul. R. Pratt, 'The Thai-Burma Railway – 30 years after', *Railway World*, February 1976, p. 67.

27 'The Death Railway', *After the Battle*, no. 26, 1979, p. 8. It has not been possible to confirm the suggestion that Japanese POWs were used in this task.

28 G. V. Gill and D. R. Bell, 'Strongyloids stercoralis infection in former Far Eastern prisoners of war', *British Medical Journal*, vol. 2, 1979, pp. 572–4; 'Correspondence' *British Medical Journal*, 31 May 1980, and 'Persisting tropical diseases amongst former prisoners of war of the Japanese', *The Practitioner*, vol. 224, August 1980, pp. 801–3. See also: D. L. Patrick and P. J. D. Heaf, op. cit.

29 The appeal was organized by the 18th Division Association with the aid of other officers including Lieutenant-Colonel Owtram (PJDT.32).

30 Mr Boon Pong Sirivejjabhandu GM, died on 29 January 1982 (his obituary is in *The Times* of 17 February 1982).

31 Foreword to Sir John Smyth, 'The Life Story of Brigadier P. J. D. Toosey', unpublished mss, pp. xi–xii (PJDT.2).

Photograph acknowledgements

Frontispiece: Mr Nicholas Toosey. Sleeve of dust jacket: Dr P. N. Davies. Photo No. 27: Y. Futamatso. Photo No. 37: The late Mr Boon Pong. Photo No. 38: Mr Lee Soon. Photo No. 39: Mr Carl Fritsche. Photo No. 40: Dr P. N. Davies. Photos Nos 41 and 42: The late Mr T. Saito. Photos Nos 43 and 44: Dr P. N. Davies.

The following photographs are taken from *Record of the Thai-Burma Railway* by Ren-ichi Sugano, published privately by the 9th Railway Regiment, I. J. A., Tokyo, 1971: Dust jacket (back cover), photos 6, 7, 8, 9, 16, 17, 18, 19, 24, 25, 26, 28, 29, 30, 31, 32, 33, 34, 35, 36.

The remaining photographs were obtained from the Toosey Collection: Dust jacket (front cover), photos 3, 4, 5, 10, 11, 12, 13, 14, 15, 20, 21, 22, 23, 45, 46, 47.

Index of persons

Index of subjects

Index of places